Wine Folly

LIFE IS TOO SHORT TO DRINK BAD WINE.

–Anonymous

Wine Folly

A Visual Guide to the World of Wine

MADELINE PUCKETTE AND JUSTIN HAMMACK

MICHAEL JOSEPH
an imprint of
PENGUIN BOOKS

Madeline Puckette is a certified sommelier with the Court of Master Sommeliers and has worked in several restaurants as a sommelier or a server before creating WineFolly.com. Her writing and visual design work in infographics has been applied in organizations such as Wines of France, Wines of Bordeaux, Wines of Beaujolais, the Court of Master Sommeliers, the Guild of Sommeliers, the Washington State Wine Commission, and Rhône Valley Wines. In 2013, Wine Folly was named Wine Blogger of the Year for the 2013–2014 year by International Wine & Spirits Competition.

Justin Hammack is a founding partner of Wine Folly and leads conceptual development, interactive tools, and marketplace branding. Justin also handles all videography and photography.

MICHAEL JOSEPH

UK | USA | Canada | Ireland | Australia
India | New Zealand | South Africa

Michael Joseph is part of the Penguin Random House group of companies whose addresses can be found at global.penguinrandomhouse.com.

First published in the United States of America by Avery, an imprint of Penguin Random House LLC
First published in Great Britain by Michael Joseph
001

Text and images copyright © Wine Folly LLC, 2015
Book design and illustration by Madeline Puckette

www.winefolly.com

The moral right of the authors and illustrators has been asserted

Printed in China by C&C Offset Printing Co., Ltd.

A CIP catalogue record for this book is available from the British Library

ISBN: 978-0-718-18307-3

www.greenpenguin.co.uk

Penguin Random House is committed to a sustainable future for our business, our readers and our planet. This book is made from Forest Stewardship Council® certified paper.

Contents

INTRODUCTION

Like wine? Want to know more about it? This book is for those of us who need simple guidance to get over the challenges of getting into wine. It contains practical knowledge that is immediately useful to help you find and enjoy great wine.

This guide is small on purpose. It's a visual reference guide designed specifically for everyday wine drinkers. Within these pages you'll find:

› Wine fundamentals
› How to taste, handle and store wine
› A compendium of 55 different types of wine
› 20 detailed wine maps

Want more? Go online.

http://winefolly.com/book

› Hundreds of articles
› How-to videos
› In-depth resources
› Poster guides and maps

Access Wine Folly's extensive resources free online. The site is supported by hundreds of thousands of subscribers and is used by consumers and professionals alike.

WHY LEARN ABOUT WINE

Perhaps you want to stock up on delicious value wines. Or maybe you want to navigate a restaurant wine list with confidence. Learning about wine starts with the realization that the wine world is a lot bigger than we think:

There are over a thousand wine varieties to choose from . . .

There are thousands of wine regions with unique wines . . .

Every day, an average of 600 new wines are released . . .

Fortunately, wine isn't overwhelming when you have a solid foundation. A good foundation leads to informed purchases and better-tasting wine.

THE CHALLENGE

Complete the following challenges and you will gain confidence both in choosing and tasting wine.

Taste at least 34 of the 55 wines included in this book (just not all at once!). Take great **tasting notes** (pg. 21).

Try at least 1 wine from each of the **12 countries** (pgs. 176–217).

Learn how to **blind taste** (pgs. 12–21) your favourite single-varietal wine.

Fundamentals

Wine Basics

WHAT IS WINE

Definition of wine, grape varieties, regions, and what's inside a single bottle of wine.

WINE BOTTLE FACTS

On drinking, sulphites, bottle sizes, and ways that bottles are labelled.

BASIC WINE CHARACTERISTICS

Definitions of the 5 basic traits of wine: alcohol, acidity, tannin, sweetness and body.

INSIDE A BOTTLE
OF WINE

5 GLASSES
150 ML

WATER

ALCOHOL

ACIDS, MINERALS
GLYCEROL, SUGAR

1 GLASS
DRY WINE

10%	11%	12%	13%	14%	15%	16%	ABV
105	120	135	150	165	180	195	CALORIES

WHAT IS WINE?

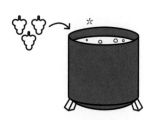

Wine is an alcoholic beverage made with fermented grapes. Technically, wine can be made with any fruit, but most wines are made with wine grapes.

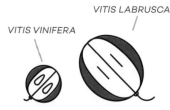

VITIS LABRUSCA

VITIS VINIFERA

Wine grapes are different than table grapes. They are much smaller, they have seeds, and they are also sweeter than table grapes.

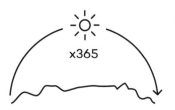

x365

Grapevines take a year to grow grapes. The harvest in the northern hemisphere is Aug.–Oct., and the harvest in the southern hemisphere is Feb.–Apr.

2010 2007 2012 1990 1985

Vintage refers to the year when the grapes were harvested. Non-vintage (NV) wines are a blend of several harvests.

A **single-varietal wine** is made with one grape variety (e.g., Pinot Noir, pg. 100).

A **wine blend** is made by mixing several wines together (e.g., Bordeaux blend, pg. 134).

A temperate climate is where grapes grow best. In North America, grapes grow from northern Mexico to southern Canada.

Regions with **cooler climates** make wines that taste more tart.

Regions with **warmer climates** make wines that taste more ripe.

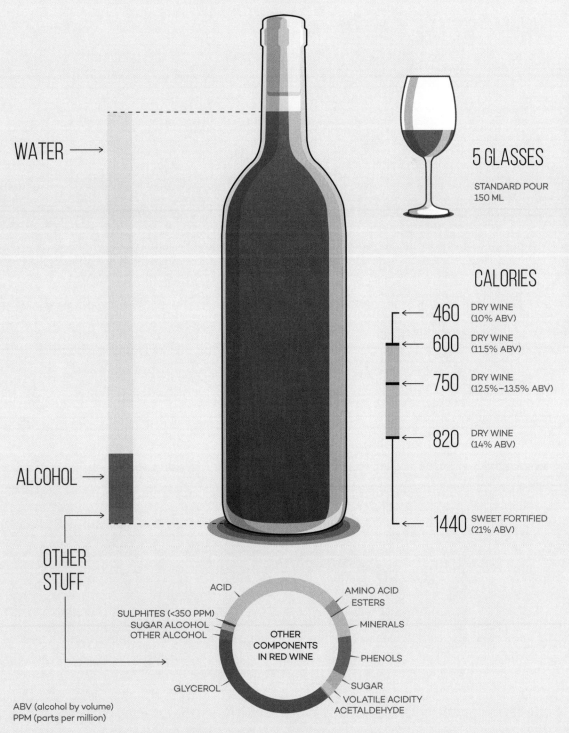

WATER →

ALCOHOL →

OTHER
STUFF

5 GLASSES

STANDARD POUR
150 ML

CALORIES

460 ← DRY WINE
(10% ABV)

600 ← DRY WINE
(11.5% ABV)

750 ← DRY WINE
(12.5%–13.5% ABV)

820 ← DRY WINE
(14% ABV)

1440 ← SWEET FORTIFIED
(21% ABV)

OTHER
COMPONENTS
IN RED WINE

ACID
AMINO ACID
ESTERS
MINERALS
PHENOLS
SUGAR
VOLATILE ACIDITY
ACETALDEHYDE
GLYCEROL
SULPHITES (<350 PPM)
SUGAR ALCOHOL
OTHER ALCOHOL

ABV (alcohol by volume)
PPM (parts per million)

5

WINE BOTTLE FACTS

DRINKING FACTS

⌀ STANDARD BOTTLE SIZE
A standard 750 ml bottle contains 5 servings of wine.

♀ STANDARD WINE POUR
A standard pour is 150 ml and contains an average of 150 calories and 0–2 grams of carbs.

♡ HEALTHY DRINKING
NHS Change 4 Life recommends that women have no more than 1 drink per day and men have no more than 2.

♀ A GLASS A DAY
If you drink a glass of wine every night of your adult life, you will drink over 4,000 bottles of wine.

A bottle of wine contains the fermented juice of *Vitis vinifera* grapes. Besides fermented grape juice, there is also a small portion of sulphur dioxide (aka 'sulphites') added as a preservative.

SULPHITE FACTS

Sulphites affect about 1% of the general population, and wineries are required to label their wines if they contain more than 10 ppm (parts per million). In the US, wine has no more than 350 ppm sulphites and organic wine has no more than 100 ppm. In comparison, a can of Coke contains 350 ppm of sulphites, french fries contain 1,900 ppm, and dried fruit contains about 3,500 ppm.

WINE BOTTLE SIZES

187.5 ml — SPLIT	
375 ml — DEMI/HALF	
500 ml — JENNIE	
750 ml — STANDARD	
1.5 L (2) — MAGNUM	
3 L (4) — DOUBLE MAGNUM	
4.5 L — 6 STANDARD BOTTLES — JEROBOAM	
6 L — 8 STANDARD BOTTLES — IMPERIAL	
9 L — 12 STANDARD BOTTLES — SALMANAZAR	
12 L — 16 STANDARD BOTTLES — BALTHAZAR	
15 L — 20 STANDARD BOTTLES — NEBUCHADNEZZAR	

3 EXAMPLES OF HOW WINE IS LABELLED

BY VARIETY

Wines can be labelled by grape variety. This German wine has the name of the grape variety— Riesling—listed on the label. Each country requires a minimum percentage of the variety in the wine in order for it to be listed on the label:

75% USA, CHILE, SOUTH AFRICA, AUSTRALIA

80% ARGENTINA

85% ITALY, FRANCE, GERMANY, AUSTRIA, PORTUGAL, NEW ZEALAND, UK

BY REGION

Wines can be labelled by region. This French wine is labelled as a Bordeaux Supérieur. If you learn about Bordeaux, you will learn that this region grows primarily Merlot and Cabernet Sauvignon and blends them together. Wines labelled by region are common in:

FRANCE

ITALY

SPAIN

PORTUGAL

BY NAME

Wines can be labelled with a made-up name. More often than not, a named wine is a blend of grape varieties that is unique to the producer. Named wines are occasionally found on single-varietal wines in order to differentiate between the wines that the producers make.

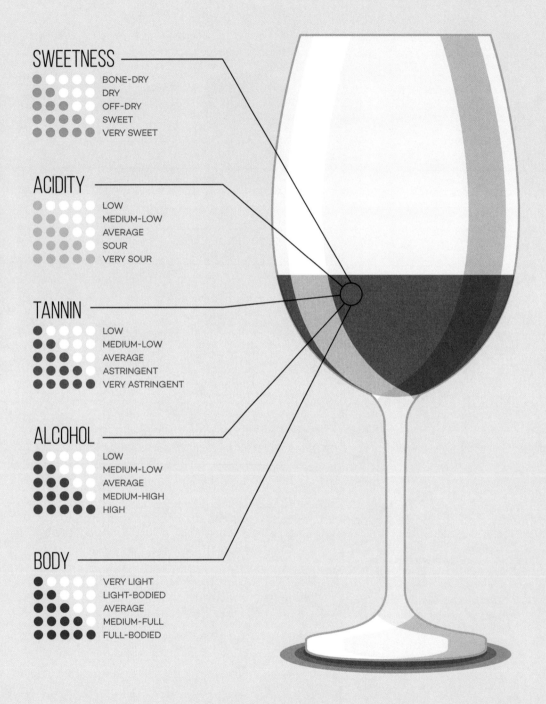

SWEETNESS
- ●○○○○ BONE-DRY
- ●●○○○ DRY
- ●●●○○ OFF-DRY
- ●●●●○ SWEET
- ●●●●● VERY SWEET

ACIDITY
- ●○○○○ LOW
- ●●○○○ MEDIUM-LOW
- ●●●○○ AVERAGE
- ●●●●○ SOUR
- ●●●●● VERY SOUR

TANNIN
- ●○○○○ LOW
- ●●○○○ MEDIUM-LOW
- ●●●○○ AVERAGE
- ●●●●○ ASTRINGENT
- ●●●●● VERY ASTRINGENT

ALCOHOL
- ●○○○○ LOW
- ●●○○○ MEDIUM-LOW
- ●●●○○ AVERAGE
- ●●●●○ MEDIUM-HIGH
- ●●●●● HIGH

BODY
- ●○○○○ VERY LIGHT
- ●●○○○ LIGHT-BODIED
- ●●●○○ AVERAGE
- ●●●●○ MEDIUM-FULL
- ●●●●● FULL-BODIED

BASIC WINE CHARACTERISTICS

There are 5 characteristics that help define the profile of a wine: sweetness, acidity, tannin, alcohol, and body.

SWEETNESS

Sweetness in wine is derived from residual sugar (RS). Residual sugar is the leftover sweetness when not all the grape must is fermented into alcohol.

We describe sweetness as a taste that ranges from bone-dry to very sweet. It's good to know that a technically dry wine can contain up to a half tea-spoon of sugar per glass. See the chart below for standardized vocabulary to describe sweetness.

LOWER ACIDITY   HIGHER ACIDITY

PERCEIVED SWEETNESS: At the same sweetness level, wines with lower acidity taste sweeter than wines with higher acidity.

SWEETNESS LEVELS

Sweetness levels in still wines can result in additional calories per 150 ml glass:

BONE DRY	DRY	OFF-DRY	SWEET	VERY SWEET
●●●●●	●●●●●	●●●●●	●●●●●	●●●●●
0 cal.	0–6 cal.	10–21 cal.	21–72 cal.	72–130 cal.
less than 1 g/L RS	*1–10 g/L RS*	*17–35 g/L RS*	*35–120 g/L RS*	*120–220 g/L RS*

Sparkling wine sweetness levels shown in teaspoons of sugar and calorie levels per 150 ml glass:

BRUT NATURE	EXTRA BRUT	BRUT	EXTRA DRY	DRY	DEMI-SEC	DOUX
0–2 cal.	0–5 cal.	0–7 cal.	7–10 cal.	10–20 cal.	20–30 cal.	30+ cal.
0–3 g/L RS	*0–6 g/L RS*	*0–12 g/L RS*	*12–17 g/L RS*	*17–32 g/L RS*	*32–50 g/L RS*	*50+ g/L RS*

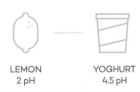

LEMON
2 pH

YOGHURT
4.5 pH

ACIDITY RANGE OF WINE:
Wine ranges in acidity from
2.5 pH to 4.5 pH. A wine with
a pH level of 3 has ten times
more acidity than a wine with
a pH level of 4.

STEMS
SKINS
SEEDS

GRAPE TANNIN: Tannin comes
from skins, seeds, and stems.
Grape tannin is bitter and
astringent but contains high
levels of antioxidants.

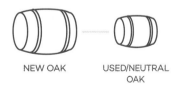

NEW OAK

USED/NEUTRAL
OAK

OAK TANNIN: New oak barrels
impart more tannin into wine than
used oak barrels.

ACIDITY

Acids are the primary attribute that contribute to wine's tart and sour flavor. Most acids in wine come from grapes including tartaric, malic and citric acid. Like many fruits, wine lies on the acid side of the pH scale, ranging from about 2.5–4.5 pH (7 is neutral).

One useful thing to know about acidity in wine is that, as grapes ripen, they become less acidic. Thus, a wine from a cooler climate where it's hard to ripen grapes will produce wines with higher acidity.

TANNIN

Tannin is a naturally occurring polyphenol found in plants. Tannin is unique to red wine, since white wines ferment without skins. In wine, tannin is not necessarily a flavour but a textural astringent taste.

Tannin comes from two sources: grape skins and seeds, and from new wood barrels.

To taste tannin in wine, focus on the texture on your tongue. A high tannin wine will remove proteins from your tongue, causing a drying and puckering sensation. This sensation is often described as 'grippy'. High tannin wines act as palate cleansers to rich, fatty meats; cheeses; and pasta dishes. This is why they are often served with food.

ALCOHOL

The alcohol in wine comes from yeast converting grape must (sugar) into ethanol. Alcohol may also be added to a wine, which is called fortifying.

Alcohol plays an important role in wine aromas. It's the vehicle by which aromas travel from the surface of the wine to your nose. Alcohol also adds viscosity and body to wine. You can sense alcohol in the back of your throat as a burning sensation.

A 'HOT' WINE: Alcohol level is often described as a temperature because of how it feels in your throat. A 'hot' wine has higher alcohol.

LOW	MEDIUM-LOW	MEDIUM	MEDIUM-HIGH	HIGH
●○○○○	●●○○○	●●●○○	●●●●○	●●●●●
Below 10% ABV	10–11.5% ABV	11.5–13.5% ABV	13.5–15% ABV	Over 15% ABV

BODY

Body is not a scientific term, but a categorization of style from lightest to boldest. The four characteristics of sweetness, acidity, tannin and alcohol each affect how light or bold a wine will taste.

TIP: Imagine the difference between light- and full-bodied wines like the difference between skimmed and full-fat milk.

LIGHTER WINES
MORE ACIDITY
LOWER ALCOHOL
LESS TANNIN
LESS SWEET

BOLDER WINES
LESS ACIDITY
HIGHER ALCOHOL
MORE TANNIN
SWEETER

You can use terms like 'light-bodied' or 'full-bodied' to describe the style of wine you want to drink.

Tasting Wine

HOW TO TASTE: LOOK

HOW TO TASTE: SMELL

HOW TO TASTE: TASTE

HOW TO TASTE:
CONCLUDE

The 4-step wine tasting method is a professional tasting technique that focuses a taster's ability to separate and identify key characteristics in a wine and improve flavour and taste memory.

HOW TO TASTE
WINE

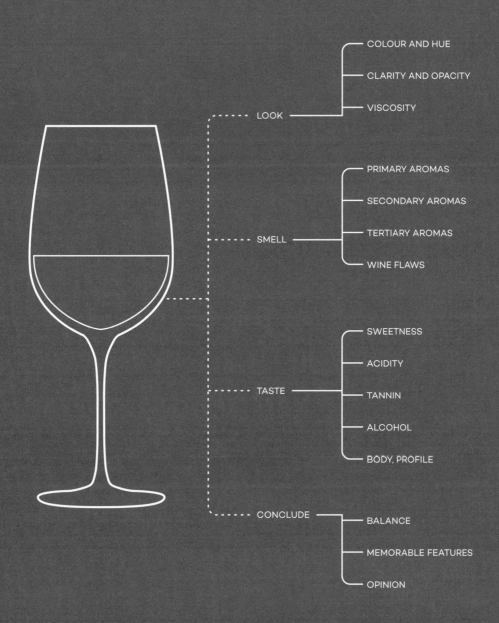

LOOK
- COLOUR AND HUE
- CLARITY AND OPACITY
- VISCOSITY

SMELL
- PRIMARY AROMAS
- SECONDARY AROMAS
- TERTIARY AROMAS
- WINE FLAWS

TASTE
- SWEETNESS
- ACIDITY
- TANNIN
- ALCOHOL
- BODY, PROFILE

CONCLUDE
- BALANCE
- MEMORABLE FEATURES
- OPINION

HOW TO TASTE: LOOK

The 4 steps of wine tasting are: **look**, **smell**, **taste** and **conclude**.

HOW TO TASTE WINE: LOOK

The colour in wine is a scientif-ically complex topic. Fortunately, a seasoned taster can learn to identify clues about a wine just from inspecting the **colour**, **intensity**, **opacity** and **viscosity**.

For a tasting size, pour a 75 ml serving. Attempt to view the wine with natural light over a white surface, such as a napkin or a piece of paper.

INSPECT: Angle the glass over a white backdrop and inspect the colour, intensity and hue at the rim of the glass.

SWIRL: Swirl the wine to see the viscosity. Viscous wines have higher alcohol and/or residual sugar.

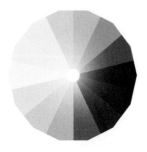  

COLOUR: We look at the hue and compare it not necessarily to all wines but to other examples of the same wine—in that way we can see how it differs in terms of both variety and production.

INTENSITY: Observe the wine from the rim to the middle. You will see small differences in colour and clarity of a wine based on several factors, including variety, production and age.

WINE TEARS: Wine 'legs' or 'tears' is a phenomenon called the Marangoni effect caused by fluid surface tension. Slow-moving 'tears' indicate higher alcohol levels but do not signify quality.

THE COLOUR OF WINE

CLEAR: UN-OAKED AND
COOL CLIMATE WINES

HUE: GREEN TO COPPER

DEEP GOLD: OAK-AGED
AND LATE HARVEST WINES

winefolly.com / learn / basics / tasting-wine / wine-color

PALE PLATINUM: A nearly clear white wine that refracts in the light will likely be young and not aged in oak.

MEDIUM LEMON: Several white wines have green hints in their colour, including Grüner Veltliner and Sauvignon Blanc.

DEEP GOLD: Oak aging will often give a white wine a deeper golden hue due to the natural oxidation that happens while it ages in barrels.

PALE COLOUR:
LESS PIGMENT

A RED TINT:
HIGHER ACIDITY

A BLUE-VIOLET TINT:
LOWER ACIDITY

PALE GARNET: Pale red wines contain less of the red pigment anthocyanin. Pinot Noir, Gamay, Grenache and Zinfandel are naturally more pale in colour.

MEDIUM RED: Wines that tint red typically have higher acidity than wines that tint blue-violet. Merlot, Sangiovese, Tempranillo and Nebbiolo tend to tint red.

DEEP PURPLE: Opaque red wines contain more pigment. Aglianico, Malbec, Mourvèdre, Petite Sirah, Syrah and Touriga Nacional contain more anthocyanin.

HOW TO TASTE: SMELL

SMELL: Hold your glass just under your nose and sniff once to 'prime' your nose. Then swirl your wine once and smell again. This time, smell the wine longer and slower but just as delicately. Switch between sniffing and thinking.

AROMAS: Move your nose to different positions around the glass. Rich fruit aromas are generally found on the lower lip, and floral aromas and volatile esters can be smelled on the upper lip of the glass.

LEARN TO SWIRL: Swirling wine releases aroma compounds into the air.

OVERLOADED?: Neutralize your nose by sniffing your forearm.

PERFUME: Avoid wearing strong scents when actively tasting wine.

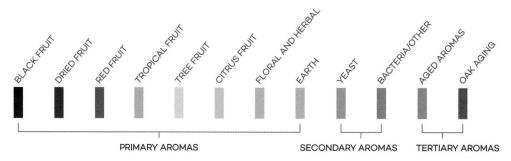

BLACK FRUIT — DRIED FRUIT — RED FRUIT — TROPICAL FRUIT — TREE FRUIT — CITRUS FRUIT — FLORAL AND HERBAL — EARTH — YEAST — BACTERIA/OTHER — AGED AROMAS — OAK AGING

PRIMARY AROMAS   SECONDARY AROMAS   TERTIARY AROMAS

PRIMARY AROMAS: Primary aromas come from grapes. Each variety has a range of possible aromas. For example, the white wine variety Sauvignon Blanc often smells like gooseberry or fresh-cut grass. Primary aromas range depending on the climate where the wine was made and how long the wine has aged.

SECONDARY AROMAS: Secondary aromas come from winemaking, specifically from reactions caused by wine yeast and bacteria.

For example, the aroma of butter found in Chardonnay is from a special bacteria.

TERTIARY AROMAS: Tertiary aromas come from ageing and controlled interaction with oxygen. For example, the nutty flavours in vintage Champagne and Sherry are from years of ageing.

WINE FAULTS: Some aromas you will encounter are faults. It's useful to learn them in order to know a good wine from a bad one.

HOW TO IDENTIFY WINE FAULTS

winefolly.com / learn / basics / tasting-wine / wine-faults

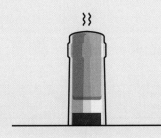

'Corked'

aka TCA Taint, 2,4,6-Trichloroanisole

Most corked wines smell strongly of wet cardboard, wet dog or a musty cellar. Sometimes, however, a corked wine will just lack aromas and have very subtle musty aromas. Don't worry, you can return a faulty wine.

Reduction

aka Mercaptans, Sulphur Compounds

Reduction in wines smells like boiled garlic and cabbage. It happens when a wine doesn't receive enough oxygen in bottle. Decanting should improve the smell, or you can stir your wine with a pure silver spoon.

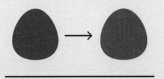

Oxidized

aka 'Maderized'

Oxidized wines smell flat and are brown in colour, much like an apple. Red wines will taste dry and bitter due to phenols (e.g., tannin) interacting with oxygen. Oxidized white wines typically have an apple cider-like odour.

UV Damage

aka 'Light Strike'

Light strike happens when wines sit under supermarket lighting for too long or are exposed to sun. Light strike causes reduction. Avoid light damage by storing your wines in the dark, and avoid 'shelf-aged' bottles.

Heat Damage

aka 'Cooked', 'Maderized'

Wine starts to deteriorate quickly at 82°F and cooks at around 90°F (32°C). Cooked wines can smell pleasant, like caramel and cooked fruits, but they will taste flat with no beginning, middle or end. Heat damage also causes browning.

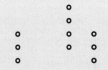

Spritz and Bubbles

(in a non-sparkling wine)

Occasionally, wines will ferment again in the bottle. This is easy to identify by the presence of spritz in a wine that's supposed to be still. These wines will also typically be a little hazy, due to yeast and protein particles.

HOW TO TASTE: TASTE

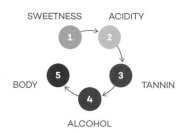

SWEETNESS   ACIDITY
1   2
BODY   5   3   TANNIN
4
ALCOHOL

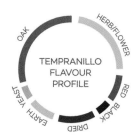

TEMPRANILLO FLAVOUR PROFILE

OAK · HERB/FLOWER · RED · BLACK · DRIED · EARTH · YEAST

TASTE: Try coating your mouth with a larger sip of wine followed by several smaller sips so that you can isolate and pick out flavours.

Try to pick out at least 3 fruit flavours and 3 other flavours— one at a time.

TIP: Spitting is more common at professional tastings.

IDENTIFY: Identify where the basic wine traits hit your palate:

Sweetness is toward the front.

Acidity makes your mouth water.

Tannin is textural and dries your mouth out like a wet tea bag.

Alcohol feels like heat in the back of your throat.

PROFILE: Now that you've tasted the wine, create a mental profile (or write one down) of the wine. Try to organize the flavours and aromas by their category. For example, if you taste vanilla, it might be due to oak.

TIP: You can cross-reference the variety section of this book for hints on how to categorize flavours.

WINE EVOLVES ON YOUR PALATE

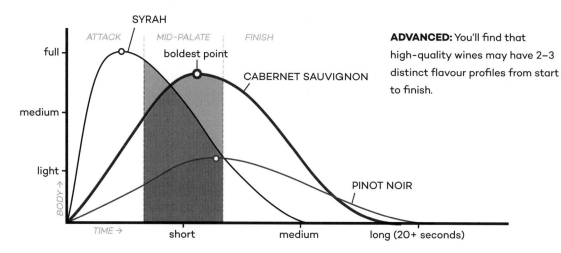

ATTACK   MID-PALATE   FINISH

SYRAH

full

boldest point

CABERNET SAUVIGNON

medium

light

PINOT NOIR

BODY →

TIME →   short   medium   long (20+ seconds)

ADVANCED: You'll find that high-quality wines may have 2–3 distinct flavour profiles from start to finish.

TASTE PREFERENCES ARE GENETIC

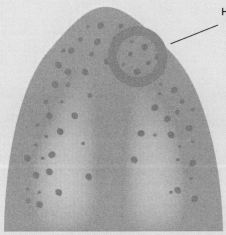

How many taste buds are within the area of one hole punch on your tongue?

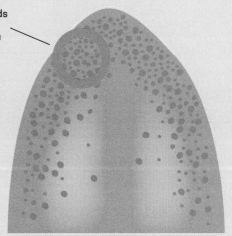

NON-SENSITIVE

HYPERSENSITIVE

Non-sensitive

10–25% of people

Less than 15 taste buds. You can handle spicy food and love the richest, boldest flavours. Bitterness doesn't bother you because you can't taste it at all. You're primed for drinking the most intense wines in the world.

Average Taster

50–75% of people

15–30 taste buds. You can taste bitterness like tannin just fine, but it doesn't make you wince in pain. You're capable of loving most wines. Improve your palate simply by slowing down and paying attention to nuances.

Hypersensitive

"Supertaster": 10–25% of people

30+ taste buds. Everything tastes intense: salty, sweet, sour, oily and bitter. You are not a fan of bitterness. The good thing is, sensitivity makes you a more conscientious eater. You'll lean toward delicate, smooth wines.

FACT: Asians, Africans and South Americans have a higher proportion of supertasting genetics than Caucasians.

FACT: Women are over two times more likely to be supertasters than men.

IDEA: The #1 way to improve your sense of taste is to spend more time smelling and identifying aromas.

HOW TO TASTE: CONCLUDE

bleh   meh   yeah   last meal

BALANCE: Now that you've tasted the wine, you can evaluate it. Do all the traits in the wine balance one another?

TIP: A wine that's out of balance will have characteristics that overpower other flavours in the wine, for example, a jarring acidic flavour that dominates the taste.

IMPROVE YOUR MEMORY: Note a few key traits of the wine and commit them to memory:

Traits or flavours specific to the grape variety.

Flavours or traits unique to the region, vintage, or producer.

YOUR OPINION: Take your time with wines that you enjoy. Identify what you prefer about them over other wines. You'll find yourself to be more articulate when seeking new wines.

At Wine Folly, we use a simple 4-point rating system with a focus on drinkability. A 'last meal' is so good you can die happy.

BLIND TASTING

Practise blind tasting with your friends. Have your friends each bring a bottle of wine in a bag or wrapped in tin foil. Then pour tastes of each wine and go around the table discussing characteristics to identify each wine.

TIP: It's easiest to start blind tasting with single-varietal wines. Then work up to blends.

TIP: Set up your tasting in a well-lit room to improve your visual assessment.

TASTING IDEAS

REGIONAL COMPARISON: Try the same variety over several regions to see how geography influences flavour.

VINTAGE COMPARISON: Find a series of vintages by a producer for a specific wine to learn how wine changes year to year.

QUALITY COMPARISON: Put together a lineup of similar wines that vary in price to see how quality varies.

DUNN VINEYARDS CAB. HOWELL MTN.
2002, TASTED 2009 w/ J. & D.

HAZY RUBY TO GARNET RIM.
VERY BRIGHT. MED. VISCOSITY WITH
STAINED TEARS.

BOLD AROMAS. DRIED BLACK CURRANT,
RED PLUM, TRICOLOR PEPPER, SAGE,
CRUSHED GRAVEL, CEDAR PLANK &
LICORICE. ALL WRAPPED UP IN
WINTERGREEN.

TASTED   LIGHTER THAN EXPECTED
MODERATE ACIDITY, MODERATE FINE
TANNIN. TASTED OF BLACK CHERRY,
WINTERGREEN & RARE STEAK.
SMOKY SWEET FINISH.

DRANK ON EQUINOX. WONDER IF THAT
HAS ANYTHING TO DO WITH IT. SERVER
BUTCHERED THE CAPSULE. IT WAS
CUTE.

WILL TRY TO SAVE NEXT BOTTLE FOR 2015!

WHAT YOU TASTED/DRANK
Producer, region, variety, vintage,
and any special designation.

WHEN YOU TASTED IT
Wine changes as it ages.

YOUR OPINION
This is what really matters.

WHAT YOU SAW
Will help identify winning themes.

WHAT YOU SMELLED
Be specific.

TIP: Try listing the most obvious
flavours first. This helps create a
hierarchy of importance.

WHAT YOU TASTED
Since we 'taste' so much with our
nose, add structural notes here, as
well as anything unique that you
didn't get in the smell.

WHAT YOU DID
Because wine is an experience.

TASTING PLACE MATS: Available
in our resources section online:

http://winefolly.com/resources/tasting-mats

Handling Wine

WINE GLASSES — Different types of wine glasses and tips on picking glassware.

SERVING WINE — How to open and decant still and sparkling wines.

WINE TEMPERATURE — Wine temperature best practices.

WINE STORAGE — Tips on storing wine short and long term.

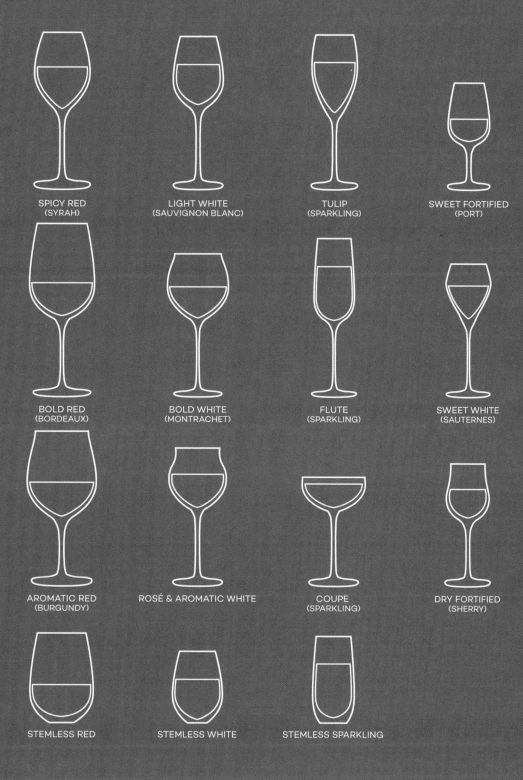

SPICY RED
(SYRAH)

LIGHT WHITE
(SAUVIGNON BLANC)

TULIP
(SPARKLING)

SWEET FORTIFIED
(PORT)

BOLD RED
(BORDEAUX)

BOLD WHITE
(MONTRACHET)

FLUTE
(SPARKLING)

SWEET WHITE
(SAUTERNES)

AROMATIC RED
(BURGUNDY)

ROSÉ & AROMATIC WHITE

COUPE
(SPARKLING)

DRY FORTIFIED
(SHERRY)

STEMLESS RED

STEMLESS WHITE

STEMLESS SPARKLING

WINE GLASSES

There are many different wine glasses to choose from.   Here are a few facts about wine glasses to help you decide what glassware is best for you.

Hold stemmed glasses by the stem and close to the foot.

Lead-free crystal glassware is dishwasher-safe.

Leaded crystal contains anywhere from 1% to 30% lead oxide. Fine crystal is 24% or more. Leaded crystal is not hazardous unless wine is stored in it for many days.

Buying wine glasses? Stick to 2 glass styles most suited to your drinking habits.

Stemmed v. stemless? Stems do not affect aroma or taste.

CRYSTAL V. GLASS

Crystal stemware refracts light due to its mineral content. Minerals also strengthen crystal, allowing it to be spun very thin. Traditionally, crystal glassware is leaded, but today there are several lead-free options made with magnesium and zinc. Most lead-free crystal is dishwasher safe. However, leaded crystal glasses are porous and should be hand washed with fragrance-free soap.

Standard glass is technically more fragile than crystal but it's spun thicker to make it more durable. Regular glass is dishwasher-safe.

HOW THE SHAPE AFFECTS TASTE

The bowl of a glass affects aroma intensity while the rim affects how much wine hits your palate.

IDEAL FOR DELICATE, AROMATIC WINES

A LARGE ROUND BOWL collects more aromas from the larger exposed wine surface.

IDEAL FOR SPICY, BOLD WINES

A NARROW BOWL collects less aromas and has less wine surface exposed to air.

CHOOSING GLASSWARE

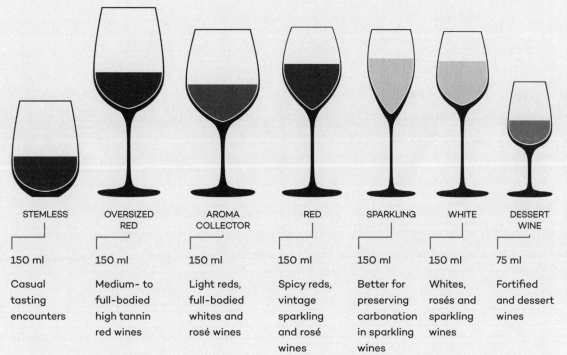

winefolly.com / learn / basics / handling / wine glasses

STEMLESS	OVERSIZED RED	AROMA COLLECTOR	RED	SPARKLING	WHITE	DESSERT WINE
150 ml	150 ml	150 ml	150 ml	150 ml	150 ml	75 ml
Casual tasting encounters	Medium- to full-bodied high tannin red wines	Light reds, full-bodied whites and rosé wines	Spicy reds, vintage sparkling and rosé wines	Better for preserving carbonation in sparkling wines	Whites, rosés and sparkling wines	Fortified and dessert wines

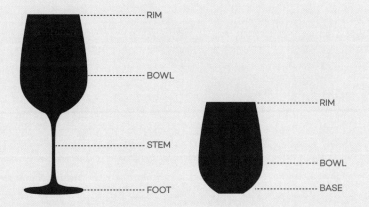

RIM

BOWL

STEM

FOOT

RIM

BOWL

BASE

SERVING WINE

The fundamentals of opening, pouring, serving and decanting wine:

OPENING STILL WINE

INSERT SLIGHTLY
OFF-CENTRE

95%

150 ML

REMOVE THE FOIL: It doesn't matter if you cut the foil above or below the lip, although tradition is to cut below.

THE WORM: Insert the worm off-centre and rotate the screw until the worm is about 95% of the way in. Slowly pull the cork out to reduce breakage.

STANDARD POUR: The standard serving size for wine is about 150–180 ml. Dry wines average 130–175 calories per glass depending on alcohol level.

OPENING SPARKLING WINE

CORK

CAGE

TAB

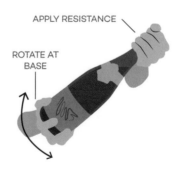

APPLY RESISTANCE

ROTATE AT
BASE

HOLD BOTTLE
AT AN ANGLE
AND IT WON'T
BUBBLE OVER

45°

THE CAGE: Remove the foil and untwist tab 6 times. Keep your thumb on cage and cork—they will come off together.

TWIST: With 1 hand firmly holding the cork and cage, use your other hand to rotate the bottom of the bottle.

RELEASE: When the cork pushes, resist it and slowly release it. Keep bottle at an angle for a second or two after you remove the cork.

AERATING WINE TO IMPROVE FLAVOUR

Decanting introduces oxygen to wine. This simple step oxidizes stinky aroma compounds into less detectable smells. It also reduces the concentration of certain acids and tannins, making wine taste smoother. In short, it's magic.

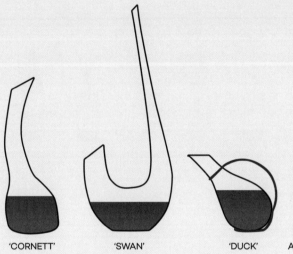

'CORNETT'   'SWAN'   'DUCK'   AERATOR   STANDARD

WHICH DECANTER?: Get one you love. It's wise to get one that's easy to fill, pour and rinse. A wine aerator is technically more efficient although not as stately.

POUR: For increased air-to-wine contact, pour wine so it distributes on the sides of the glass as it fills.

WAIT: The bolder and more concentrated the wine, the longer you should wait. 15–30 minutes is a good starting point.

WHAT TO DECANT: All red wines can be aerated. An aerated wine won't store open for long, so be sure to decant only what you plan to drink.

TIP: Smell sulphur? Don't worry, it's not sulphites. It just means your wine is 'reductive' (see Wine Faults, pg. 17). Decanting will improve the smell and so will stirring the wine with a silver spoon.

WINE TEMPERATURE

SERVING TEMPERATURE

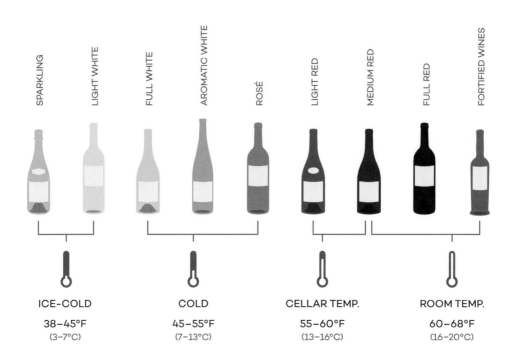

| SPARKLING | LIGHT WHITE | FULL WHITE | AROMATIC WHITE | ROSÉ | LIGHT RED | MEDIUM RED | FULL RED | FORTIFIED WINES |

ICE-COLD
38–45°F
(3–7°C)

COLD
45–55°F
(7–13°C)

CELLAR TEMP.
55–60°F
(13–16°C)

ROOM TEMP.
60–68°F
(16–20°C)

It's useful to note that wines served at room temperature are served at 60–68°F, which is cooler than most homes.

TOO COLD: Your wine might be served too cold if it's lacking aroma and tastes sour. This is a common problem for white wines stored in the refrigerator. Cup the bowl with your hands to warm your glass.

TOO HOT: Your wine might be too hot if the aroma burns your nose and smells medicinal. This is common with higher alcohol red wines that are stored in ambient home temperatures. Cool the bottle for 15 minutes.

WINE STORAGE

STORING OPEN WINE

Wines quickly deteriorate when exposed to oxygen or ambient home temperatures. So store open wines in a chiller at 50–55°F (10–13°C). If you don't have a wine chiller, store open wines in your fridge and let them warm up for about an hour before serving.

VACUUM CAP

Recorking a wine stops outside oxygen from getting in, but it won't remove the oxygen inside. A wine preserver such as a vacuum pump or argon gas preserver will keep your wine fresh longer.

	1–3 DAYS
	1 WEEK
	3–5 DAYS
	1 WEEK
	1 WEEK
	3–5 DAYS
	3–5 DAYS
	3–5 DAYS
	1 MONTH

AGEING WINE

The ideal storage temperature is 50–55°F and 75% humidity.

Wine ages four times faster stored in a pantry or closet. Bottles stored in variable temperature environments are also more likely to develop wine faults. So if you plan to age wine for longer than a year, look into purchasing a wine fridge or related cellaring solution.

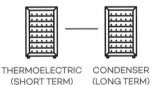

THERMOELECTRIC (SHORT TERM)   CONDENSER (LONG TERM)

There are 2 types of wine fridges: thermoelectric and condenser. Thermoelectric chillers fluctuate with temperature but are quieter. Condenser-type chillers are louder and require maintenance intervals but are more temperature accurate.

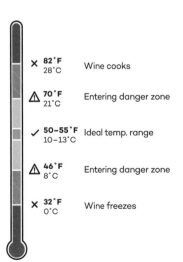

✕ 82°F 28°C   Wine cooks
⚠ 70°F 21°C   Entering danger zone
✓ 50–55°F 10–13°C   Ideal temp. range
⚠ 46°F 8°C   Entering danger zone
✕ 32°F 0°C   Wine freezes

Food and Wine Pairing

FLAVOUR PAIRING THEORY

CHEESE PAIRING

MEAT PAIRING

VEGETABLE PAIRING

HERB/SPICE PAIRING

Food pairing is the practice of creating harmonious pairings by considering flavour, texture, aroma and intensity. Learning to pair wine with food opens up a new range of wines to enjoy and explore.

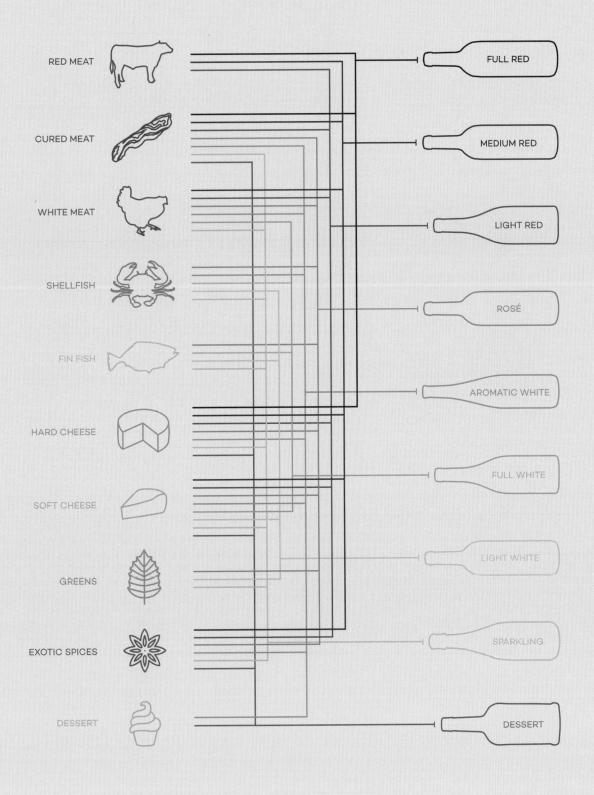

RED MEAT

CURED MEAT

WHITE MEAT

SHELLFISH

FIN FISH

HARD CHEESE

SOFT CHEESE

GREENS

EXOTIC SPICES

DESSERT

FULL RED

MEDIUM RED

LIGHT RED

ROSÉ

AROMATIC WHITE

FULL WHITE

LIGHT WHITE

SPARKLING

DESSERT

FLAVOUR PAIRING THEORY

Flavour pairing is the practice of finding what foods go well together by paying attention to taste, aroma, texture, colour, temperature and intensity.

MANY SHARED COMPOUNDS

FEW SHARED COMPOUNDS

CONGRUENT V. COMPLEMENTARY

Flavours match together in a congruent or complementary manner. Congruent pairings have many shared compounds that combine together and intensify. Complementary pairings oppose and counteract each other to create balance.

You can create amazing pairings by employing congruent pairings to amplify harmonious flavours and complementary pairings to counteract discordant flavours.

FOOD AND WINE PAIRING TIPS

ACIDIC FOOD: High acidity foods make lower acidity wines taste flat. Match high acidity foods with high acidity wines.

RICH FOOD: A high tannin red wine acts as a palate cleanser to rich, fatty proteins.

SPICY FOOD: A cold sweet wine with low alcohol will counteract the burn of spiciness.

PUNGENT FOOD: Pungent flavours like Gorgonzola match with wines that have higher acidity and sweetness.

BITTER FOOD: Bitter foods magnify the bitterness of tannin. Try pairing bitter foods with low or no tannin wines with salinity and sweetness.

SWEET FOOD: Sweet foods often make dry wines taste bitter. Try matching sweet foods with a sweet wine.

WINE PAIRING CONSIDERATIONS

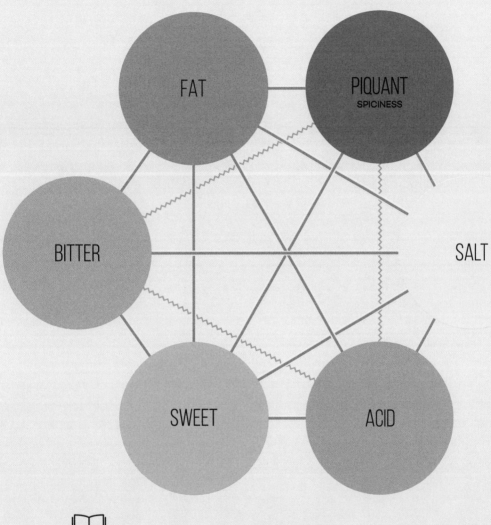

FAT

PIQUANT
SPICINESS

BITTER

SALT

SWEET

ACID

The 6 tastes are just a portion of what humans sense. Other tastes include fizziness, umami (meaty), numbness, electricity, soapiness, calcium and coolness (menthol).

—— HARMONIOUS MATCH
〰〰 DISCORDANT MATCH

BALANCE: Create balanced pairings by matching the intensity of the wine with the intensity of the food.

33

CHEESE PAIRING

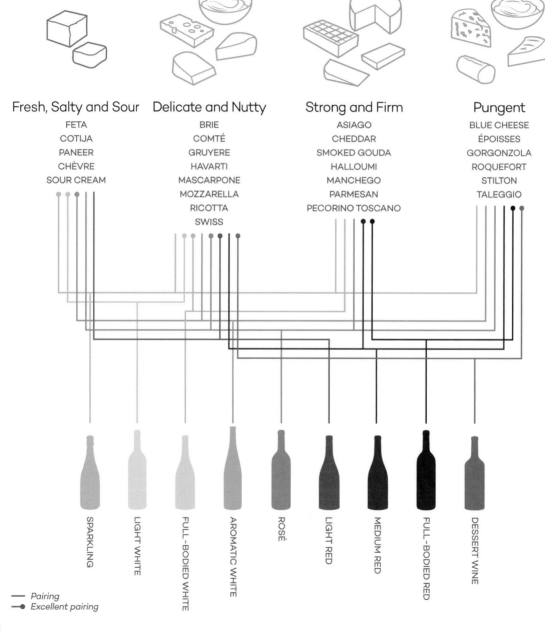

Fresh, Salty and Sour
FETA
COTIJA
PANEER
CHÈVRE
SOUR CREAM

Delicate and Nutty
BRIE
COMTÉ
GRUYERE
HAVARTI
MASCARPONE
MOZZARELLA
RICOTTA
SWISS

Strong and Firm
ASIAGO
CHEDDAR
SMOKED GOUDA
HALLOUMI
MANCHEGO
PARMESAN
PECORINO TOSCANO

Pungent
BLUE CHEESE
ÉPOISSES
GORGONZOLA
ROQUEFORT
STILTON
TALEGGIO

SPARKLING
LIGHT WHITE
FULL-BODIED WHITE
AROMATIC WHITE
ROSÉ
LIGHT RED
MEDIUM RED
FULL-BODIED RED
DESSERT WINE

—— Pairing
—● Excellent pairing

MEAT PAIRING

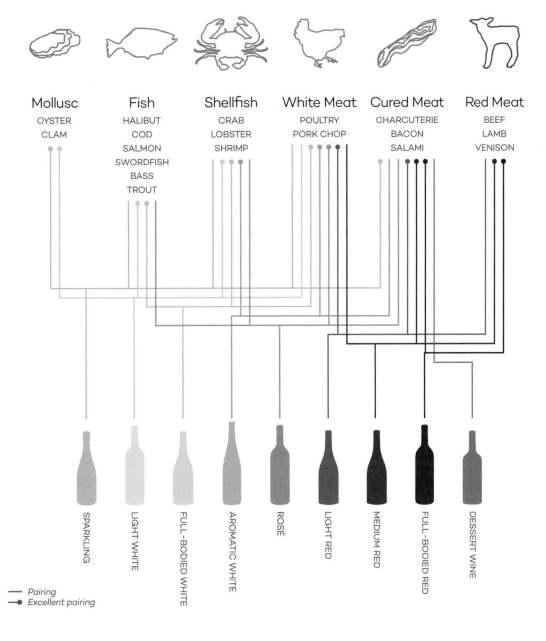

winefolly.com / learn / basics / food-and-wine / meat

Mollusc
OYSTER
CLAM

Fish
HALIBUT
COD
SALMON
SWORDFISH
BASS
TROUT

Shellfish
CRAB
LOBSTER
SHRIMP

White Meat
POULTRY
PORK CHOP

Cured Meat
CHARCUTERIE
BACON
SALAMI

Red Meat
BEEF
LAMB
VENISON

SPARKLING

LIGHT WHITE

FULL-BODIED WHITE

AROMATIC WHITE

ROSÉ

LIGHT RED

MEDIUM RED

FULL-BODIED RED

DESSERT WINE

— Pairing
—•— Excellent pairing

35

VEGETABLE PAIRING

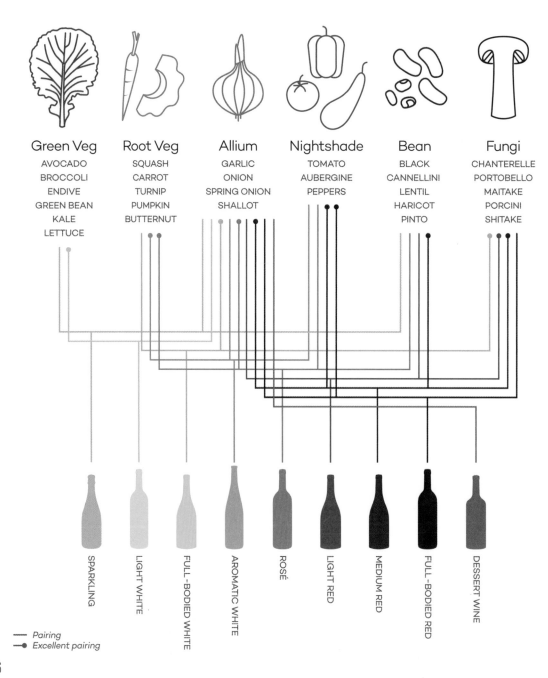

Green Veg
AVOCADO
BROCCOLI
ENDIVE
GREEN BEAN
KALE
LETTUCE

Root Veg
SQUASH
CARROT
TURNIP
PUMPKIN
BUTTERNUT

Allium
GARLIC
ONION
SPRING ONION
SHALLOT

Nightshade
TOMATO
AUBERGINE
PEPPERS

Bean
BLACK
CANNELLINI
LENTIL
HARICOT
PINTO

Fungi
CHANTERELLE
PORTOBELLO
MAITAKE
PORCINI
SHITAKE

SPARKLING
LIGHT WHITE
FULL-BODIED WHITE
AROMATIC WHITE
ROSÉ
LIGHT RED
MEDIUM RED
FULL-BODIED RED
DESSERT WINE

— Pairing
—● Excellent pairing

HERB/SPICE PAIRING

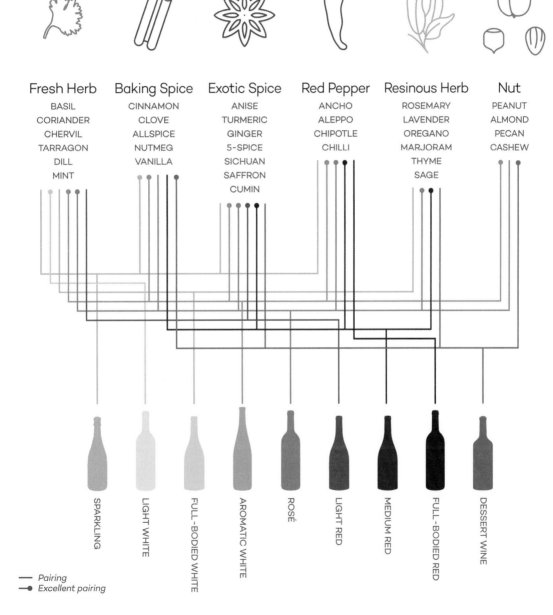

Fresh Herb
BASIL
CORIANDER
CHERVIL
TARRAGON
DILL
MINT

Baking Spice
CINNAMON
CLOVE
ALLSPICE
NUTMEG
VANILLA

Exotic Spice
ANISE
TURMERIC
GINGER
5-SPICE
SICHUAN
SAFFRON
CUMIN

Red Pepper
ANCHO
ALEPPO
CHIPOTLE
CHILLI

Resinous Herb
ROSEMARY
LAVENDER
OREGANO
MARJORAM
THYME
SAGE

Nut
PEANUT
ALMOND
PECAN
CASHEW

SPARKLING
LIGHT WHITE
FULL-BODIED WHITE
AROMATIC WHITE
ROSÉ
LIGHT RED
MEDIUM RED
FULL-BODIED RED
DESSERT WINE

— Pairing
—● Excellent pairing

Styles of Wine

Styles of Wine

SPARKLING WINE

LIGHT-BODIED WHITE WINE

FULL-BODIED WHITE WINE

AROMATIC WHITE WINE

ROSÉ WINE

LIGHT-BODIED RED WINE

MEDIUM-BODIED RED WINE

FULL-BODIED RED WINE

DESSERT WINE

Wines in this book are organized from lightest to boldest within nine different styles. This categorization method is designed to help you quickly identify what a wine tastes like without having to try it. Occasionally, you may come across a wine that doesn't fit neatly into this categorization method. It is an exception to the rule.

SECTION DETAILS

NAME

PRIMARY FLAVOURS

aka (ALSO KNOWN AS)
Other varietal names or regional names that are synonymous with wine.

PRONUNCIATION

CHARACTERISTICS
See pgs. 8–11 for details.

🌩 VARIETY

🍷 WINE/BLEND

WINE FOLLY LINK
Where to go online for more information.

ADDITIONAL FLAVOURS
See pg. 16 for details.

POSSIBLE FLAVOURS
Find out more about flavours and aromas on pg 16.

PRIMARY
- ■ BLACK FRUIT
- ■ DRIED FRUIT
- ■ RED FRUIT
- TROPICAL FRUIT
- TREE FRUIT
- CITRUS FRUIT
- FLORAL / HERBAL
- EARTH / OTHER

SECONDARY
- ■ YEAST
- ■ BACTERIA / OTHER

TERTIARY
- ■ OAK
- OTHER TERTIARY

SANGIOVESE

🔊 'San-jo Vay-zay'
aka: Chianti, Brunello, Nielluccio, Morellino

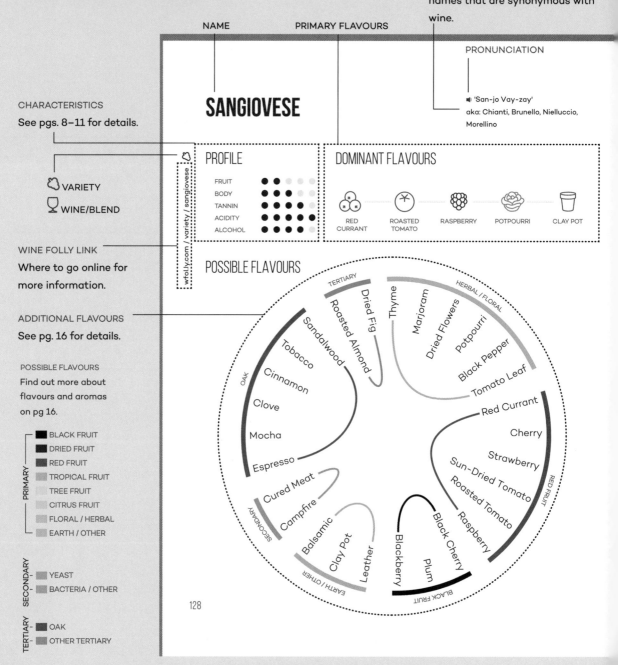

PROFILE

FRUIT	●●●○○
BODY	●●●●○
TANNIN	●●●●○
ACIDITY	●●●●●
ALCOHOL	●●●●○

wfolly.com / variety / sangiovese

DOMINANT FLAVOURS

RED CURRANT · ROASTED TOMATO · RASPBERRY · POTPOURRI · CLAY POT

POSSIBLE FLAVOURS

TERTIARY — Roasted Almond, Dried Fig
OAK — Sandalwood, Tobacco, Cinnamon, Clove, Mocha, Espresso
SECONDARY — Cured Meat, Campfire, Balsamic
EARTH / OTHER — Clay Pot, Leather
BLACK FRUIT — Blackberry, Plum, Black Cherry
RED FRUIT — Raspberry, Roasted Tomato, Sun-Dried Tomato, Strawberry, Cherry, Red Currant
HERBAL / FLORAL — Tomato Leaf, Black Pepper, Potpourri, Dried Flowers, Marjoram, Thyme

128

42

ORIGIN

WINE STATISTICS
Distribution and total world
acres based on statistics
from 2010–2014.

Origin: Italy

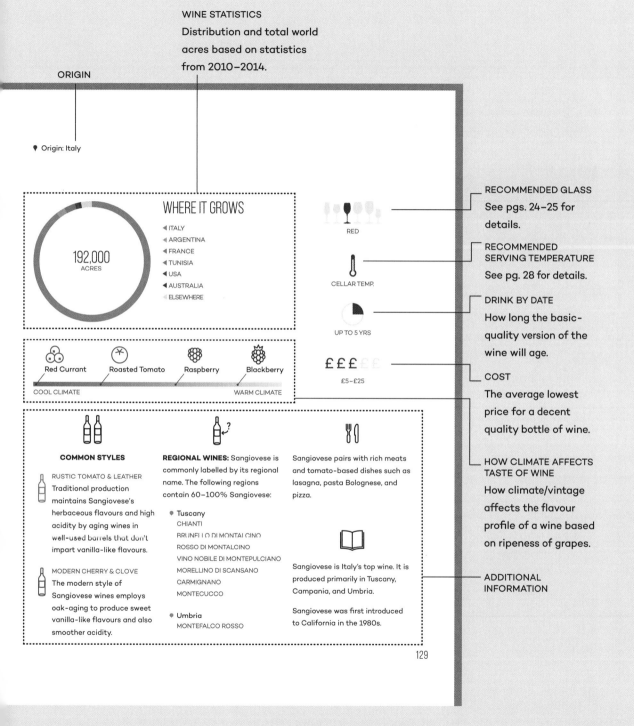

WHERE IT GROWS

192,000
ACRES

◀ ITALY
◀ ARGENTINA
◀ FRANCE
◀ TUNISIA
◀ USA
◀ AUSTRALIA
◀ ELSEWHERE

Red Currant   Roasted Tomato   Raspberry   Blackberry

COOL CLIMATE   WARM CLIMATE

RED

CELLAR TEMP.

UP TO 5 YRS

£ £ £ £ £
£5–£25

RECOMMENDED GLASS
See pgs. 24–25 for
details.

RECOMMENDED
SERVING TEMPERATURE
See pg. 28 for details.

DRINK BY DATE
How long the basic-
quality version of the
wine will age.

COST
The average lowest
price for a decent
quality bottle of wine.

HOW CLIMATE AFFECTS
TASTE OF WINE
How climate/vintage
affects the flavour
profile of a wine based
on ripeness of grapes.

ADDITIONAL
INFORMATION

COMMON STYLES

RUSTIC TOMATO & LEATHER
Traditional production
maintains Sangiovese's
herbaceous flavours and high
acidity by aging wines in
well-used barrels that don't
impart vanilla-like flavours.

MODERN CHERRY & CLOVE
The modern style of
Sangiovese wines employs
oak-aging to produce sweet
vanilla-like flavours and also
smoother acidity.

REGIONAL WINES: Sangiovese is
commonly labelled by its regional
name. The following regions
contain 60–100% Sangiovese:

● Tuscany
CHIANTI
BRUNELLO DI MONTALCINO
ROSSO DI MONTALCINO
VINO NOBILE DI MONTEPULCIANO
MORELLINO DI SCANSANO
CARMIGNANO
MONTECUCCO

● Umbria
MONTEFALCO ROSSO

Sangiovese pairs with rich meats
and tomato-based dishes such as
lasagna, pasta Bolognese, and
pizza.

Sangiovese is Italy's top wine. It is
produced primarily in Tuscany,
Campania, and Umbria.

Sangiovese was first introduced
to California in the 1980s.

129

43

Sparkling Wine

CAVA

CHAMPAGNE

LAMBRUSCO

PROSECCO

Sparkling wine is carbonated by yeast fermenting in an airtight container. The 2 most common sparkling winemaking methods are called 'traditional method' and 'tank method'. Sparkling wine is produced throughout the world and often follows the same winemaking methods and grape varieties found in Champagne.

DIFFERENT SPARKLING WINEMAKING METHODS

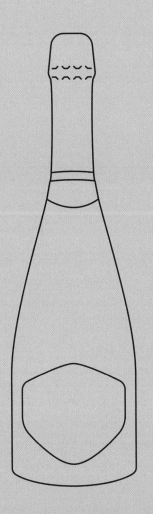

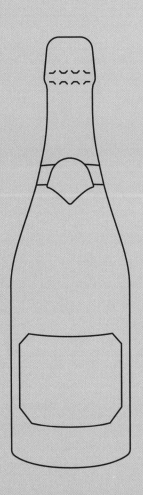

TANK 'CHARMAT' METHOD

EXAMPLE: Prosecco, Lambrusco

BUBBLES: Medium-size, spritzy bubbles and 2–4 atmospheres of pressure

TRADITIONAL METHOD

EXAMPLE: Champagne, Cava, Crémant, US sparkling wine, Metodo Classico (Italy), Cap Classique (South Africa)

BUBBLES: Small, persistent bubbles and 6–7 atmospheres of pressure

CAVA

winefolly.com / learn / wine / cava

PROFILE

FRUIT
BODY
DRY
ACIDITY
ALCOHOL

DOMINANT FLAVOURS

QUINCE — LIME — YELLOW APPLE — PEAR — ALMOND

POSSIBLE FLAVOURS

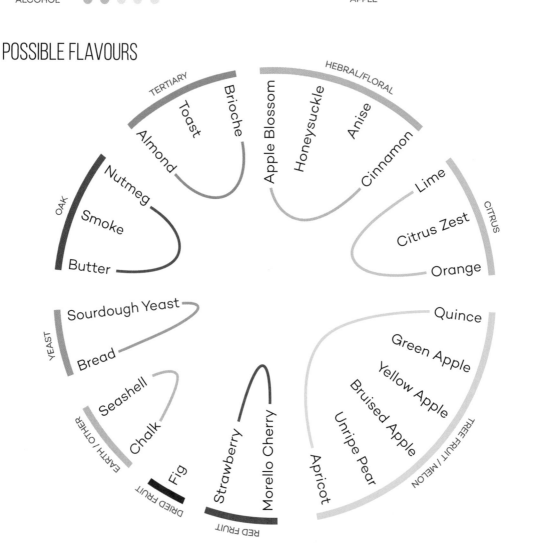

TERTIARY
Brioche
Toast
Almond

HEBRAL/FLORAL
Apple Blossom
Honeysuckle
Anise
Cinnamon

OAK
Nutmeg
Smoke
Butter

Lime
Citrus Zest
Orange
CITRUS

YEAST
Sourdough Yeast
Bread

Quince
Green Apple
Yellow Apple
Bruised Apple
Unripe Pear
Apricot
TREE FRUIT / MELON

EARTH / OTHER
Seashell
Chalk

Fig
DRIED FRUIT

Strawberry
Morello Cherry
RED FRUIT

46

📍 Origin: Spain

79,000
ACRES

WHERE IT'S MADE

◀ PENEDÈS, SPAIN
◀ [ELSEWHERE IN SPAIN]

Quince   Lemon   Orange   Apricot

COOL VINTAGE   WARM VINTAGE

SPARKLING

ICE-COLD

UP TO 2 YRS

£5–£10

winefolly.com / learn / winefolly.com / learn / wine / cava

CAVA GRAPES: There are 3 primary grapes of Cava:

 MACABEO
(aka Viura, Macabeu)
Adds floral, apricot and berry flavours.

 XARELLO
Adds acidity.

 PARELLADA
Adds quince, apple and citrus flavours.

QUALITY LEVELS: There are 3 quality levels, indicated by a sticker or band on the bottle:

 CAVA (STANDARD)
9 months min. ageing

 RESERVA
15 months min. ageing

 GRAN RESERVA
30 months min. ageing and vintage dated

Cava is versatile with food because of its palate-cleansing effect. Try it with chilli, huevos rancheros, nachos and tacos.

Cava DO (Denominación de Origen) is the only Spanish wine classification for a style of wine rather than a region. Still, around 95% of the production is in the Penedès region of Spain.

CHAMPAGNE

🔊 'sham-pain'
🛢 Traditional Method

PROFILE

FRUIT
BODY
BONE-DRY
ACIDITY
ALCOHOL

DOMINANT FLAVOURS

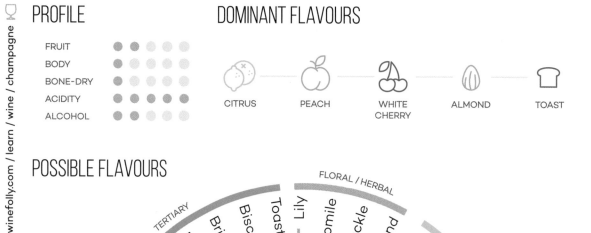

CITRUS　　PEACH　　WHITE CHERRY　　ALMOND　　TOAST

POSSIBLE FLAVOURS

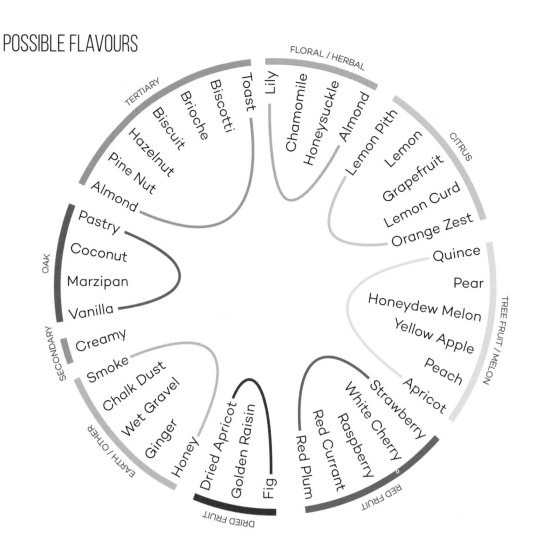

FLORAL / HERBAL

TERTIARY

Toast
Biscotti
Brioche
Biscuit
Hazelnut
Pine Nut
Almond
Pastry
Coconut
Marzipan
Vanilla
Creamy
Smoke
Chalk Dust
Wet Gravel
Ginger
Honey
Dried Apricot
Golden Raisin
Fig

Lily
Chamomile
Honeysuckle
Almond
Lemon Pith
Lemon
Grapefruit
Lemon Curd
Orange Zest
Quince
Pear
Honeydew Melon
Yellow Apple
Peach
Apricot
Strawberry
White Cherry
Raspberry
Red Currant
Red Plum

OAK

SECONDARY

EARTH / OTHER

DRIED FRUIT

RED FRUIT

TREE FRUIT / MELON

CITRUS

48

📍 Origin: Champagne, France

winefolly.com / learn / winefolly.com / learn / wine / champagne

WHERE IT'S MADE

◀ CHAMPAGNE, FRANCE

83,000
ACRES

Quince · Apple · Raspberry · Peach

COOL VINTAGE — WARM VINTAGE

FLUTE OR WHITE

ICE-COLD

10 YRS

£20+

GRAPES: Champagne produces both white and rosé wines using just these 3 grapes:

PINOT NOIR
Adds orange and red fruit flavours.

PINOT MEUNIER
Adds richness and yellow apple flavours.

CHARDONNAY
Adds citrus flavours and marzipan flavours.

COMMON STYLES

NON-VINTAGE
Consistent house-style wines

BLANC DE BLANCS
100% Chardonnay wines

BLANC DE NOIRS
P. Noir and P. Meunier wines

ROSÉ
Rosé wines with red fruit flavours

VINTAGE & SPECIAL CUVÉE
Aged Champagne wines

Non-vintage wines age for a minimum of 15 months.

Vintage Champagne ages for a minimum of 36 months.

Special cuvée Champagnes age an average of 6–7 years to develop nutty tertiary aromas.

More than 90% of Champagne is made in the brut style—with less than a half gram of sugar per glass.

49

LAMBRUSCO

🔊 'lam-broos-co'

🛢 Tank 'Charmat' Method

PROFILE

FRUIT ● ● ● ● ●
BODY ● ● ● ● ●
OFF-DRY ● ● ● ● ●
ACIDITY ● ● ● ● ●
ALCOHOL ● ● ● ● ●

DOMINANT FLAVOURS

STRAWBERRY   CHERRY   BLACKBERRY   RHUBARB   HIBISCUS

POSSIBLE FLAVOURS

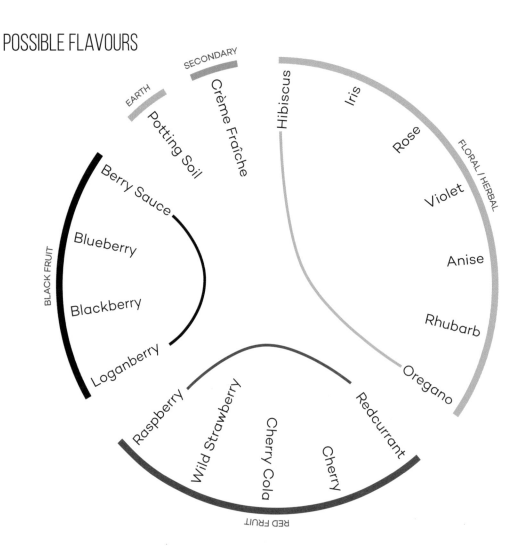

SECONDARY

EARTH

Crème Fraîche

Potting Soil

Hibiscus

Iris

Rose

FLORAL / HERBAL

Violet

Anise

Rhubarb

Berry Sauce

Blueberry

BLACK FRUIT

Blackberry

Loganberry

Oregano

Raspberry

Wild Strawberry

Cherry Cola

Cherry

Redcurrant

RED FRUIT

50

📍 Origin: northern Italy

WHERE IT GROWS

33,000
ACRES

◀ EMILIA-ROMAGNA AND LOMBARDY, ITALY

WHITE OR RED

COLD

UP TO 2 YRS

£5–£15

Rhubarb

Wild Strawberry

Sweet Cherry

Blackberry

COOL VINTAGE   WARM VINTAGE

SWEETNESS LEVELS

 DRY LAMBRUSCO
Look for the word 'Secco' on the label for a dry style.

OFF-DRY LAMBRUSCO
The word 'Semisecco' indicates an off-dry style.

SWEET LAMBRUSCO
The words 'Dolce' and 'Amabile' indicate a sweet style.

COMMON STYLES

 RED FRUIT & FLOWERS
A lighter style with these varieties/styles:

LAMBRUSCO DI SORBARA
LAMBRUSCO ROSATO (ROSÉ)

BLACK FRUIT & POTTING SOIL
A bolder style with these varieties:

LAMBRUSCO GRASPAROSSA
LAMBRUSCO SALAMINO DI SANTA CROCE
LAMBRUSCO REGGIANO

Quality Lambrusco wines are labeled DOC or 'Denominazione di Origine Controllata'. The other common classification is IGT, 'Indicazione Geografica Tipica'.

Lambrusco is the name of more than 13 indigenous wine grapes, each with unique characteristics. The 2 most planted Lambrusco varieties are Lambrusco Salamino and Lambrusco Grasparossa.

winefolly.com / learn / winefolly.com / learn / wine / lambrusco

PROSECCO

🔊 'pro-seh-co'
🛢 Tank 'Charmat' Method

PROFILE

FRUIT
BODY
DRY
ACIDITY
ALCOHOL

DOMINANT FLAVOURS

GREEN APPLE — HONEYDEW MELON — PEAR — HONEYSUCKLE — CREAM

POSSIBLE FLAVOURS

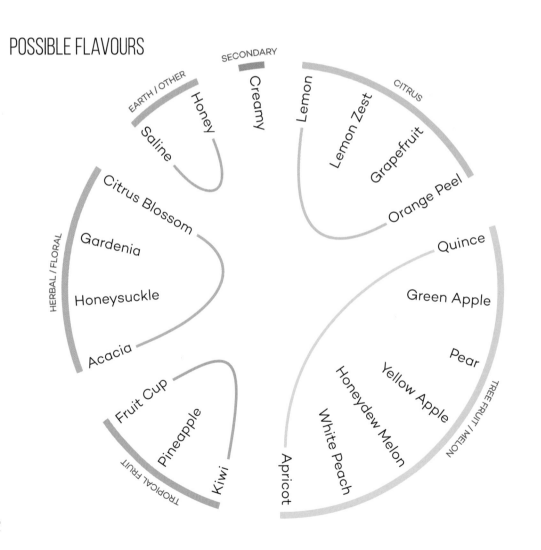

SECONDARY

Creamy

EARTH / OTHER

Honey
Saline

CITRUS

Lemon
Lemon Zest
Grapefruit
Orange Peel

HERBAL / FLORAL

Citrus Blossom
Gardenia
Honeysuckle
Acacia

TREE FRUIT / MELON

Quince
Green Apple
Pear
Yellow Apple
Honeydew Melon
White Peach
Apricot

TROPICAL FRUIT

Fruit Cup
Pineapple
Kiwi

♥ Origin: northern Italy

15,000
ACRES

WHERE IT'S MADE

◄ VENETO AND FRUILI, ITALY

WHITE

ICE-COLD

UP TO 2 YRS

£ £ £ £ £

£5–£10

| Quince | Green Apple | Ripe Pear | Apricot |

COOL VINTAGE   WARM VINTAGE

SWEETNESS LEVELS

 BRUT: 0–12 G/L RS
Up to a half gram of sugar
per glass

EXTRA DRY: 12–17 G/L RS
Just over a half gram of
sugar per glass

DRY: 17–32 G/L RS
Up to 1 gram of sugar per
glass

QUALITY LEVELS: There are 3
main quality levels of Prosecco:

⊘ PROSECCO
The most common type of
Prosecco available

⊘ PROSECCO SUPERIORE
A higher quality level based on
production standards

⊘ CONEGLIANO VALDOBBIADENE
AND COLLI ASOLANI
Two exceptional Prosecco
subregions offering
'millesimato' (single vintage)
Prosecco wines

Prosecco has about 3
atmospheres of pressure.

Try pairing with cured meats and
fruit-driven appetizers such as
prosciutto-wrapped melon.
Prosecco also pairs well with
middleweight Asian dishes such
as pad thai and Vietnamese
vermicelli noodles.

53

Light-Bodied White Wine

ALBARIÑO

GRÜNER VELTLINER

MUSCADET

PINOT GRIS (GRIGIO)

SAUVIGNON BLANC

SOAVE

VERMENTINO

Light-bodied white wines are known for their dry and refreshingly tart flavour. Most light-bodied white wines are meant to be enjoyed young when they have maximum acidity and bold fruit.

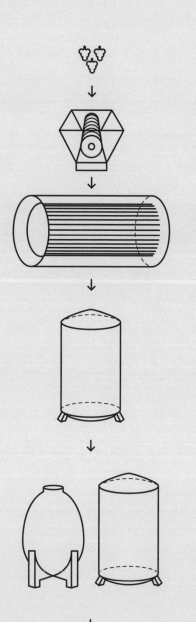

White or red wine grapes are collected and sorted.

Grape bunches are destemmed.

Grapes are pressed and separated from skins and seeds.

Juice ferments into wine without skins.

Wine is kept cool in storage tanks to settle and stabilize for a short period of time.

Wines are clarified, bottled and released shortly thereafter.

ALBARIÑO

🔊 'alba-reen-yo'
aka: Alvarinho

PROFILE

FRUIT	● ● ● ● ●
BODY	● ● ● ● ●
DRY	● ● ● ● ●
ACIDITY	● ● ● ● ●
ALCOHOL	● ● ● ● ●

DOMINANT FLAVOURS

LEMON — GRAPEFRUIT — NECTARINE — MELON — WET GRAVEL

POSSIBLE FLAVOURS

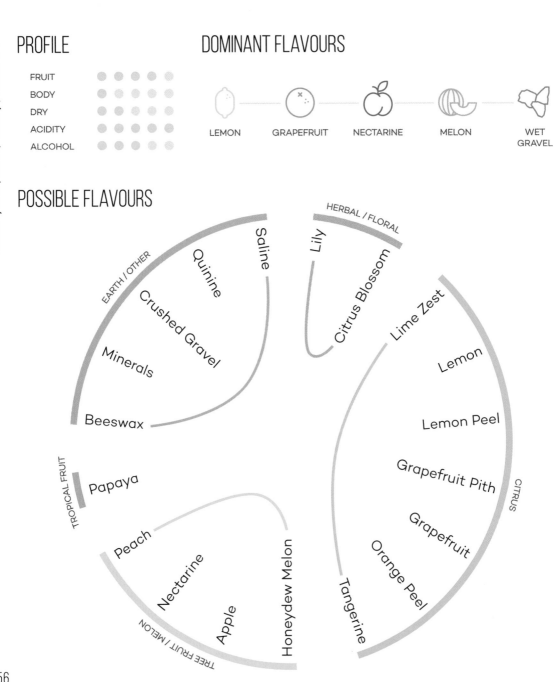

HERBAL / FLORAL
- Lily
- Citrus Blossom

EARTH / OTHER
- Saline
- Quinine
- Crushed Gravel
- Minerals
- Beeswax

CITRUS
- Lime Zest
- Lemon
- Lemon Peel
- Grapefruit Pith
- Grapefruit
- Orange Peel
- Tangerine

TROPICAL FRUIT
- Papaya
- Peach

TREE FRUIT / MELON
- Nectarine
- Apple
- Honeydew Melon

📍 Origin: Northern Portugal

19,000
ACRES

WHERE IT GROWS

◀ SPAIN
◀ PORTUGAL
◀ USA
◀ ELSEWHERE

WHITE

ICE-COLD

UP TO 2 YRS

£ £ £ £ £
£5–£15

Lemon   Grapefruit   Melon   Peach

COOL CLIMATE   WARM CLIMATE

REGIONS

RIAS BAIXAS, SPAIN
90% of the vineyards here are dedicated to Albariño. The Val do Salnés area is noted as one of the most classic subregions.

MINHO, PORTUGAL
Alvarinho is one of the grapes in Vinho Verde, which is a crisp, aromatic white wine that often has some spritz.

AROMAS

The melon and grapefruit aromas found in Albariño come from a group of aroma compounds called thiols. Thiols are commonly found in light white wines from cooler-climate growing regions, such as Sauvignon Blanc from New Zealand and France and Pinot Grigio from northern Italy.

Albariño is particularly well suited to Thai, Moroccan, and Indian cuisine.

THAI

MOROCCAN

INDIAN

57

GRÜNER VELTLINER

🔊 'GREW-ner FELT-lee-ner'

PROFILE

FRUIT
BODY
DRY
ACIDITY
ALCOHOL

DOMINANT FLAVOURS

YELLOW APPLE — GREEN PEAR — GREEN BEAN — CHERVIL — WHITE PEPPER

POSSIBLE FLAVOURS

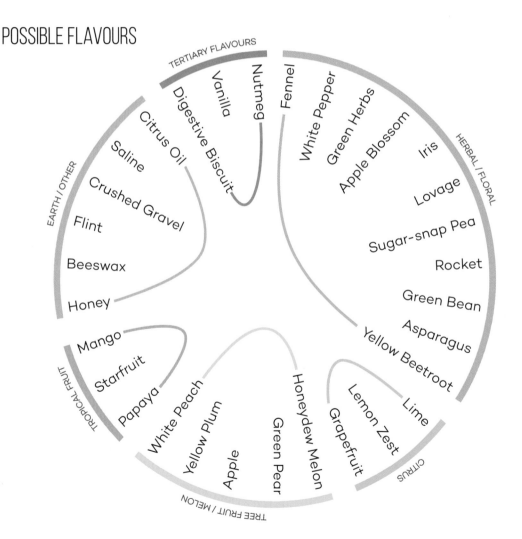

TERTIARY FLAVOURS

Nutmeg
Vanilla
Digestive Biscuit
Citrus Oil
Saline
Crushed Gravel
Flint
Beeswax
Honey

EARTH / OTHER

Mango
Starfruit
Papaya

TROPICAL FRUIT

White Peach
Yellow Plum
Apple
Green Pear
Honeydew Melon

TREE FRUIT / MELON

Grapefruit
Lemon Zest
Lime

CITRUS

Fennel
White Pepper
Green Herbs
Apple Blossom
Iris
Lovage
Sugar-snap Pea
Rocket
Green Bean
Asparagus
Yellow Beetroot

HERBAL / FLORAL

♥ Origin: Austria

WHERE IT GROWS

50,000 ACRES

◄ AUSTRIA
◄ SLOVAKIA
◄ CZECH REPUBLIC
◄ HUNGARY
◄ ELSEWHERE

WHITE

ICE-COLD

UP TO 2 YRS

£ £ £ £ £

£25–£30

winefolly.com/learn/winefolly.com/learn/variety/gruner-veltliner

Lime | Green Pear | Yellow Apple | Peach

COOL VINTAGE — WARM VINTAGE

QUALITY: There are 3 main quality levels of Austrian Grüner Veltliner:

LANDWEIN
Typically low alcohol wines made in bulk

QUALITÄTSWEIN
Austria's mark of quality for Grüner Veltliner

DAC

DAC
Subregional Qualitätswein with a light style, Classic, and a rich style, Reserve

COMMON STYLES

LIGHT & ZESTY
The most common and affordable style, known for tingling acidity and simple melon/lime flavours. DAC wines are labelled 'Classic'.

RICH, FRUITY AND PEPPERY
A richer style often labelled 'Reserve (DAC)' or 'Smaragd (from Wachau)' in Austria. Wines are dry and taste of honey, apple, smoke, mango and white pepper.

Grüner Veltliner pairs particularly well with aromatic vegetables, tofu, and Japanese cuisine.

GINGER

YUZU

WASABI

GREEN ONION

59

MUSCADET

PROFILE

FRUIT	●●●○○
BODY	●●●○○
BONE-DRY	●●●●●
ACIDITY	●●●●●
ALCOHOL	●●●○○

DOMINANT FLAVOURS

LIME — LEMON — GREEN APPLE — PEAR — SEASHELL

POSSIBLE FLAVOURS

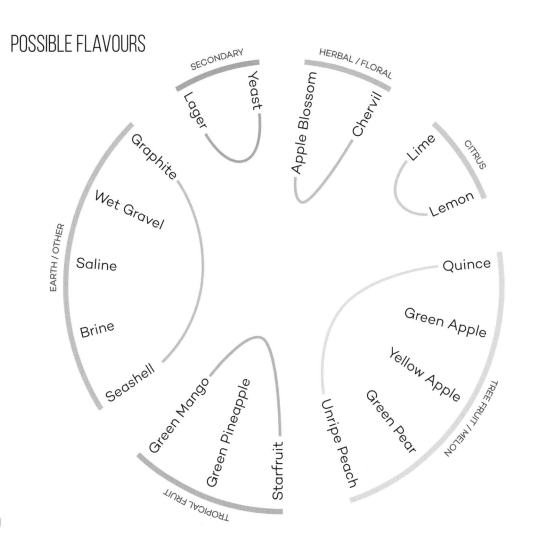

SECONDARY
Lager · Yeast

HERBAL / FLORAL
Apple Blossom · Chervil

CITRUS
Lime · Lemon

TREE FRUIT / MELON
Quince · Green Apple · Yellow Apple · Green Pear · Unripe Peach

TROPICAL FRUIT
Green Mango · Green Pineapple · Starfruit

EARTH / OTHER
Graphite · Wet Gravel · Saline · Brine · Seashell

● Origin: Loire, France

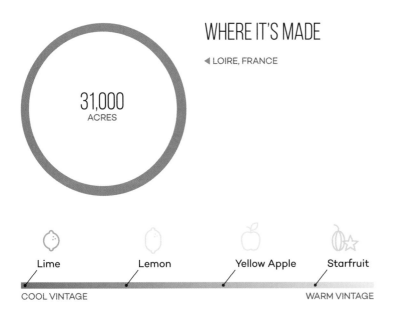

WHERE IT'S MADE

◀ LOIRE, FRANCE

31,000
ACRES

WHITE

ICE-COLD

UP TO 2 YRS

£ £ £ £ £
£5–£10

| Lime | Lemon | Yellow Apple | Starfruit |

COOL VINTAGE — WARM VINTAGE

winefolly.com / learn / winefolly.com / learn / wine / muscadet

MUSCADET GRAPE: Melon de Bourgogne or just Melon is the grape of the Muscadet region in France. Two regions make up over 90% of Muscadet wine:

 MUSCADET SÈVRE-ET-MAINE
This appellation produces over 70% of Muscadet wine.

 MUSCADET
This appellation has lower quality standards than Muscadet Sèvre-et-Maine.

ON THE LABEL: It's common to see the words 'sur lie' on a bottle of Muscadet. 'Sur lie' means 'on the lees', which is a term used to describe a process where wine is aged on the dead yeast particles for a period of time.

Lees ageing adds an oily mouthfeel as well as yeasty bread-like flavours to wine. It's common to find it in white wines such as Muscadet, Viognier and Marsanne, as well as many sparkling wines.

Muscadet is a classic match with shellfish, and fish and chips. Due to its high acidity, Muscadet pairs with pickled ingredients and vinegar-based sauces.

SHELLFISH

LEMON

FRIED FOOD

61

PINOT GRIS

◀ 'pee-no gree'
aka: Pinot Grigio, Grauburgunder

PROFILE

FRUIT	●●●○○
BODY	●●○○○
DRY	●●○○○
ACIDITY	●●●○○
ALCOHOL	●●●○○

DOMINANT FLAVOURS

LEMON — YELLOW APPLE — MELON — NECTARINE — PEACH

POSSIBLE FLAVOURS

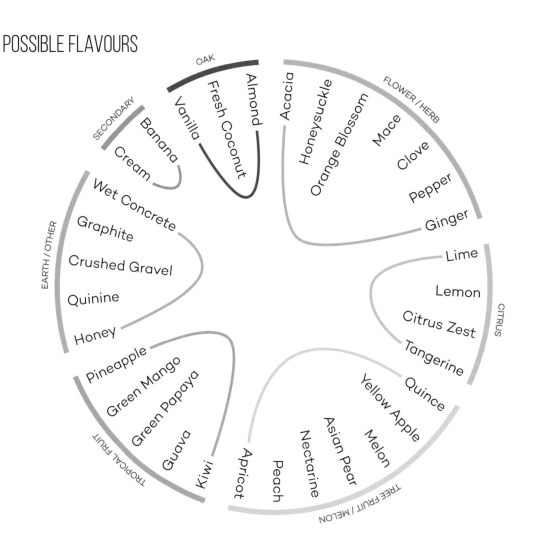

OAK: Vanilla, Fresh Coconut, Almond

SECONDARY: Cream, Banana

FLOWER / HERB: Acacia, Honeysuckle, Orange Blossom, Mace, Clove, Pepper, Ginger

EARTH / OTHER: Wet Concrete, Graphite, Crushed Gravel, Quinine, Honey

CITRUS: Lime, Lemon, Citrus Zest, Tangerine, Quince

TROPICAL FRUIT: Pineapple, Green Mango, Green Papaya, Guava, Kiwi

TREE FRUIT / MELON: Apricot, Peach, Nectarine, Asian Pear, Yellow Apple, Melon

📍 Origin: France and Italy

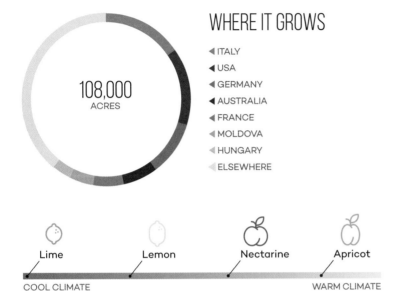

WHERE IT GROWS

108,000 ACRES

◄ ITALY
◄ USA
◄ GERMANY
◄ AUSTRALIA
◄ FRANCE
◄ MOLDOVA
◄ HUNGARY
◄ ELSEWHERE

WHITE

ICE-COLD

UP TO 5 YRS

£ £ £ £ £
£5–£10

Lime

Lemon

Nectarine

Apricot

COOL CLIMATE → WARM CLIMATE

PINOT GRIS: Pinot Gris is 1 of 4 common types of Pinot:

🍇 **PINOT BLANC**
A white wine grape.

🍇 **PINOT GRIS**
A grey-purple grape used for white and rosé wine.

🍇 **PINOT NOIR**
A black grape for red and rosé wine.

🍇 **PINOT MEUNIER**
A black grape used mainly in Champagne.

COMMON STYLES

🍾 **MINERALLY & DRY**
Mostly known as Pinot Grigio, from northern Italy, with citrus notes and salinity.

🍾 **FRUITY & DRY**
This style is found in USA, Australia and other warmer climate regions.

🍾 **FRUITY & SWEET**
This style is found mostly in Alsace, France, and offers flavours of lemon, peach and honey.

In the Friuli-Venezia Giulia region of Italy there is a unique style of Pinot Grigio called Ramato in which the juice macerates on the grape skins for about 2–3 days to make a pale-copper-hued rosé.

Try pairing Pinot Gris with light flaky fish dishes, crab, and softer cow's milk cheeses such as a triple-cream cheese.

SAUVIGNON BLANC

PROFILE

FRUIT ●●●●●
BODY   ●●●●●
DRY   ●●●●●
ACIDITY ●●●●●
ALCOHOL ●●●●●

DOMINANT FLAVOURS

GOOSEBERRY — GREEN MELON — GRAPEFRUIT — WHITE PEACH — PASSION FRUIT

POSSIBLE FLAVOURS

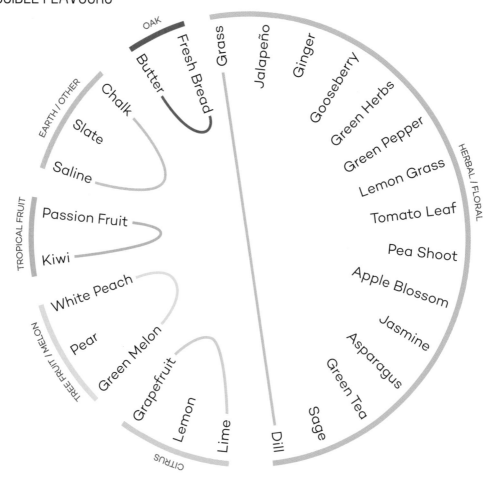

OAK
Butter
Fresh Bread

Grass
Jalapeño
Ginger
Gooseberry
Green Herbs
Green Pepper
Lemon Grass
Tomato Leaf
Pea Shoot
Apple Blossom
Jasmine
Asparagus
Green Tea
Sage
Dill

HERBAL / FLORAL

EARTH / OTHER
Chalk
Slate
Saline

TROPICAL FRUIT
Passion Fruit
Kiwi

TREE FRUIT / MELON
White Peach
Pear
Green Melon

Grapefruit
Lemon
Lime

CITRUS

Origin: France

WHERE IT GROWS

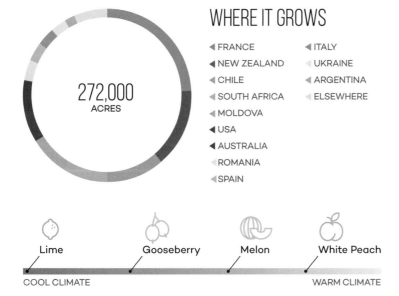

272,000 ACRES

◄ FRANCE
◄ NEW ZEALAND
◄ CHILE
◄ SOUTH AFRICA
◄ MOLDOVA
◄ USA
◄ AUSTRALIA
◄ ROMANIA
◄ SPAIN

◄ ITALY
◄ UKRAINE
◄ ARGENTINA
◄ ELSEWHERE

WHITE

ICE-COLD

UP TO 2 YRS

£ £ £ £
£3–£6

Lime Gooseberry Melon White Peach

COOL CLIMATE   WARM CLIMATE

REGIONAL DIFFERENCES: Every region produces a different taste of Sauvignon Blanc. Here are a few examples of dominant fruit flavours by region:

 WHITE PEACH
North Coast, CA, USA

 LIME
Loire Valley, FR

 PASSION FRUIT
Marlborough, NZ

BARREL-AGED: A style made famous by Robert Mondavi in the 1970s when he renamed his barrel-aged Sauvignon Blanc Fumé Blanc ('foom-aye blonk'). Barrel-aged Sauvignon Blanc tastes creamy while still exhibiting the variety's trademark 'green' notes.

 PEAR   TARRAGON   CREAM

Like Sauvignon Blanc? You'll find similar flavours in Austrian Grüner Veltliner, Spanish Verdejo, French Gros Manseng and Colombard, and Italian Vermentino.

Sauvignon Blanc is a parent of Cabernet Sauvignon. The cross happened naturally between Cabernet Franc and Sauvignon Blanc sometime during the 17th century in western France.

winefolly.com/learn/winefolly.com/learn/variety/sauvignon-blanc

SOAVE

🔊 'swa-vay'
aka: Garganega

PROFILE

FRUIT	● ● ● ● ●
BODY	● ● ● ● ●
BONE-DRY	● ● ● ● ●
ACIDITY	● ● ● ● ●
ALCOHOL	● ● ● ● ●

DOMINANT FLAVOURS

PRESERVED LEMON — HONEYDEW MELON — SALINE — GREEN ALMOND — CHERVIL

POSSIBLE FLAVOURS

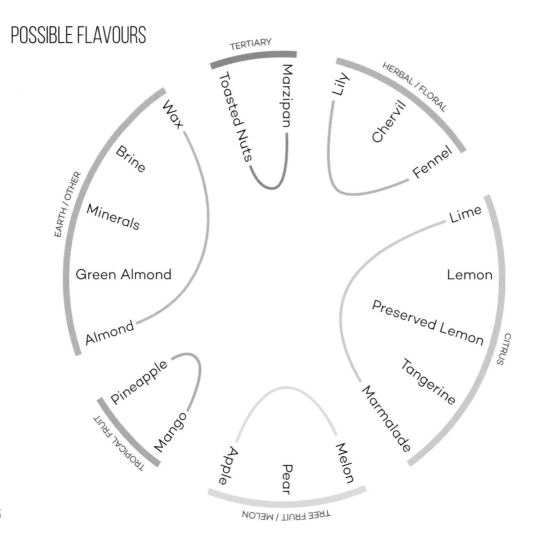

TERTIARY
Toasted Nuts
Marzipan

HERBAL / FLORAL
Lily
Chervil
Fennel

CITRUS
Lime
Lemon
Preserved Lemon
Tangerine
Marmalade

TREE FRUIT / MELON
Apple
Pear
Melon

TROPICAL FRUIT
Pineapple
Mango

EARTH / OTHER
Wax
Brine
Minerals
Green Almond
Almond

📍 Made in Veneto, Italy

WHERE IT GROWS

◀ VENETO, ITALY

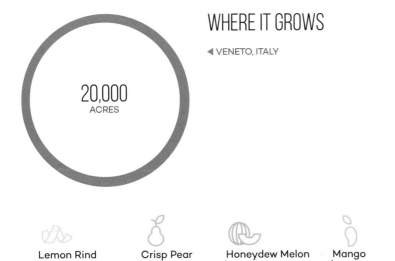

20,000 ACRES

Lemon Rind   Crisp Pear   Honeydew Melon   Mango

COOL VINTAGE   WARM VINTAGE

WHITE

ICE COLD

UP TO 2 YRS

£ £ £ £ £
£5–£10

SOAVE GRAPE: Garganega ('gar-GAN-neh-gah') is the grape of Soave. The best vineyards are located on slopes in the hills above the walled city of Soave.

SOAVE & SOAVE SUPERIORE
A larger production zone. Soave Superiore has longer aging reqs.

SOAVE CLASSICO
The original classic growing zone located in the hills.

SOAVE COLLI SCALIGERI
Wines from hillside vineyards outside the classic zone.

COMMON STYLES

LIGHT & ZESTY
Young Soave wines taste of honeydew melon, saline, marmalade and white peach, often with a subtle note of green almond.

RICH, HONEYED & FLORAL
Older vintage Soave wines taste of candied fennel, saffron, honey, baked apple and preserved lemon. Look for Soave aged for 4 or more years.

Soave pairs very well with shellfish, chicken, tofu and hard-to-pair foods including split peas, lentils and asparagus.

Garganega is the same grape as Grecanico in Sicily. Grecanico wines tend to be bolder and more fruity, and Soave wines tend to be more lean and crisp.

67

VERMENTINO

🔊 'vur-men-tino'
aka: Rolle, Favorita, Pigato

PROFILE

FRUIT
BODY
DRY
ACIDITY
ALCOHOL

DOMINANT FLAVOURS

LIME   GRAPEFRUIT   GREEN APPLE   ALMOND   DAFFODIL

POSSIBLE FLAVOURS

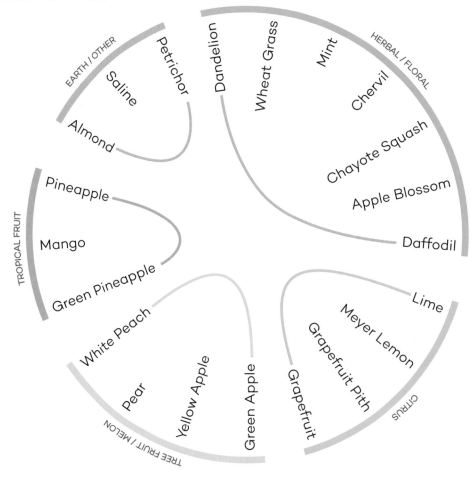

EARTH / OTHER
- Petrichor
- Saline
- Almond

HERBAL / FLORAL
- Dandelion
- Wheat Grass
- Mint
- Chervil
- Chayote Squash
- Apple Blossom
- Daffodil

TROPICAL FRUIT
- Pineapple
- Mango
- Green Pineapple

TREE FRUIT / MELON
- White Peach
- Pear
- Yellow Apple
- Green Apple

CITRUS
- Lime
- Meyer Lemon
- Grapefruit Pith
- Grapefruit

📍 Origin: Italy

22,000
ACRES

WHERE IT GROWS

◀ SOUTHERN FRANCE AND CORSICA
◀ CENTRAL ITALY AND SARDINIA
◀ ELSEWHERE

WHITE

ICE-COLD

UP TO 2 YRS

£ £ £ £ £

£5–£10

| Lime | Grapefruit | Yellow Apple | Mango |

COOL CLIMATE — WARM CLIMATE

winefolly.com/learn/winefolly.com/learn/variety/vermentino

REGIONS

SARDINIA, ITALY
Vermentino is the second most planted grape in Sardinia. Fine Vermentino wines come from the northern part of the island.

TUSCANY, ITALY
Vermentino grows primarily along the coast of Tuscany and extends up into Liguria.

BITTERNESS: Vermentino is often noted for having a bitter note on the finish that tastes similar to grapefruit pith. This type of flavour is referred to as phenolic bitterness, which is a common feature in several Italian white wines, including Verdicchio, Grechetto di Orvieto and Vernaccia di San Gimignano.

Due to its complexity, Vermentino stands up well to richer foods, including seafood gumbo, fried calamari, and tomato-based sauces.

In Southern France, Vermentino is called Rolle and is a key blending grape in Provence Rosé.

Full-Bodied White Wine

CHARDONNAY

MARSANNE BLEND

SÉMILLON

VIOGNIER

Full-bodied white wines are known for their rich, bold flavours. These wines are often aged on their lees or in oak barrels to add unctuous flavours of cream, vanilla and butter.

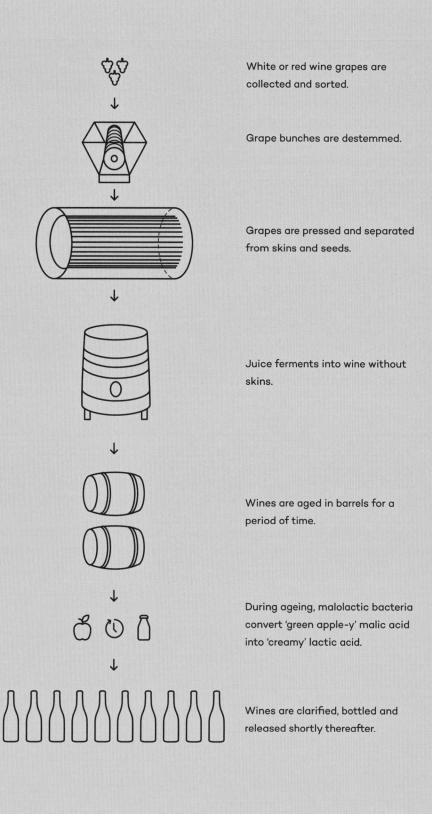

White or red wine grapes are collected and sorted.

Grape bunches are destemmed.

Grapes are pressed and separated from skins and seeds.

Juice ferments into wine without skins.

Wines are aged in barrels for a period of time.

During ageing, malolactic bacteria convert 'green apple-y' malic acid into 'creamy' lactic acid.

Wines are clarified, bottled and released shortly thereafter.

CHARDONNAY

'shar-dun-nay'

PROFILE

FRUIT

BODY

DRY

ACIDITY

ALCOHOL

DOMINANT FLAVOURS

YELLOW APPLE — STARFRUIT — PINEAPPLE — BUTTER — CHALK

POSSIBLE FLAVOURS

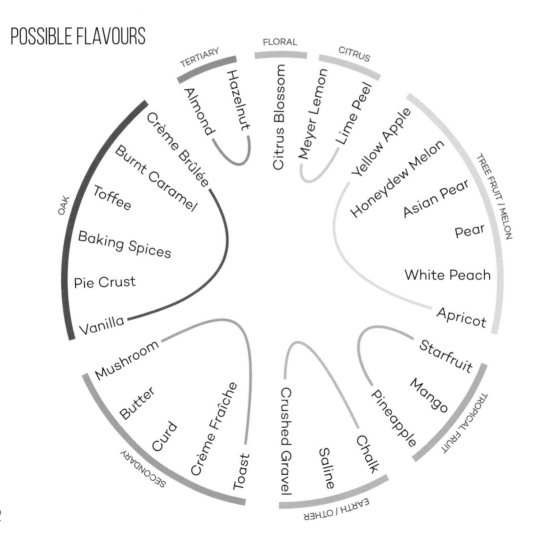

TERTIARY
- Almond
- Hazelnut

FLORAL
- Citrus Blossom

CITRUS
- Meyer Lemon
- Lime Peel

TREE FRUIT / MELON
- Yellow Apple
- Honeydew Melon
- Asian Pear
- Pear
- White Peach
- Apricot

OAK
- Crème Brûlée
- Burnt Caramel
- Toffee
- Baking Spices
- Pie Crust
- Vanilla

TROPICAL FRUIT
- Starfruit
- Mango
- Pineapple

SECONDARY
- Mushroom
- Butter
- Curd
- Crème Fraîche
- Toast

EARTH / OTHER
- Crushed Gravel
- Saline
- Chalk

♥ Origin: France

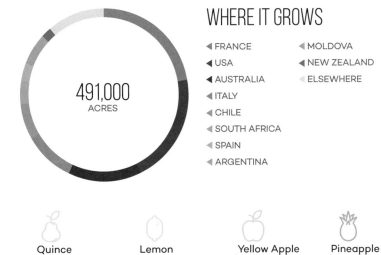

491,000
ACRES

WHERE IT GROWS

◀ FRANCE
◀ USA
◀ AUSTRALIA
◀ ITALY
◀ CHILE
◀ SOUTH AFRICA
◀ SPAIN
◀ ARGENTINA

◀ MOLDOVA
◀ NEW ZEALAND
◀ ELSEWHERE

WHITE

COLD

UP TO 5 YRS

Quince   Lemon   Yellow Apple   Pineapple

COOL CLIMATE   WARM CLIMATE

£££££
£10–£15

REGIONAL DIFFERENCES

COMMON STYLES

Try serving a rich creamy Chardonnay warmer at 55°F (13°C). Warming it slightly will release more aromas into the bowl of the glass and make the wine bolder.

PINEAPPLE & YELLOW APPLE
● CALIFORNIA
● SOUTH AUSTRALIA
● SPAIN
● SOUTH AFRICA
● ARGENTINA
● SOUTHERN ITALY

QUINCE & STARFRUIT
● BURGUNDY, FRANCE
● NORTHERN ITALY
● COASTAL CHILE
● NEW ZEALAND
● WESTERN AUSTRALIA
● OREGON

OAKED RICH & CREAMY
Found in California, Chile, Australia, Argentina, Spain & Côte de Beaune, Burgundy.

UNOAKED LIGHT & ZESTY
Unoaked styles can be found in Mâconnais, Chablis and western Australia.

SPARKLING
'Blanc de Blancs' labelled sparkling wines are made with Chardonnay.

Chardonnay is the world's most planted white grape.

Bourgogne Blanc is normally 100% Chardonnay.

MARSANNE BLEND

'mar-sahn'
aka: Châteauneuf-du-Pape
Blanc, Côtes du Rhône Blanc

PROFILE

FRUIT
BODY
DRY
ACIDITY
ALCOHOL

DOMINANT FLAVOURS

QUINCE — MANDARIN ORANGE — APRICOT — ACACIA — BEESWAX

POSSIBLE FLAVOURS

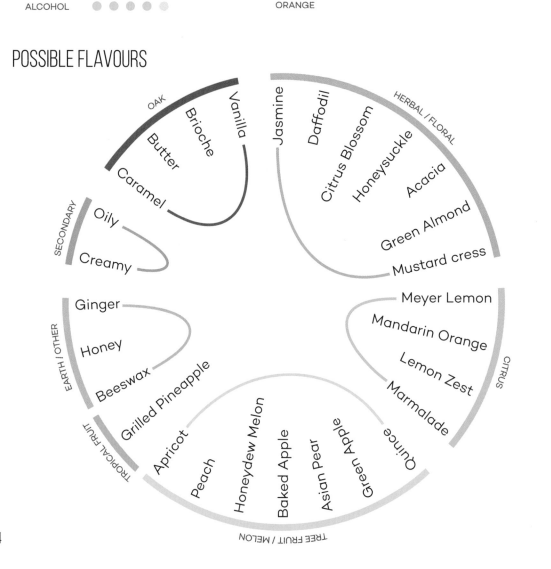

OAK
Vanilla
Brioche
Butter
Caramel

SECONDARY
Oily
Creamy

EARTH / OTHER
Ginger
Honey
Beeswax

TROPICAL FRUIT
Grilled Pineapple

HERBAL / FLORAL
Jasmine
Daffodil
Citrus Blossom
Honeysuckle
Acacia
Green Almond
Mustard cress

CITRUS
Meyer Lemon
Mandarin Orange
Lemon Zest
Marmalade
Quince

TREE FRUIT / MELON
Apricot
Peach
Honeydew Melon
Baked Apple
Asian Pear
Green Apple

120,000
ACRES

THE BLEND

◄ MARSANNE
◄ ROUSSANNE
◄ VIOGNIER
◄ GRENACHE BLANC
◄ CLAIRETTE
◄ BOURBOULENC
◄ PIQUEPOUL
◄ OTHERS

WHITE

COLD

UP TO 5 YRS

£ £ £ £ £
£10–£15

Quince   Lemon   Peach   Apricot

COOL CLIMATE   WARM CLIMATE

FRANCE: Generally, French white Rhône blends are light bodied because they are a blend of many varieties, including Marsanne, Roussanne, Grenache Blanc, Clairette, Bourboulenc and Viognier.

USA: Marsanne and other white Rhône varieties became popular in the US after Tablas Creek winery in Paso Robles imported cuttings from Château de Beaucastel in Châteauneuf-du-Pape.

THE BLEND: Because of the wide range of grape varieties that contribute to this blend, the secret to the flavour of a particular wine lies in its dominant grape.

PEACH & FLOWERS
Viognier

PEAR & BEESWAX
Marsanne & Roussanne

CITRUS FRUIT
Others

If you prefer a richer style, look for white Rhône blends with higher proportions of Viognier and Marsanne grapes in the blend.

As its name implies, the original white Rhône blend is from the Rhône in southern France, where today just 6% of the regional production is dedicated to white wine.

SÉMILLON

PROFILE

FRUIT	●●●●○
BODY	●●●●○
DRY	●●●●○
ACIDITY	●●●●○
ALCOHOL	●●●○○

DOMINANT FLAVOURS

LEMON — BEESWAX — YELLOW PEACH — CHAMOMILE — SALINE

POSSIBLE FLAVOURS

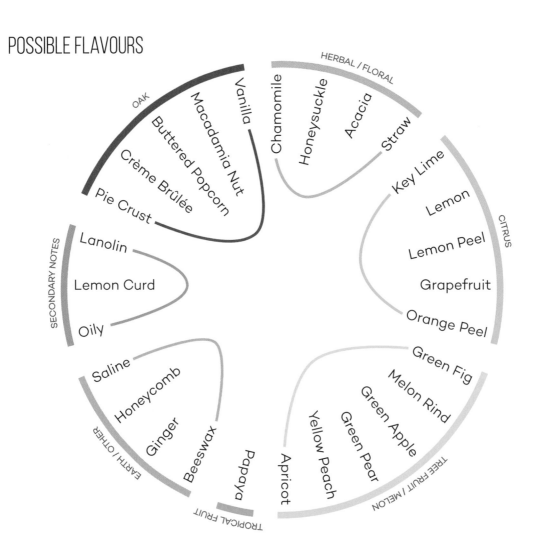

OAK: Vanilla, Macadamia Nut, Buttered Popcorn, Crème Brûlée, Pie Crust

HERBAL / FLORAL: Chamomile, Honeysuckle, Acacia, Straw

CITRUS: Key Lime, Lemon, Lemon Peel, Grapefruit, Orange Peel

TREE FRUIT / MELON: Green Fig, Melon Rind, Green Apple, Green Pear, Yellow Peach, Apricot

TROPICAL FRUIT: Papaya

EARTH / OTHER: Saline, Honeycomb, Ginger, Beeswax

SECONDARY NOTES: Lanolin, Lemon Curd, Oily

Origin: France

57,000
ACRES

WHERE IT GROWS

◀ FRANCE
◀ AUSTRALIA
◀ CHILE
◀ SOUTH AFRICA
◀ ARGENTINA
◀ USA
◀ TURKEY
◀ ELSEWHERE

WHITE

COLD

UP TO 10 YRS

£££££
£15-£20

Lime · Yellow Apple · Papaya · Fig

COOL CLIMATE · WARM CLIMATE

REGIONAL DIFFERENCES: When comparing Sémillon wines from different regions, you'll notice some taste differences:

 LIME, SALINE & CHAMOMILE
  ● BORDEAUX, FRANCE
  ● HUNTER VALLEY, AUSTRALIA
  ● WASHINGTON STATE

 PAPAYA, APPLE & LEMON CURD
  ● SOUTH AUSTRALIA
  ● CALIFORNIA

COMMON STYLES

WHITE BORDEAUX BLEND
A zesty white of Sauvignon Blanc and Sémillon found in Graves, Bordeaux; Hunter Valley, Australia, and Washington State.

BARREL-AGED SÉMILLON
Just a few Sémillon wines are aged in oak. Look into Sémillon wines from Péssac-Leognan, Bordeaux, France; Barossa Valley, South Australia; and Washington State.

DESSERT WINE
Sémillon is the key varietal in Sauternes, which is a honeyed dessert wine from Bordeaux, France, made of Sémillon, Sauvignon Blanc, and Muscadelle.

77

VIOGNIER

PROFILE

FRUIT
BODY
OFF-DRY
ACIDITY
ALCOHOL

DOMINANT FLAVOURS

TANGERINE   PEACH   MANGO   HONEYSUCKLE   ROSE

POSSIBLE FLAVOURS

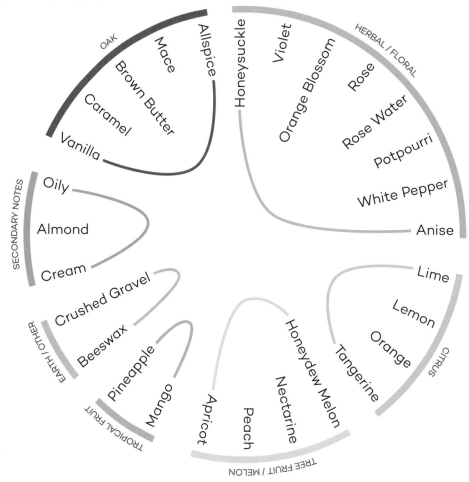

OAK
Allspice
Mace
Brown Butter
Caramel
Vanilla

HERBAL / FLORAL
Honeysuckle
Violet
Orange Blossom
Rose
Rose Water
Potpourri
White Pepper
Anise

SECONDARY NOTES
Oily
Almond
Cream

EARTH / OTHER
Crushed Gravel
Beeswax

CITRUS
Lime
Lemon
Orange
Tangerine

TROPICAL FRUIT
Pineapple
Mango

TREE FRUIT / MELON
Apricot
Peach
Nectarine
Honeydew Melon

♦ Origin: Southern France

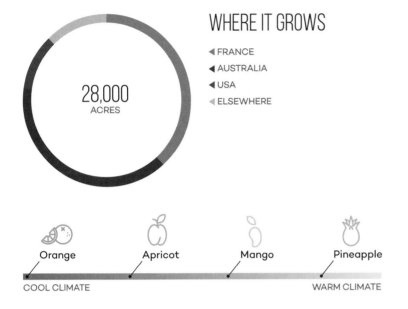

WHERE IT GROWS

28,000 ACRES

◄ FRANCE
◄ AUSTRALIA
◄ USA
◄ ELSEWHERE

WHITE

COLD

UP TO 2 YRS

£10–£20

| Orange | Apricot | Mango | Pineapple |

COOL CLIMATE   WARM CLIMATE

REGIONS

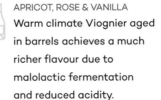

COMMON STYLES

FRANCE
The Rhône Valley and Languedoc-Roussillon

AUSTRALIA
South Australia, including Barossa Valley

USA
Central Coast, California, including Paso Robles

LIME, FLOWERS & MINERALS
Common in cool climate regions where wines do not undergo malolactic fermentation in stainless steel.

APRICOT, ROSE & VANILLA
Warm climate Viognier aged in barrels achieves a much richer flavour due to malolactic fermentation and reduced acidity.

SWEET PEACH & FLOWER
The small Condrieu region in the northern Rhône of France produces a very rare off-dry style of Viognier.

Aromatic White Wine

CHENIN BLANC

GEWÜRZTRAMINER

MUSCAT BLANC

RIESLING

TORRONTÉS

Aromatic white wines have highly perfumed and sweet-fruit aromas but can range from dry to sweet in taste. Aromatic whites are ideal pairing partners with Asian and Indian cuisine because they match well with sweet-and-sour flavors and quench spicy sauces.

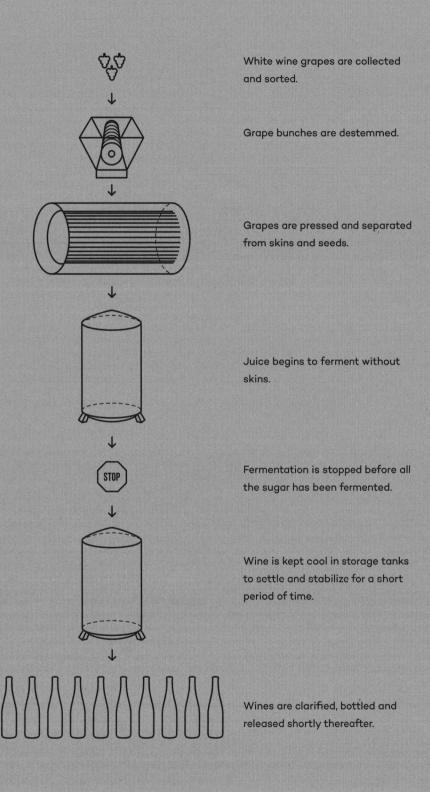

White wine grapes are collected and sorted.

Grape bunches are destemmed.

Grapes are pressed and separated from skins and seeds.

Juice begins to ferment without skins.

Fermentation is stopped before all the sugar has been fermented.

Wine is kept cool in storage tanks to settle and stabilize for a short period of time.

Wines are clarified, bottled and released shortly thereafter.

CHENIN BLANC

🔊 'shen-in blonk'
aka: Steen, Pineau, Vouvray

PROFILE

FRUIT	●	●	●	●	●
BODY	●	●	●	●	●
OFF-DRY	●	●	●	●	●
ACIDITY	●	●	●	●	●
ALCOHOL	●	●	●	●	●

DOMINANT FLAVOURS

LEMON · YELLOW APPLE · PEAR · HONEY · CHAMOMILE

POSSIBLE FLAVOURS

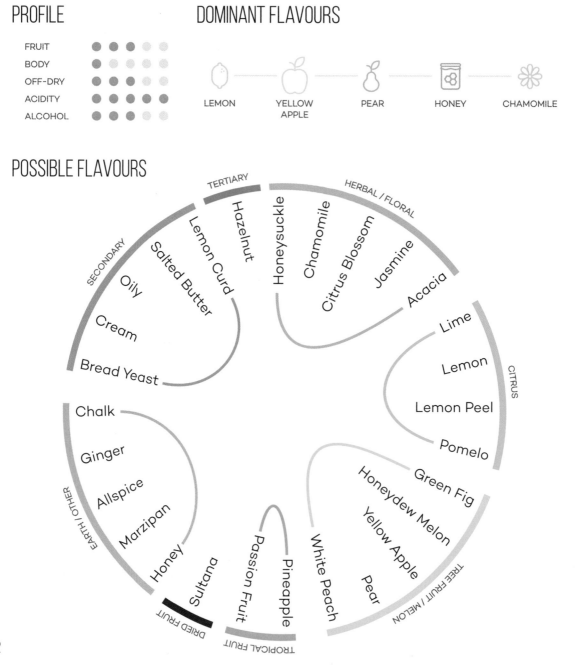

TERTIARY
Hazelnut
Lemon Curd

SECONDARY
Salted Butter
Oily
Cream
Bread Yeast

HERBAL / FLORAL
Honeysuckle
Chamomile
Citrus Blossom
Jasmine
Acacia

CITRUS
Lime
Lemon
Lemon Peel
Pomelo

TREE FRUIT / MELON
Green Fig
Honeydew Melon
Yellow Apple
Pear
White Peach

TROPICAL FRUIT
Pineapple
Passion Fruit

DRIED FRUIT
Sultana

EARTH / OTHER
Chalk
Ginger
Allspice
Marzipan
Honey

♦ Origin: France

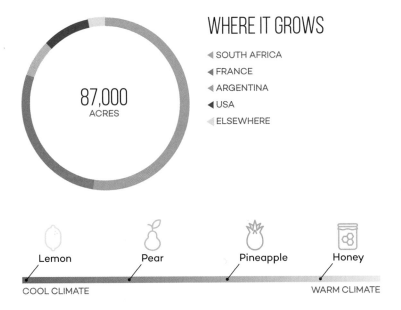

WHERE IT GROWS

87,000
ACRES

◄ SOUTH AFRICA
◄ FRANCE
◄ ARGENTINA
◄ USA
◄ ELSEWHERE

WHITE

COLD

UP TO 2 YRS

£££££
£3–£5

winefolly.com/learn/winefolly.com/learn/variety/chenin-blanc

Lemon   Pear   Pineapple   Honey

COOL CLIMATE   WARM CLIMATE

COMMON STYLES

 SPARKLING
Sparkling wines come from the Loire Valley in Vouvray, Saumur and Montlouis, and in South Africa they are blended into Method Cap Classique.

 LIGHT & ZESTY
Tasting of lime and tarragon, this dry style is common in value-priced South African Chenin and in Loire wines labelled 'Sec'.

 PEACHES & FLOWERS
South Africa offers a rich style with nectarine, honey, and meringue notes. Also available on warm vintages in Anjou, Montlouis and Vouvray in the Loire.

 NOBLE ROT DESSERT WINE
In Anjou, close to the river where the fog collects on certain years, noble rot adds candied ginger notes.

Occasionally, you'll come across a Chenin Blanc with bruised apple flavours—a sign of oxidation. Some Chenin Blanc wines are made in an oxidative style on purpose, including a region in the Loire called Savennières.

Much of the Chenin Blanc grown in South Africa is used for brandy production.

83

GEWÜRZTRAMINER

🔊 'ge-voortz-tram-ee-ner'

PROFILE

FRUIT
BODY
OFF-DRY
ACIDITY
ALCOHOL

DOMINANT FLAVOURS

LYCHEE — ROSE — PINK GRAPEFRUIT — TANGERINE — GUAVA

POSSIBLE FLAVOURS

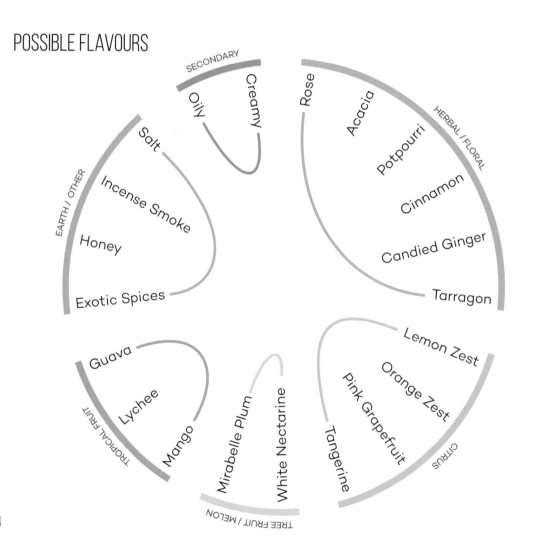

SECONDARY
Oily
Creamy

Rose
Acacia
Potpourri
Cinnamon
Candied Ginger
Tarragon

HERBAL / FLORAL

Salt
Incense Smoke
Honey
Exotic Spices

EARTH / OTHER

Lemon Zest
Orange Zest
Pink Grapefruit
Tangerine

CITRUS

Guava
Lychee
Mango

TROPICAL FRUIT

Mirabelle Plum
White Nectarine

TREE FRUIT / MELON

Origin: Germany and France

WHERE IT GROWS

35,000
ACRES

◀ FRANCE
◀ MOLDOVA
◀ UKRAINE
◀ AUSTRALIA
◀ GERMANY
◀ USA
◀ HUNGARY
◀ ELSEWHERE

Tangerine   Rose   Lychee   Guava

COOL CLIMATE   WARM CLIMATE

WHITE

COLD

UP TO 2 YRS

£ £ £ £
£5–£10

COMMON STYLES

DRY & OFF-DRY
There are several Gewürztraminer with sweet and floral aromas and a completely dry taste. This dry style can be found in Trento-Alto Adige, Italy; Alsace, France; and cooler areas in California including Mendocino and Monterey. Dry Gewürztraminer from Alsace, France, has a rich, oily texture and subtle salinity.

DESSERT WINE
In Alsace, there are two very high-quality dessert wines produced with Gewürztraminer: Vendanges Tardives and Sélection de Grains Nobles (SGN). SGN is produced with noble rot grapes and Vendanges Tardives means 'late harvest'. These wines are generally rare and command high prices.

Try a dry Gewürztraminer with dim sum, Vietnamese cuisine, won ton, and dumpling soup.

As a general rule, Gewürztraminer tastes best within a year or two of release. This is to ensure it has the highest possible acidity, which gives Gewürztraminer a crisp, fresh flavour.

85

MUSCAT BLANC

PROFILE

FRUIT
BODY
SWEET
ACIDITY
ALCOHOL

DOMINANT FLAVOURS

MEYER LEMON — MANDARIN ORANGE — PEAR — ORANGE BLOSSOM — HONEYSUCKLE

POSSIBLE FLAVOURS

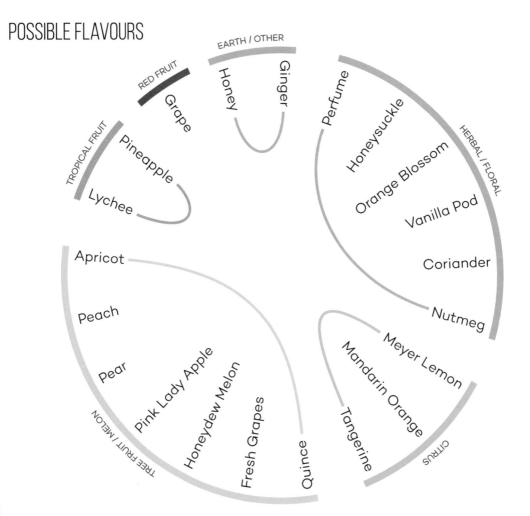

RED FRUIT
- Grape

EARTH / OTHER
- Honey
- Ginger

TROPICAL FRUIT
- Pineapple
- Lychee

HERBAL / FLORAL
- Perfume
- Honeysuckle
- Orange Blossom
- Vanilla Pod
- Coriander
- Nutmeg

TREE FRUIT / MELON
- Apricot
- Peach
- Pear
- Pink Lady Apple
- Honeydew Melon
- Fresh Grapes
- Quince

CITRUS
- Meyer Lemon
- Mandarin Orange
- Tangerine

📍 Origin: Ancient Greece and Italy

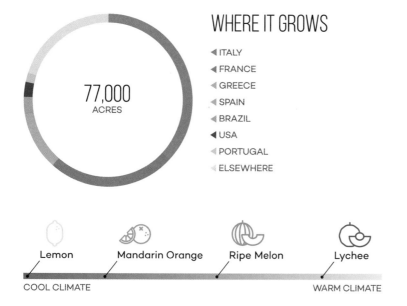

77,000
ACRES

WHERE IT GROWS

◄ ITALY
◄ FRANCE
◄ GREECE
◄ SPAIN
◄ BRAZIL
◄ USA
◄ PORTUGAL
◄ ELSEWHERE

DEPENDS ON STYLE

COLD

UP TO 2 YRS

£5–£10

winefolly.com/learn/winefolly.com/learn/variety/learn/variety/muscat-blanc

Lemon   Mandarin Orange   Ripe Melon   Lychee

COOL CLIMATE   WARM CLIMATE

MUSCAT: Muscat Blanc is an ancient grape with several closely related varieties:

MUSCAT OF ALEXANDRIA
The oldest—Cleopatra supposedly loved it.

MUSCAT GIALLO
The Italian version from Roman times.

MUSCAT OTTONEL
Hailing from the Ottoman Empire, a dry Muscat.

COMMON STYLES

DRY & AROMATIC
This style is most classically associated with Alto Adige, Italy; Germany; and Alsace, France.

SWEET & LIGHTLY SPARKLING
The most famous Muscat Blanc is Moscato d'Asti, which comes from the Piedmont region in northern Italy.

SWEET DESSERT MUSCAT
Several regions produce Muscat-based dessert wines, which can have upward of 200 g/L of residual sugar with a viscosity like hot maple syrup.

RIESLING

PROFILE

FRUIT
BODY
OFF-DRY
ACIDITY
ALCOHOL

DOMINANT FLAVOURS

LIME   GREEN APPLE   BEESWAX   JASMINE   PETROLEUM

POSSIBLE FLAVOURS

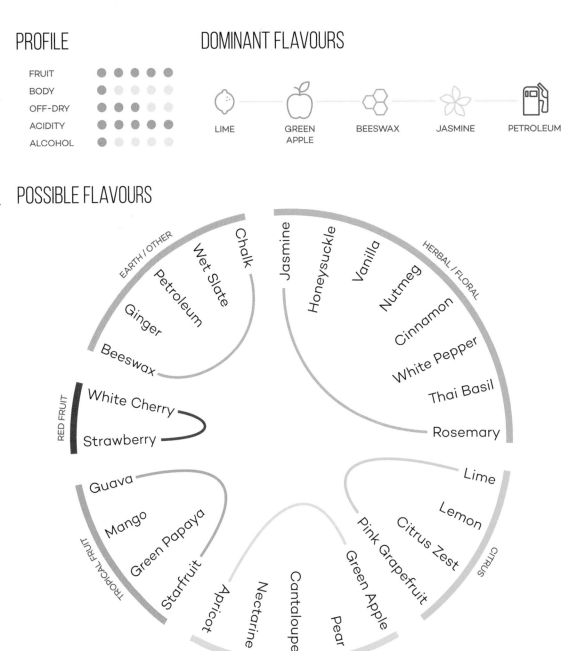

EARTH / OTHER
Chalk
Wet Slate
Petroleum
Ginger
Beeswax

RED FRUIT
White Cherry
Strawberry

Jasmine
Honeysuckle
Vanilla
Nutmeg
Cinnamon
White Pepper
Thai Basil
Rosemary
HERBAL / FLORAL

Lime
Lemon
Citrus Zest
Pink Grapefruit
Green Apple
Pear
CITRUS

Guava
Mango
Green Papaya
Starfruit
TROPICAL FRUIT

Apricot
Nectarine
Cantaloupe
TREE FRUIT / MELON

88

● Origin: Germany

WHERE IT GROWS

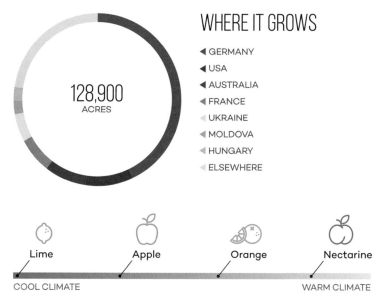

128,900
ACRES

◀ GERMANY
◀ USA
◀ AUSTRALIA
◀ FRANCE
◀ UKRAINE
◀ MOLDOVA
◀ HUNGARY
◀ ELSEWHERE

WHITE

COLD

UP TO 10 YRS

£ £ £ £
£5–£10

Lime   Apple   Orange   Nectarine

COOL CLIMATE   WARM CLIMATE

REGIONS

○ GERMANY
Germany is known for the world's best Riesling ranging in style from dry to sweet.

GERMAN LABEL TERMS:

TROCKENBEERENAUSLESE (TBA)
BEERENAUSLESE (BA) — VERY SWEET
AUSLESE — SWEET
SPÄTLESE
KABINETT — OFF-DRY
HALBTROCKEN
FEINHERB
TROCKEN — DRY

○ USA
Washingon State and New York produce dry and sweet Riesling.

○ AUSTRALIA
Clare and Eden Valley produce dry Riesling with lime and petrol aromas.

○ FRANCE
Riesling from Alsace is typically made in a dry style.

Not sure if the wine is dry or sweet? As a general rule, if the wine is low alcohol (below 9% ABV) you can assume that it's on the sweeter side of the spectrum.

Sweet Riesling pairs very well with spicy and spice-driven dishes, including Indian and Thai cuisine. Dry Riesling has enough acidity to pair wonderfully with oily lighter meats, like duck and bacon.

89

TORRONTÉS

PROFILE

FRUIT
BODY
DRY
ACIDITY
ALCOHOL

DOMINANT FLAVOURS

MEYER LEMON · PEACH · LEMON PEEL · ROSE PETAL · GERANIUM

POSSIBLE FLAVOURS

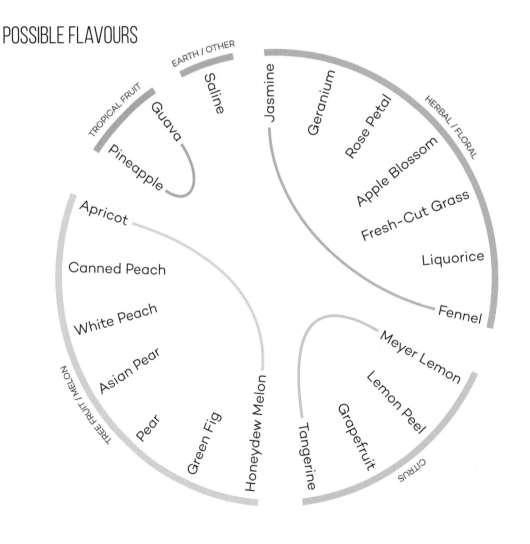

EARTH / OTHER
Saline

TROPICAL FRUIT
Guava
Pineapple

Apricot
Canned Peach
White Peach
Asian Pear
Pear
Green Fig
Honeydew Melon
TREE FRUIT / MELON

Jasmine
Geranium
Rose Petal
Apple Blossom
Fresh-Cut Grass
Liquorice
Fennel
HERBAL / FLORAL

Meyer Lemon
Lemon Peel
Grapefruit
Tangerine
CITRUS

📍 Origin: Argentina

21,000
ACRES

WHERE IT GROWS

◄ ARGENTINA
◄ ELSEWHERE

WHITE

COLD

UP TO 2 YRS

£ £ £ £ £

£3–£6

 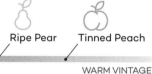

| Meyer Lemon | Honeydew Melon | Ripe Pear | Tinned Peach |

COOL VINTAGE   WARM VINTAGE

COMMON STYLES

 DRY & ZESTY
The Argentine region of
Salta is known for making
dry Torrontés with flavours
of grapefruit, lemon peel,
nutmeg and saline.

A TOUCH SWEET
The Torrontés from the
warmer regions in Mendoza
and San Juan taste sweeter,
with flavours of peach
and guava.

The high-altitude vineyards in
Salta are known for producing
high-quality Torrontés.

Torrontés is an indigenous
Argentine grape that is a natural
cross with Muscat of Alexandria
and the Chilean grape called País.

Try Torrontés with delicately
flavoured meats and sweet-sour
sauces such as miso-glazed
sea bass or teriyaki-braised
sesame tofu.

FISH & SUSHI

BRAISED TOFU

91

Rosé Wine

ROSÉ

Rosé wine is produced when red grape skins macerate in their juices for a period of time. Rosé is produced in every major country and is made of nearly every grape variety, both red and white. Rosé wines range in taste from dry to sweet. For example, a rosé of Tempranillo is usually dry and savoury. Whereas White Zinfandel is almost always sweet and fruity.

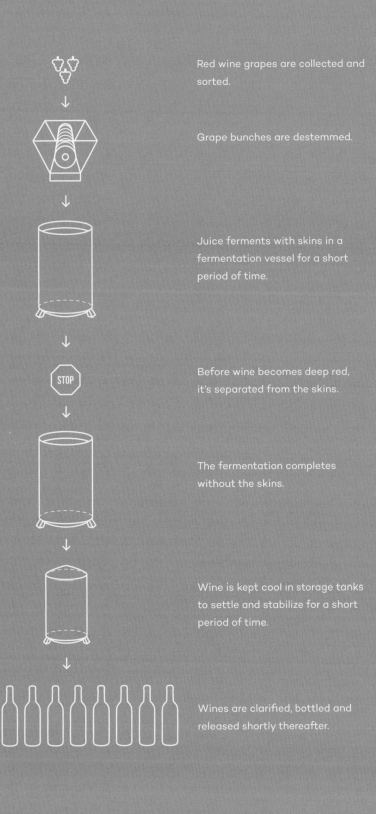

Red wine grapes are collected and sorted.

Grape bunches are destemmed.

Juice ferments with skins in a fermentation vessel for a short period of time.

Before wine becomes deep red, it's separated from the skins.

The fermentation completes without the skins.

Wine is kept cool in storage tanks to settle and stabilize for a short period of time.

Wines are clarified, bottled and released shortly thereafter.

ROSÉ

🔊 'rose-aye'
aka: Rosado, Rosato, Vin Gris

PROFILE

FRUIT	●	●	●	●	●
BODY	●	●	●	○	○
DRY / SWEET	●	●	○	○	○
ACIDITY	●	●	●	○	○
ALCOHOL	●	●	●	○	○

DOMINANT FLAVOURS

STRAWBERRY — HONEYDEW MELON — ROSE PETAL — CELERY — ORANGE PEEL

POSSIBLE FLAVOURS

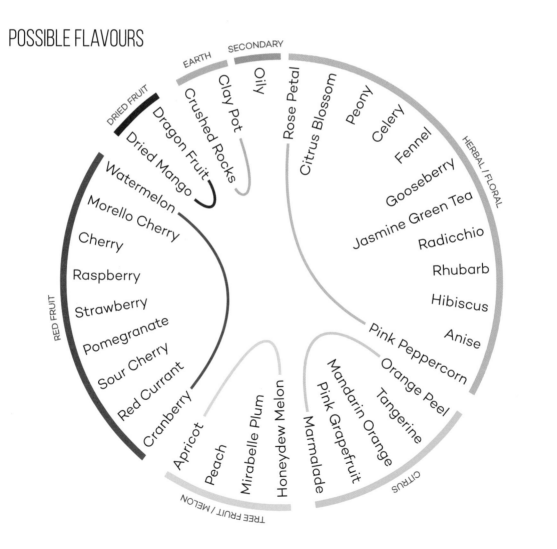

EARTH
- Clay Pot
- Crushed Rocks

SECONDARY
- Oily

DRIED FRUIT
- Dragon Fruit
- Dried Mango

RED FRUIT
- Watermelon
- Morello Cherry
- Cherry
- Raspberry
- Strawberry
- Pomegranate
- Sour Cherry
- Red Currant
- Cranberry

TREE FRUIT / MELON
- Apricot
- Peach
- Mirabelle Plum
- Honeydew Melon

CITRUS
- Marmalade
- Pink Grapefruit
- Mandarin Orange
- Tangerine
- Orange Peel
- Pink Peppercorn

HERBAL / FLORAL
- Rose Petal
- Citrus Blossom
- Peony
- Celery
- Fennel
- Gooseberry
- Jasmine Green Tea
- Radicchio
- Rhubarb
- Hibiscus
- Anise

● Origin: unknown

3 BILLION
BOTTLES

WHERE IT'S MADE

◄ FRANCE
◄ ITALY
◄ USA
◄ SPAIN
◄ ELSEWHERE

AROMA COLLECTOR

COLD

UP TO 2 YRS

£3–£6

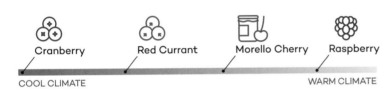

Cranberry   Red Currant   Morello Cherry   Raspberry

COOL CLIMATE   WARM CLIMATE

REGIONS

FRANCE
The rosé wines of France are dry and come mainly from Provence and Languedoc-Roussillon. The blend typically includes Grenache and Syrah.

ITALY
Rosato is made all over Italy using one or several of the country's indigenous grape varieties.

USA
Many new styles of rosé wine are introduced every year, but the largest rosé production is dedicated to White Zinfandel.

SPAIN
Spanish rosés include Tempranillo, with a meaty note; and Garnacha, with candied grapefruit flavours and a brilliant ruby hue.

An aroma collector glass will capture the subtle floral aromas that are harder to pick up in a regular white wine glass.

In the US, the majority of Zinfandel grapes go toward the production of White Zinfandel.

winefolly.com / learn / winefolly.com / learn / style / rose

Light-Bodied Red Wine

GAMAY

PINOT NOIR

Light-bodied red wines are translucent in colour and tend to have moderately high acidity. They are known for their perfumed aromas that are best collected in a large globe-shaped glass.

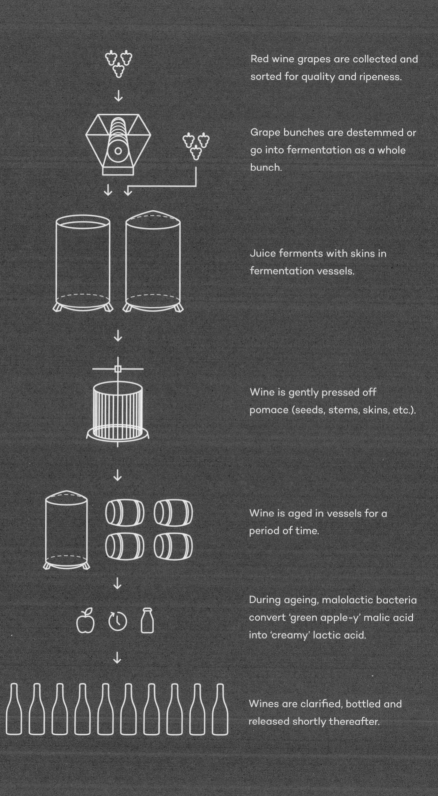

Red wine grapes are collected and sorted for quality and ripeness.

Grape bunches are destemmed or go into fermentation as a whole bunch.

Juice ferments with skins in fermentation vessels.

Wine is gently pressed off pomace (seeds, stems, skins, etc.).

Wine is aged in vessels for a period of time.

During ageing, malolactic bacteria convert 'green apple-y' malic acid into 'creamy' lactic acid.

Wines are clarified, bottled and released shortly thereafter.

GAMAY

winefolly.com / learn / variety / gamay

PROFILE

FRUIT	● ● ● ○ ○
BODY	● ● ○ ○ ○
TANNIN	● ○ ○ ○ ○
ACIDITY	● ● ● ● ○
ALCOHOL	● ● ○ ○ ○

DOMINANT FLAVOURS

HUCKLEBERRY — RASPBERRY — VIOLET — POTTING SOIL — BANANA

POSSIBLE FLAVOURS

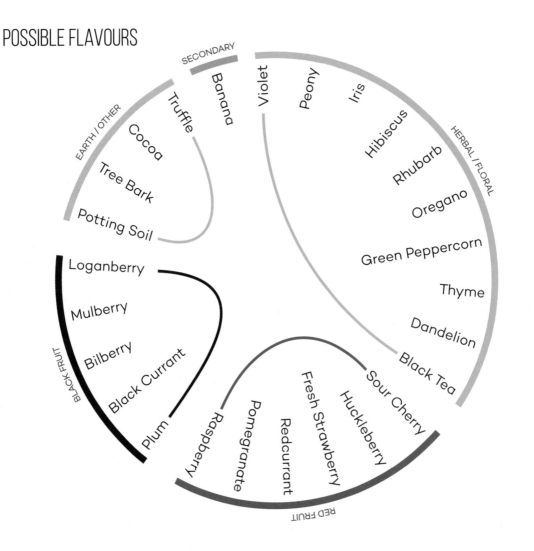

SECONDARY: Banana, Truffle

EARTH / OTHER: Cocoa, Tree Bark, Potting Soil

HERBAL / FLORAL: Violet, Peony, Iris, Hibiscus, Rhubarb, Oregano, Green Peppercorn, Thyme, Dandelion, Black Tea

BLACK FRUIT: Loganberry, Mulberry, Bilberry, Black Currant, Plum

RED FRUIT: Raspberry, Pomegranate, Redcurrant, Fresh Strawberry, Huckleberry, Sour Cherry

📍 Origin: France

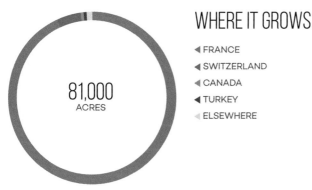

81,000
ACRES

WHERE IT GROWS

◀ FRANCE
◀ SWITZERLAND
◀ CANADA
◀ TURKEY
◀ ELSEWHERE

AROMA COLLECTOR

CELLAR TEMP.

UP TO 5 YRS

£ £ £ £ £
£5–£10

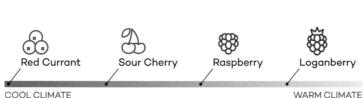

Red Currant — Sour Cherry — Raspberry — Loganberry

COOL CLIMATE   WARM CLIMATE

BEAUJOLAIS QUALITY LEVELS

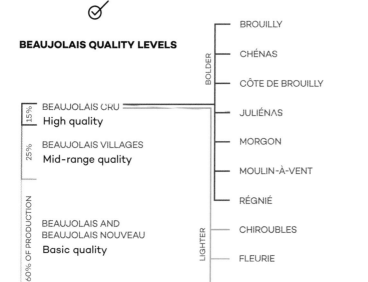

BOLDER

BROUILLY

CHÉNAS

CÔTE DE BROUILLY

JULIÉNAS

MORGON

MOULIN-À-VENT

RÉGNIÉ

CHIROUBLES

FLEURIE

SAINT-AMOUR

LIGHTER

15% — BEAUJOLAIS CRU
High quality

25% — BEAUJOLAIS VILLAGES
Mid-range quality

60% OF PRODUCTION — BEAUJOLAIS AND BEAUJOLAIS NOUVEAU
Basic quality

Around 75% of Gamay from France comes from the Beaujolais region.

Looking for quality? Seek out Gamay Noir from a Beaujolais Cru. A cru is a designated quality zone. There are 10 Beaujolais Crus.

Beaujolais Nouveau is meant to be drunk during its vintage year and doesn't age well.

winefolly.com / learn / winefolly.com / learn / variety / gamay

99

PINOT NOIR

'pee-no nwar'
aka: Spätburgunder

PROFILE

FRUIT	●●●●○
BODY	●●●○○
TANNIN	●●●○○
ACIDITY	●●●●○
ALCOHOL	●●●○○

DOMINANT FLAVOURS

CRANBERRY — CHERRY — RASPBERRY — CLOVE — MUSHROOM

POSSIBLE FLAVOURS

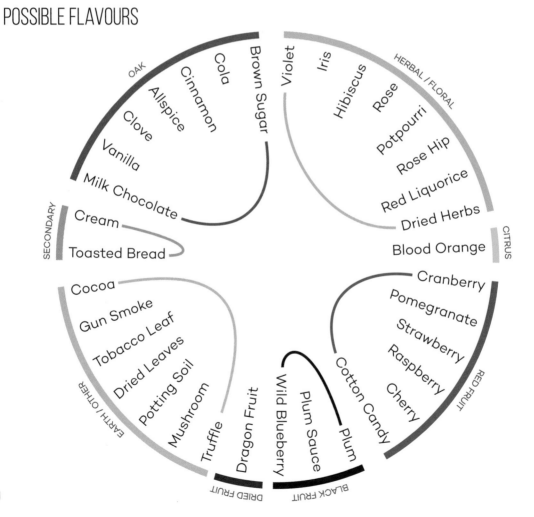

OAK: Brown Sugar, Cola, Cinnamon, Allspice, Clove, Vanilla, Milk Chocolate

SECONDARY: Cream, Toasted Bread

EARTH / OTHER: Cocoa, Gun Smoke, Tobacco Leaf, Dried Leaves, Potting Soil, Mushroom, Truffle

DRIED FRUIT: Dragon Fruit

BLACK FRUIT: Wild Blueberry, Plum Sauce, Plum, Cotton Candy

RED FRUIT: Cranberry, Pomegranate, Strawberry, Raspberry, Cherry

CITRUS: Blood Orange

HERBAL / FLORAL: Violet, Iris, Hibiscus, Rose, Potpourri, Rose Hip, Red Liquorice, Dried Herbs

📍 Origin: France

214,000
ACRES

WHERE IT GROWS

◀ FRANCE
◀ USA
◀ GERMANY
◀ MOLDOVA
◀ ITALY
◀ NEW ZEALAND
◀ AUSTRALIA
◀ SWITZERLAND
◀ ELSEWHERE

AROMA COLLECTOR

CELLAR TEMP.

UP TO 5 YRS

£££ £ £

£10–£15

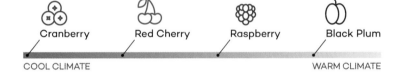

Cranberry   Red Cherry   Raspberry   Black Plum

COOL CLIMATE   WARM CLIMATE

REGIONAL DIFFERENCES: When comparing Pinot Noir wines from different regions, you'll notice some taste differences:

 RASPBERRY & CLOVE
  ● CALIFORNIA
  ● CENTRAL OTAGO, NZ
  ● SOUTH AUSTRALIA
  ● CHILE
  ● ARGENTINA

 CRANBERRY AND MUSHROOM
  ● FRANCE
  ● GERMANY
  ● ITALY
  ● OREGON

COMMON STYLES

 ZESTY ROSÉ
A dry rosé tasting of elderflower, green strawberry and sour plum.

 LIGHT RED
Red wines vary greatly in taste based on region, vintage and producer.

 SPARKLING
Cremant d'Alsace rosé is 100% Pinot Noir.

Looking for varieties similar to Pinot Noir? You might also enjoy St. Laurent, Cinsaut and Zweigelt.

There are 15 common clones of Pinot Noir and each has a distinct flavour.

The original home of Pinot Noir is in Burgundy, France.

Medium-Bodied Red Wine

BARBERA

CABERNET FRANC

CARIGNAN

CARMÉNÈRE

GRENACHE

MENCÍA

MERLOT

MONTEPULCIANO

NEGROAMARO

RHÔNE/GSM BLEND

SANGIOVESE

VALPOLICELLA BLEND

ZINFANDEL

Medium-bodied red wines are often referred to as 'food wines' because of their excellent ability to pair with a wide range of foods. Generally speaking, medium-bodied wines are characterized by dominant red-fruit flavours.

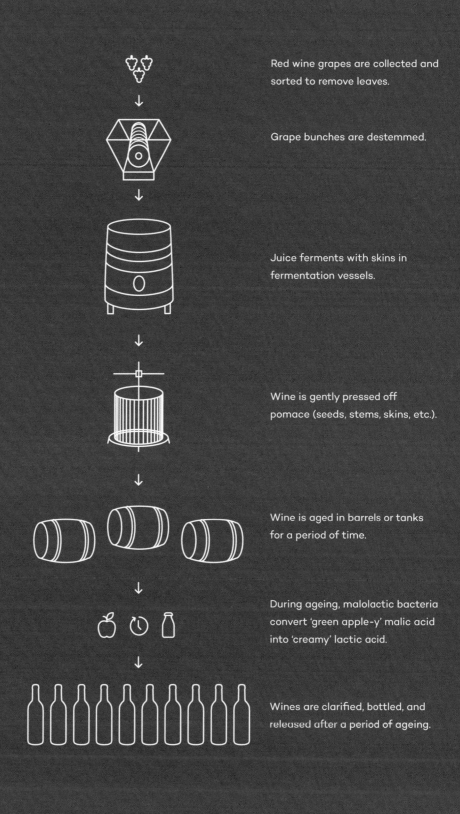

Red wine grapes are collected and sorted to remove leaves.

Grape bunches are destemmed.

Juice ferments with skins in fermentation vessels.

Wine is gently pressed off pomace (seeds, stems, skins, etc.).

Wine is aged in barrels or tanks for a period of time.

During ageing, malolactic bacteria convert 'green apple-y' malic acid into 'creamy' lactic acid.

Wines are clarified, bottled, and released after a period of ageing.

BARBERA

PROFILE

FRUIT ●●●●○
BODY ●●●●○
TANNIN ●○○○○
ACIDITY ●●●●●
ALCOHOL ●●●●○

DOMINANT FLAVOURS

SOUR CHERRY   LIQUORICE   BLACKBERRY   DRIED HERBS   TAR

POSSIBLE FLAVOURS

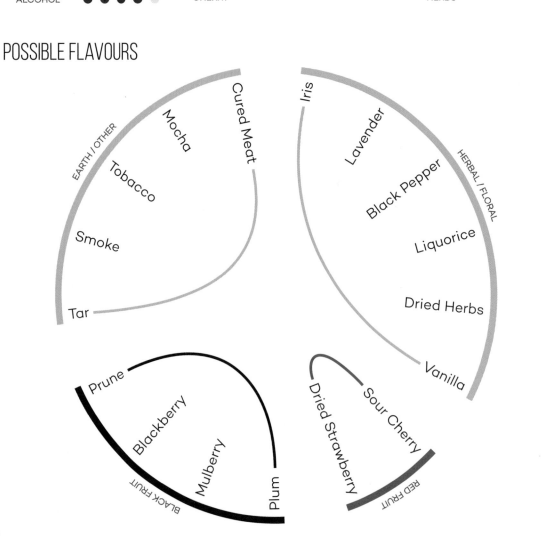

EARTH / OTHER
- Cured Meat
- Mocha
- Tobacco
- Smoke
- Tar

HERBAL / FLORAL
- Iris
- Lavender
- Black Pepper
- Liquorice
- Dried Herbs
- Vanilla

BLACK FRUIT
- Prune
- Blackberry
- Mulberry
- Plum

RED FRUIT
- Dried Strawberry
- Sour Cherry

📍 Origin: Italy

60,000
ACRES

WHERE IT GROWS

◀ ITALY
◀ USA
◀ ARGENTINA
◀ ELSEWHERE

AROMA COLLECTOR

ROOM TEMP.

UP TO 5 YRS

£5–£10

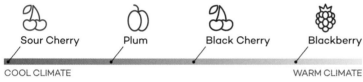

Sour Cherry   Plum   Black Cherry   Blackberry

COOL CLIMATE   WARM CLIMATE

REGIONAL DIFFERENCES: When comparing Barbera wines from different regions, you'll notice some taste differences:

 BLACKBERRY JAM & LIQUORICE
Higher alcohol wines with more fruit flavours.
● CALIFORNIA
● ARGENTINA

 MULBERRY & HERBS
Lighter wines with tart fruit and herb flavours.
● PIEDMONT, ITALY

COMMON STYLES: Barbera is produced two ways that result in two different flavour profiles:

🍷 UNOAKED = RED FRUIT
Aged in stainless steel, Barbera often has sour cherry, liquorice and herb aromas along with a brisk spicy taste.

🍫 OAKED = CHOCOLATE
Aged in oak, Barbera loses a touch of its spicy acidity and develops richer fruit flavours along with chocolate.

Looking for a particular style? Pay attention to wine descriptions when seeking out Barbera. The colour of the fruit (red v. black) often helps to identify the style.

It's useful to note that many exceptional Piedmont Barbera wines have slightly higher alcohol levels, around 14% ABV.

CABERNET FRANC

🔊 'cab-err-nay fronk'
aka: Chinon, Bourgueil, Bouchet, Breton

PROFILE

FRUIT
BODY
TANNIN
ACIDITY
ALCOHOL

DOMINANT FLAVOURS

STRAWBERRY

ROASTED PEPPER

RED PLUM

CRUSHED GRAVEL

CHILI PEPPER

POSSIBLE FLAVOURS

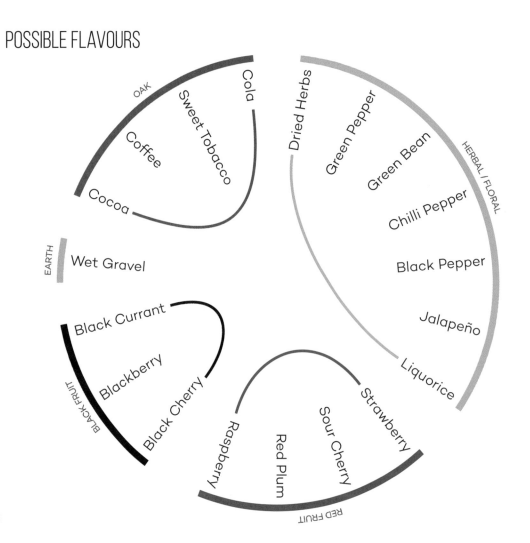

OAK
Cola
Sweet Tobacco
Coffee
Cocoa

Dried Herbs
Green Pepper
Green Bean
Chilli Pepper
Black Pepper
Jalapeño
Liquorice
HERBAL / FLORAL

EARTH
Wet Gravel

Black Currant
Blackberry
Black Cherry
BLACK FRUIT

Raspberry
Red Plum
Sour Cherry
Strawberry
RED FRUIT

📍 Origin: France

132,000
ACRES

WHERE IT GROWS

◀ FRANCE
◀ ITALY
◀ USA
◀ HUNGARY
◀ CHILE
◀ SOUTH AFRICA
◀ ELSEWHERE

RED

ROOM TEMP.

UP TO 5 YRS

£££££

£10–£15

winefolly.com/learn/winefolly.com/learn/variety/cabernet-franc

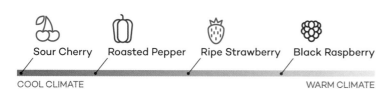

Sour Cherry   Roasted Pepper   Ripe Strawberry   Black Raspberry

COOL CLIMATE   WARM CLIMATE

REGIONAL DIFFERENCES: When comparing 100% Cabernet Franc in different regions, you'll notice these secondary flavours:

RED PEPPER
● Loire, France

STRAWBERRY JAM
● Lodi, CA

LEATHER
● Friuli, Italy

COMMON STYLES

BLENDING IN
Cabernet Franc is used in Bordeaux blends as a support character.

ZESTY & SAVOURY
At its best-tasting of red pepper, raspberry sauce, with a long tingly finish.

SWEET & SAVOURY
A fruit-forward style with sweet dried strawberry, green peppercorn and cedar.

High-quality Cabernet Franc often has high acidity and grippy tannins early on but will age beautifully for 10–15 years.

Cabernet Franc is the parent grape of Cabernet Sauvignon and Merlot.

107

CARIGNAN

🔊 'carr-in-yon'
aka: Mazuelo, Cariñena, Carignano

PROFILE

FRUIT
BODY
TANNIN
ACIDITY
ALCOHOL

DOMINANT FLAVOURS

DRIED CRANBERRY — RASPBERRY — LICORICE — BAKING SPICES — CURED MEAT

POSSIBLE FLAVOURS

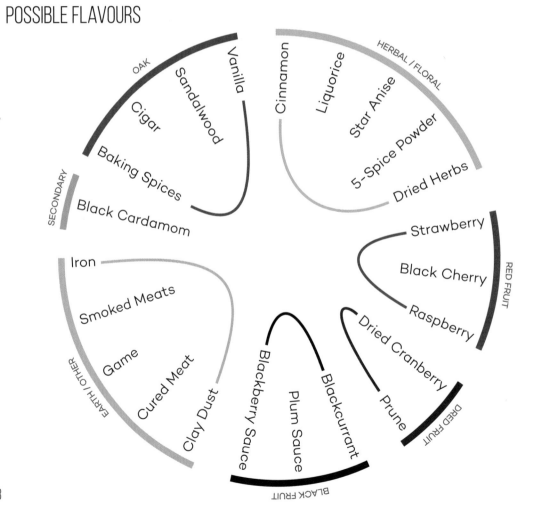

OAK
Vanilla
Sandalwood
Cigar
Baking Spices
Black Cardamom

SECONDARY

HERBAL / FLORAL
Cinnamon
Liquorice
Star Anise
5-Spice Powder
Dried Herbs

RED FRUIT
Strawberry
Black Cherry
Raspberry

DRIED FRUIT
Dried Cranberry
Prune

BLACK FRUIT
Blackberry Sauce
Plum Sauce
Blackcurrant

EARTH / OTHER
Iron
Smoked Meats
Game
Cured Meat
Clay Dust

📍 Origin: Spain

WHERE IT GROWS

198,000 ACRES

◄ FRANCE
◄ TUNISIA
◄ ALGERIA
◄ SPAIN
◄ ITALY
◄ MOROCCO
◄ USA
◄ ELSEWHERE

RED

ROOM TEMP.

UP TO 5 YRS

£ £ £ £ £
£5–£10

Strawberry   Black Currant   Blackberry   Prune

COOL CLIMATE   WARM CLIMATE

Carignan is a highly productive, drought-resistant wine grape that grows well in desert conditions. Because of this, Carignan was historically over-cropped, which produced low-quality bulk wine.

Fortunately, several quality-minded producers in Languedoc-Roussillon, France, and central Chile have resurrected the variety and use the oldest vineyards to make highly concentrated Carignan-based wines.

Try Carignan as a Christmas wine; it matches nicely with turkey, cranberries, roasted vegetables and spices.

POULTRY

CRANBERRY

BAKING SPICES

Looking for value? Look for wines from Côtes Catalanes, Faugères and Minervois appellations in Languedoc-Roussillon, France. Also, you'll find great buys from the Carignano del Sulcis region in Sardinia, Italy.

winefolly.com / learn / winefolly.com / learn / variety / carignan

109

CARMÉNÈRE

🔊 'car-men-nair'

PROFILE

FRUIT	●●●●○
BODY	●●●○○
TANNIN	●●●○○
ACIDITY	●●●○○
ALCOHOL	●●●○○

DOMINANT FLAVOURS

RASPBERRY — GREEN PEPPER — BLACK PLUM — BLACKBERRY — VANILLA

POSSIBLE FLAVOURS

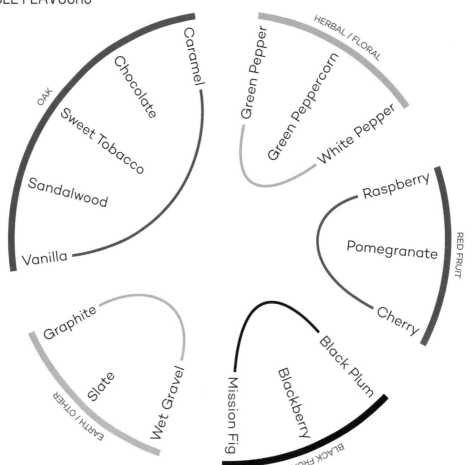

OAK: Caramel, Chocolate, Sweet Tobacco, Sandalwood, Vanilla

HERBAL / FLORAL: Green Pepper, Green Peppercorn, White Pepper

RED FRUIT: Raspberry, Pomegranate, Cherry

BLACK FRUIT: Black Plum, Blackberry, Mission Fig

EARTH / OTHER: Graphite, Slate, Wet Gravel

📍 Origin: France

WHERE IT GROWS

28,000 ACRES

◄ CHILE
◄ CHINA
◄ ITALY
◄ ELSEWHERE

RED

ROOM TEMP.

UP TO 2 YRS

£ £ £ £ £

£5–£10

Green Pepper

🍇
Raspberry

Black Plum

Jam

COOL CLIMATE   WARM CLIMATE

Carménère is a very old variety from Bordeaux, France, that has many taste similarities to Merlot and Cabernet Sauvignon.

Carménère could have become extinct had it not been mistaken for Merlot and planted in Chile during the 19th century. It wasn't until 1994 that DNA research confirmed Carménère's true identity.

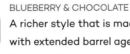

COMMON STYLES

RED FRUIT & GREEN PEPPER
A lighter style with very little oak ageing offers notes of red fruits, green pepper, paprika and cocoa powder.

BLUEBERRY & CHOCOLATE
A richer style that is made with extended barrel ageing. Tastes of blueberry, black pepper, chocolate, green peppercorn and caramel.

The region of Colchagua in Chile is well known for fine Carménère. Keep your eyes peeled for the subregions of Los Lingues or Apalta on good vintages.

Today there are less than 20 acres of Carménère in France.

111

GRENACHE

'grenn-nash'
aka: Garnacha

PROFILE

FRUIT ● ● ● ● ●
BODY ● ● ● ● ○
TANNIN ● ● ● ○ ○
ACIDITY ● ● ● ○ ○
ALCOHOL ● ● ● ● ○

DOMINANT FLAVOURS

DRIED STRAWBERRY — GRILLED PLUM — RUBY RED GRAPEFRUIT — LEATHER — LIQUORICE

POSSIBLE FLAVOURS

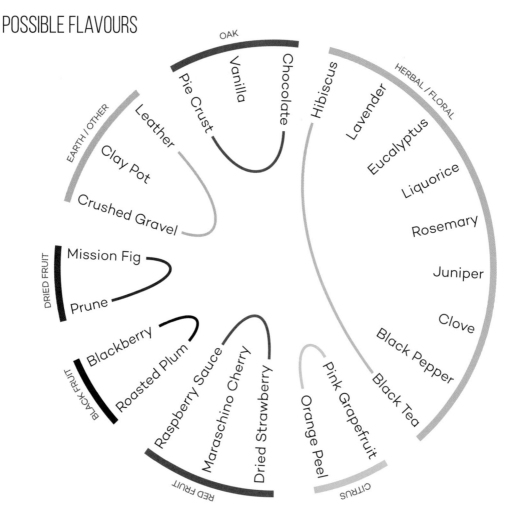

OAK
- Pie Crust
- Vanilla
- Chocolate

HERBAL / FLORAL
- Hibiscus
- Lavender
- Eucalyptus
- Liquorice
- Rosemary
- Juniper
- Clove
- Black Pepper
- Black Tea

EARTH / OTHER
- Leather
- Clay Pot
- Crushed Gravel

DRIED FRUIT
- Mission Fig
- Prune

BLACK FRUIT
- Blackberry
- Roasted Plum

RED FRUIT
- Raspberry Sauce
- Maraschino Cherry
- Dried Strawberry

CITRUS
- Orange Peel
- Pink Grapefruit

📍 Origin: Spain

456,000
ACRES

WHERE IT GROWS

◀ FRANCE
◀ SPAIN
◀ ITALY
◀ ALGERIA
◀ USA
◀ AUSTRALIA
◀ ELSEWHERE

RED

ROOM TEMP.

UP TO 5 YRS

£ £ £ £ £
£3–£6

Dried Strawberry

Raspberry Sauce

Mission Fig

Prune

COOL CLIMATE   WARM CLIMATE

REGIONAL DIFFERENCES: When comparing Grenache wines from different regions, you'll notice some taste differences:

RASPBERRY & CLOVE
Higher alcohol wines with more fruit flavours
● SPAIN
● AUSTRALIA
● USA

DRIED STRAWBERRY & HERBS
Lighter wines with more herb and tobacco flavours
● FRANCE
● ITALY

REGIONS

○ CÔTES DU RHÔNE & CHÂTEAUNEUF-DU-PAPE

○ LANGUEDOC-ROUSSILLON

○ CALATAYUD & PRIORAT

○ VINOS DE MADRID

○ CANNONAU, SARDINIA

○ PASO ROBLES, CA, USA

○ COLUMBIA VALLEY, WA, USA

○ SOUTH AUSTRALIA

In the glass, Grenache is a translucent violet-ruby hue that develops thick wine tears due to its naturally higher alcohol.

70% of the vineyards in the highly acclaimed Châteauneuf-du-Pape appellation in Rhône Valley, France, are Grenache. Quality Grenache easily ages 15–20 years.

winefolly.com / learn / winefolly.com / learn / variety / grenache

MENCÍA

🔊 'men-thee-uh'
aka: Jaen, Bierzo, Ribeira Sacra

PROFILE

FRUIT
BODY
TANNIN
ACIDITY
ALCOHOL

DOMINANT FLAVOURS

SOUR CHERRY · POMEGRANATE · BLACKBERRY · BLACK LIQUORICE · CRUSHED GRAVEL

POSSIBLE FLAVOURS

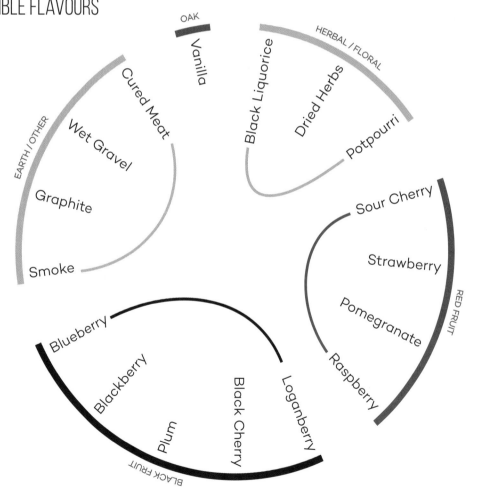

OAK
Vanilla

HERBAL / FLORAL
Black Liquorice
Dried Herbs
Potpourri

EARTH / OTHER
Cured Meat
Wet Gravel
Graphite
Smoke

RED FRUIT
Sour Cherry
Strawberry
Pomegranate
Raspberry

BLACK FRUIT
Blueberry
Blackberry
Plum
Black Cherry
Loganberry

📍 Origin: Spain

WHERE IT GROWS

◀ SPAIN
◀ PORTUGAL

26,000
ACRES

AROMA COLLECTOR

CELLAR TEMP.

UP TO 10 YRS

£ £ £ £ £
£10–£15

Pomegranate — Strawberry — Raspberry — Blueberry

COOL VINTAGE   WARM VINTAGE

RIBEIRA SACRA   BIERZO

DÃO

PORTUGAL   SPAIN

Mencía is a relatively unknown wine grape from the Iberian Peninsula that tastes remarkably similar to Merlot wines from cool climates. The grape grows mostly in the subregions of Bierzo, Ribeira Sacra and Valdeorras in Galicia, Spain and also in Dão, Portugal. (For more detail, see maps on pgs. 205 and 207.)

Highly prized Mencía wines come from old hillside vineyards.

In Portugal, Mencía is called Jaen (pronounced 'zs-eyn').

SPANISH QUALITY LEVELS: Each subregion has a different ageing system, but generally:

☐ NO CLASSIFICATION
No barrel or bottle-ageing requirements. Check with producer for specifics.

CRIANZA — CRIANZA/BARRICA
Minimal ageing in barrel and bottle (~6 months).

RESERVA — RESERVA/GRAN RESERVA
Maximum ageing in barrel and bottle before wine is released (~2–4 years).

winefolly.com / learn / winefolly.com / learn / variety / mencia

MERLOT

PROFILE

FRUIT	● ● ● ● ○
BODY	● ● ● ● ○
TANNIN	● ● ● ● ○
ACIDITY	● ● ● ○ ○
ALCOHOL	● ● ● ● ○

DOMINANT FLAVOURS

RASPBERRY — BLACK CHERRY — SUGAR PLUM — CHOCOLATE — CEDAR

POSSIBLE FLAVOURS

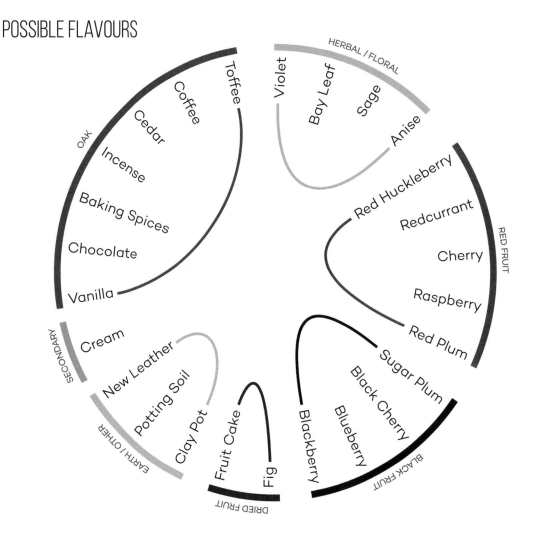

HERBAL / FLORAL: Violet, Bay Leaf, Sage, Anise

RED FRUIT: Red Huckleberry, Redcurrant, Cherry, Raspberry, Red Plum

BLACK FRUIT: Sugar Plum, Black Cherry, Blueberry, Blackberry

DRIED FRUIT: Fig, Fruit Cake

EARTH / OTHER: Clay Pot, Potting Soil, New Leather

SECONDARY: Cream

OAK: Vanilla, Chocolate, Baking Spices, Incense, Cedar, Coffee, Toffee

116

📍 Origin: France

660,000
ACRES

WHERE IT GROWS

◀ FRANCE
◀ USA
◀ SPAIN
◀ ITALY
◀ ROMANIA
◀ BULGARIA
◀ CHILE
◀ AUSTRALIA
◀ ELSEWHERE

OVERSIZED

ROOM TEMP.

UP TO 5 YRS

£ £ £ £ £
£5–£10

Red Currant   Red Plum   Sugarplum   Berry Jam

COOL CLIMATE   WARM CLIMATE

REGIONAL DIFFERENCES

When comparing Merlot wines from different regions, you'll notice some taste differences:

BLACKBERRY & VANILLA
- CALIFORNIA
- AUSTRALIA
- SOUTH AFRICA
- ARGENTINA

RED PLUM & CEDAR
- FRANCE
- ITALY
- WASHINGTON STATE
- CHILE

REGIONS

- BORDEAUX
- TUSCANY
- VENETO & FRIULI-VENEZIA GIULIA
- WASHINGTON STATE, USA
- SONOMA, CA, USA
- NAPA, CA, USA
- SOUTH AUSTRALIA
- WESTERN AUSTRALIA
- SOUTH AFRICA

Looking for quality? High-quality Merlot grapes grow in vineyards that struggle to concentrate the grapes. Look to hillside and high-elevation vineyards.

Merlot aged in American oak has rich herbaceous notes of dill and cedar.

Merlot is often misidentified as Cabernet Sauvignon in blind tasting because they're closely related (see Cabernet Franc, pgs. 106–107).

117

MONTEPULCIANO

PROFILE

FRUIT ●●●●○○
BODY ●●●●○
TANNIN ●●●●○
ACIDITY ●●●●○
ALCOHOL ●●●○○

DOMINANT FLAVOURS

RED PLUM — OREGANO — SOUR CHERRY — LOGANBERRY — TAR

POSSIBLE FLAVOURS

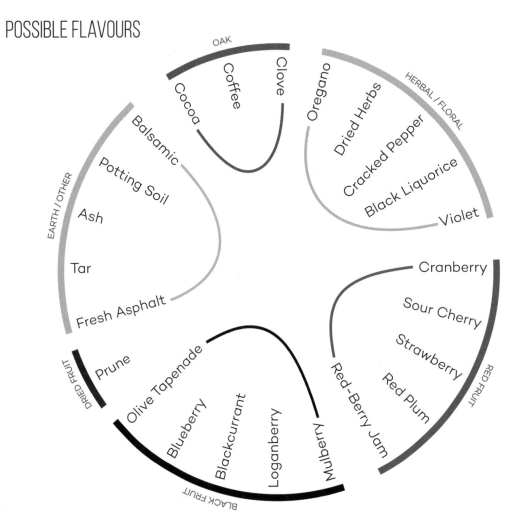

OAK
Cocoa
Coffee
Clove

HERBAL / FLORAL
Oregano
Dried Herbs
Cracked Pepper
Black Liquorice
Violet

EARTH / OTHER
Balsamic
Potting Soil
Ash
Tar
Fresh Asphalt

RED FRUIT
Cranberry
Sour Cherry
Strawberry
Red Plum
Red-Berry Jam

DRIED FRUIT
Prune

BLACK FRUIT
Olive Tapenade
Blueberry
Blackcurrant
Loganberry
Mulberry

118

📍 Origin: Southern Italy

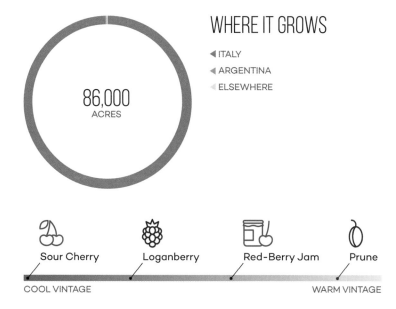

86,000
ACRES

WHERE IT GROWS

◀ ITALY
◀ ARGENTINA
◀ ELSEWHERE

OVERSIZED

ROOM TEMP.

UP TO 5 YRS

£ £ £ £ £

£3–£6

Sour Cherry

Loganberry

Red-Berry Jam

Prune

COOL VINTAGE   WARM VINTAGE

Montepulciano is the second most planted red grape in Italy. The majority of wines made from this grape are labelled 'Montepulciano d'Abruzzo' and are from Abruzzo, Italy.

Typically Montepulciano wines have red-fruit flavours similar to Merlot. High-quality producers, on the other hand, make dark-fruit full-bodied versions that will age 10+ years.

REGIONAL WINES: Montepulciano is labelled by its regional name:

● Abruzzo
MONTEPULCIANO D'ABRUZZO
CONTROGUERRA

● Marche
ROSSO CONERO
OFFIDA ROSSO DOCG
ROSSO PICENO

● Molise
BIFERNO

● Puglia
SAN SEVERO

Looking for quality? Look for a wine with at least 4 years of age and expect to spend between £15–£20 a bottle.

Montepulciano is commonly confused with Vino Nobile di Montepulciano—a wine from Tuscany made with Sangiovese.

NEGROAMARO

'neg-row-amaro'

PROFILE

FRUIT	●●●●●
BODY	●●●●○
TANNIN	●●●●○
ACIDITY	●●●○○
ALCOHOL	●●●●○

DOMINANT FLAVOURS

BLACK CHERRY · BLACK PLUM · BLACKBERRY · PRUNE · DRIED HERBS

POSSIBLE FLAVOURS

OAK: Tobacco, Clove, Chocolate, Nutmeg, Vanilla

HERBAL / FLORAL: Dried Herbs, Cinnamon, Black Liquorice

BLACK FRUIT: Black Cherry, Black Plum, Blackberry

DRIED FRUIT: Prune

EARTH / OTHER: Graphite, Potting Soil, Tar

SECONDARY: Smoke, Grilled Bread

120

📍 Origin: Puglia, Italy

WHERE IT GROWS

◀ ITALY

28,000
ACRES

Black Cherry   Black Plum   Blackberry   Prune

COOL VINTAGE   WARM VINTAGE

OVERSIZED

ROOM TEMP.

UP TO 5 YRS

£ £ £ £ £

£3–£6

winefolly.com/learn/winefolly.com/learn/variety/learn/variety/negroamaro

Negroamaro or 'black bitter' is a native grape in Puglia, Italy. It grows mostly toward the very point of the 'heel' of Puglia, Italy, along the Ionian Sea. The region is hot, so the best vineyards tend to be adjacent to the sea, where cooler night-time temperatures produce grapes with higher natural acidity and longer life.

PUGLIA

REGIONAL WINES

Negroamaro is labelled by its regional name. The following regions contain 70–100% Negroamaro:

● Puglia
   SALICE SALENTO
   ALEZIO
   NARDO
   BRINDISI
   SQUINZANO
   MATINO
   COPERTINO

Negroamaro is often blended with Primitivo (aka Zinfandel), where it complements the sweet red fruit flavours of Primitivo with tannin structure, black fruit and a smoky herbaceous quality.

Try Negroamaro with barbecued chicken and caramelized onion pizza, pulled pork sandwiches, fried mushrooms or teriyaki.

RHÔNE/GSM BLEND

🔊 'roan'
aka: Grenache-Syrah-Mourvèdre,
Côtes du Rhône

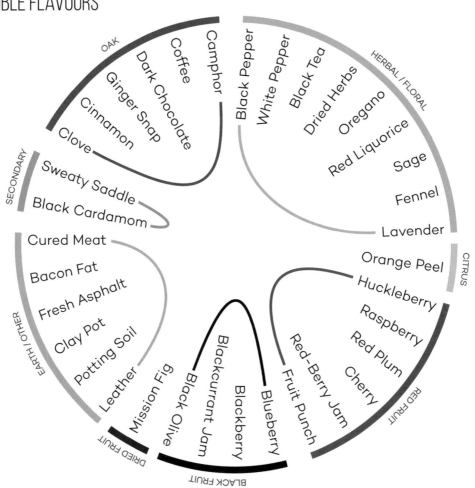

PROFILE

FRUIT ●●●●●
BODY ●●●●○
TANNIN ●●●●○
ACIDITY ●●●●○
ALCOHOL ●●●●○

DOMINANT FLAVOURS

RASPBERRY — BLACKBERRY — DRIED GREEN HERBS — BAKING SPICES — LAVENDER

POSSIBLE FLAVOURS

OAK
Camphor
Coffee
Dark Chocolate
Ginger Snap
Cinnamon
Clove

SECONDARY
Sweaty Saddle
Black Cardamom

EARTH / OTHER
Cured Meat
Bacon Fat
Fresh Asphalt
Clay Pot
Potting Soil
Leather

DRIED FRUIT
Mission Fig
Black Olive

BLACK FRUIT
Blackcurrant Jam
Blackberry
Blueberry
Fruit Punch

RED FRUIT
Red-Berry Jam
Cherry
Red Plum
Raspberry
Huckleberry

CITRUS
Orange Peel

HERBAL / FLORAL
Black Pepper
White Pepper
Black Tea
Dried Herbs
Oregano
Red Liquorice
Sage
Fennel
Lavender

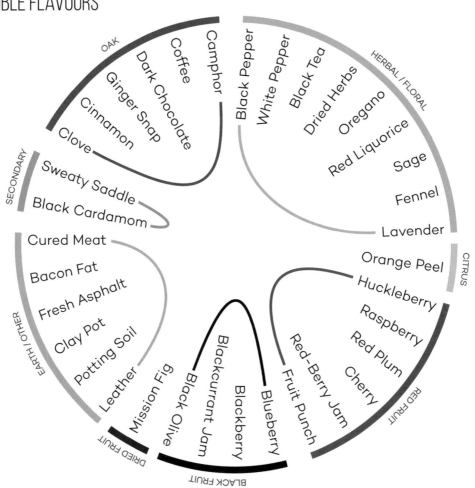

📍 Production Regions: France, Spain, Australia, USA, South Africa

THE BLEND

◀ GRENACHE
◀ SYRAH
◀ MOURVÈDRE
◀ CINSAUT
◀ CARIGNAN
◀ OTHERS

~1 MILLION ACRES

OVERSIZED

ROOM TEMP.

UP TO 5 YRS

£ £ £ £ £
£5–£10

Red Currant — Red Plum — Blackberry — Mission Fig

COOL CLIMATE   WARM CLIMATE

REGIONAL DIFFERENCES

When comparing Rhône blends from different regions, you'll notice some taste differences:

 BLACKBERRY & CLOVE
- SPAIN
- SOUTH AUSTRALIA
- SOUTH AFRICA
- CALIFORNIA, USA

 DRIED STAWBERRY & HERBS
- FRANCE
- WASHINGTON STATE, USA

REGIONS

- 🗨 CÔTES DU RHÔNE (FR)
- 🗨 LANGUEDOC-ROUSSILLON (FR)
- 🗨 CATALONIA (ESP)
- 🗨 ARAGON (ESP)
- 🗨 LA MANCHA & MADRID (ESP)
- 🗨 CENTRAL COAST, CA (USA)
- 🗨 COLUMBIA VALLEY, WA (USA)
- 🗨 SOUTH AUSTRALIA
- 🗨 SOUTH AFRICA

Looking for value? Languedoc-Roussillon, France, and La Mancha, Spain, offer good values. Look for wines with high proportions of Grenache.

The highest quality GSMs come from Priorat and Méntrida, Spain; Châteauneuf-du-Pape, France; Barossa Valley, Australia; and Santa Barbara, CA, USA.

SANGIOVESE

'san-jo vay-zay'
aka: Chianti, Brunello, Nielluccio, Morellino

PROFILE

FRUIT
BODY
TANNIN
ACIDITY
ALCOHOL

DOMINANT FLAVOURS

RED CURRANT · ROASTED TOMATO · RASPBERRY · POTPOURRI · CLAY POT

POSSIBLE FLAVOURS

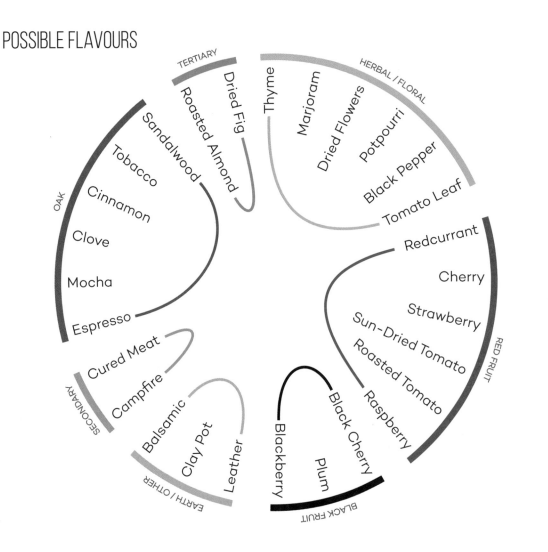

TERTIARY
Dried Fig
Roasted Almond

HERBAL / FLORAL
Thyme
Marjoram
Dried Flowers
Potpourri
Black Pepper
Tomato Leaf

OAK
Sandalwood
Tobacco
Cinnamon
Clove
Mocha
Espresso

RED FRUIT
Redcurrant
Cherry
Strawberry
Sun-Dried Tomato
Roasted Tomato
Raspberry

SECONDARY
Cured Meat
Campfire

EARTH / OTHER
Balsamic
Clay Pot
Leather

BLACK FRUIT
Blackberry
Plum
Black Cherry

Origin: Italy

192,000
ACRES

WHERE IT GROWS

◀ ITALY
◀ ARGENTINA
◀ FRANCE
◀ TUNISIA
◀ USA
◀ AUSTRALIA
◀ ELSEWHERE

RED

CELLAR TEMP.

UP TO 5 YRS

£5–£10

winefolly.com/learn/winefolly.com/learn/variety/sangiovese

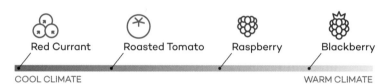

Red Currant   Roasted Tomato   Raspberry   Blackberry

COOL CLIMATE   WARM CLIMATE

COMMON STYLES

RUSTIC TOMATO & LEATHER
Traditional production maintains Sangiovese's herbaceous flavours and high acidity by aging wines in well-used barrels that don't impart vanilla-like flavours.

MODERN CHERRY & CLOVE
The modern style of Sangiovese wines employs oak ageing to produce sweet vanilla-like flavours and also smoother acidity.

REGIONAL WINES: Sangiovese is commonly labelled by its regional name. The following regions contain 60–100% Sangiovese:

● Tuscany
   CHIANTI
   BRUNELLO DI MONTALCINO
   ROSSO DI MONTALCINO
   VINO NOBILE DI MONTEPULCIANO
   MORELLINO DI SCANSANO
   CARMIGNANO
   MONTECUCCO

● Umbria
   MONTEFALCO ROSSO

Sangiovese pairs with rich meats and tomato-based dishes such as lasagna, pasta Bolognese and pizza.

Sangiovese is Italy's top wine. It is produced primarily in Tuscany, Campania, and Umbria.

VALPOLICELLA BLEND

🔊 'val-polli-chellah'
aka: Amarone

PROFILE

FRUIT	●●●○○
BODY	●●●○○
TANNIN	●●●○○
ACIDITY	●●●●●
ALCOHOL	●●●○○

DOMINANT FLAVOURS

SOUR CHERRY — CINNAMON — GREEN PEPPERCORN — CAROB — GREEN ALMOND

POSSIBLE FLAVOURS

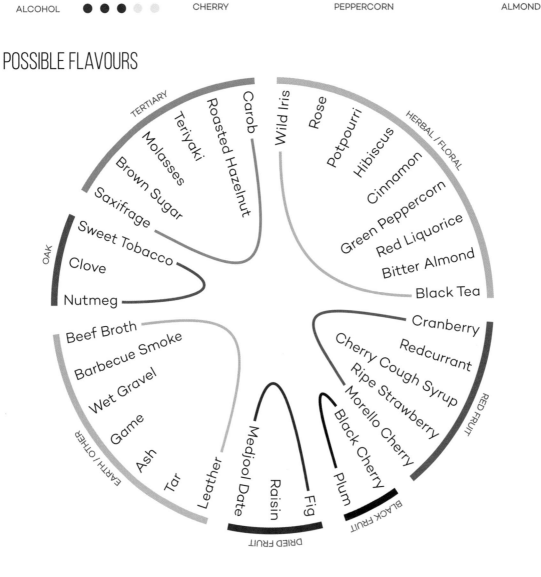

TERTIARY: Carob, Roasted Hazelnut, Teriyaki, Molasses, Brown Sugar, Saxifrage

HERBAL / FLORAL: Wild Iris, Rose, Potpourri, Hibiscus, Cinnamon, Green Peppercorn, Red Liquorice, Bitter Almond, Black Tea

OAK: Sweet Tobacco, Clove, Nutmeg

RED FRUIT: Cranberry, Redcurrant, Cherry Cough Syrup, Ripe Strawberry, Morello Cherry

EARTH / OTHER: Beef Broth, Barbecue Smoke, Wet Gravel, Game, Ash, Tar, Leather

DRIED FRUIT: Medjool Date, Raisin, Fig

BLACK FRUIT: Plum, Black Cherry

126

📍 Origin: Veneto, Italy

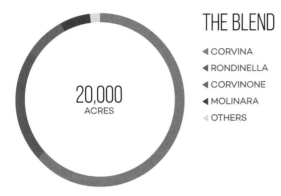

THE BLEND

◄ CORVINA
◄ RONDINELLA
◄ CORVINONE
◄ MOLINARA
◄ OTHERS

20,000
ACRES

RED

CELLAR TEMP.

UP TO 5 YRS

£ £ £ £ £

£10–£15

 Cranberry 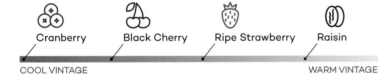 Black Cherry Ripe Strawberry Raisin

COOL VINTAGE   WARM VINTAGE

There are 4 main grapes of Valpolicella. The Corvina and Corvinone grapes are known to produce the highest quality wines.

🍇 CORVINA & CORVINONE
Spicy red fruit and green almond flavours.

🍇 RONDINELLA
Adds floral aromas and has low tannin.

🍇 MOLINARA
Known for high acidity.

QUALITY LEVELS

£ VALPOLICELLA CLASSICO
tart cherry and ash

££ VALPOLICELLA SUPERIORE
dark berries and high acidity

£££ VALPOLICELLA SUPERIORE RIPASSO
cherry sauce, green peppercorn and carob

£££££ AMARONE DELLA VALPOLICELLA
black cherry, fig, saxifrage, chocolate and brown sugar

£££££ RECIOTO DELLA VALPOLICELLA
raisin, black cherry, clove and roasted hazelnut

Looking for value? Some Ripasso taste very similar to Amarone at a fraction of the price.

Amarone and Recioto are made with the *apassimento* method. Grapes are dried on straw mats over the winter to concentrate sugars and then pressed and fermented very slowly. The resulting wines are light in colour but rich in body and flavour.

127

ZINFANDEL

🔊 'zin-fan-dell'
aka: Primitivo, Tribidrag

PROFILE

FRUIT	● ● ● ● ●
BODY	● ● ● ● ○
TANNIN	● ● ● ○ ○
ACIDITY	● ● ○ ○ ○
ALCOHOL	● ● ● ● ●

DOMINANT FLAVOURS

 BLACKBERRY

 STRAWBERRY

 PEACH PRESERVES

 5-SPICE POWDER

 SWEET TOBACCO

POSSIBLE FLAVOURS

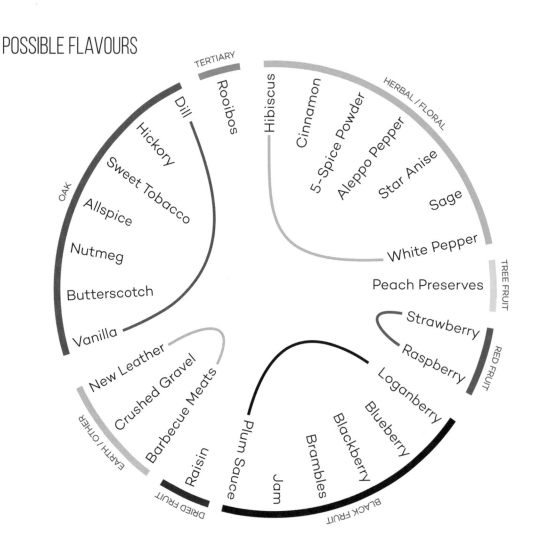

TERTIARY
- Rooibos

HERBAL / FLORAL
- Hibiscus
- Cinnamon
- 5-Spice Powder
- Aleppo Pepper
- Star Anise
- Sage
- White Pepper

TREE FRUIT
- Peach Preserves

RED FRUIT
- Strawberry
- Raspberry
- Loganberry

BLACK FRUIT
- Blueberry
- Blackberry
- Brambles
- Jam
- Plum Sauce

DRIED FRUIT
- Raisin

EARTH / OTHER
- Barbecue Meats
- Crushed Gravel
- New Leather

OAK
- Dill
- Hickory
- Sweet Tobacco
- Allspice
- Nutmeg
- Butterscotch
- Vanilla

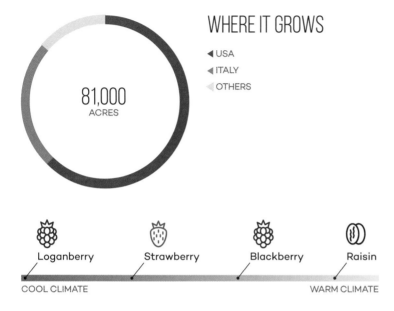

81,000
ACRES

WHERE IT GROWS

◀ USA
◀ ITALY
◀ OTHERS

RED

ROOM TEMP.

UP TO 2 YRS

£ £ £ £
£5–£10

Loganberry   Strawberry   Blackberry   Raisin

COOL CLIMATE   WARM CLIMATE

The origin of Zinfandel remained a mystery until DNA testing showed it was identical to Primitivo in Italy and Tribidrag in Croatia, where the grape originated. Zinfandel used to be prized and traded in Venice during the 1400s.

Zinfandel naturally produces a rich red wine; however, only about 15% of the US production is dedicated to this style. The rest goes into sappy-sweet rosé called White Zinfandel.

REGIONS

CALIFORNIA, USA
The best Zinfandel grows in the hills of Napa, Sonoma, Paso Robles and the Sierra Foothills. Exceptional old vineyards can be found in Lodi.

ITALY
In Puglia, most Primitivo is lighter in style but can reach incredible depth in and around Manduria. It's often blended with Negroamaro.

COMMON STYLES

RED FRUITS & SPICE
A lighter style with lower alcohol (~13.5%) has raspberry, rose petal, spice cake, sage and black pepper flavours.

JAM & SMOKED CARAMEL
A rich style with higher alcohol (~15%) offers blackberry, cinnamon, caramel, jam, chocolate and smoky tobacco flavours.

129

Full-Bodied Red Wine

AGLIANICO

BORDEAUX BLEND

CABERNET SAUVIGNON

MALBEC

MOURVÈDRE

NEBBIOLO

NERO D'AVOLA

PETIT VERDOT

PETITE SIRAH

PINOTAGE

SYRAH

TEMPRANILLO

TOURIGA NACIONAL

Full-bodied red wines typically have high tannin, opaque ruby colour from high anthocyanin content, and rich fruit flavours. Wines that are bold such as these can be enjoyed on their own or with equally bold-flavoured foods.

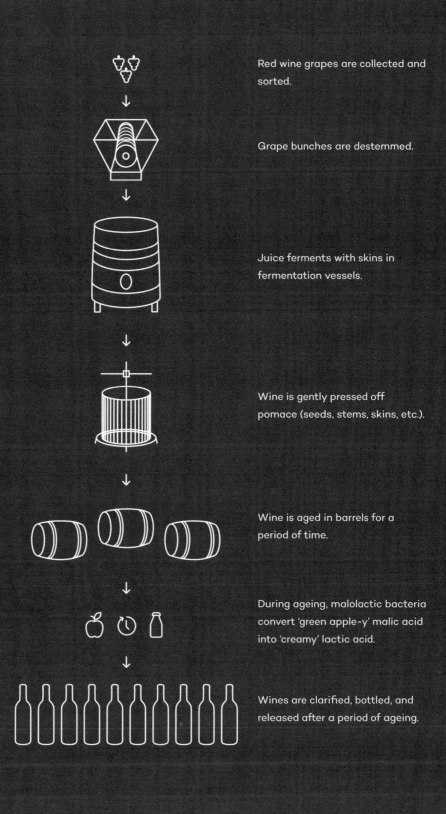

Red wine grapes are collected and sorted.

Grape bunches are destemmed.

Juice ferments with skins in fermentation vessels.

Wine is gently pressed off pomace (seeds, stems, skins, etc.).

Wine is aged in barrels for a period of time.

During ageing, malolactic bacteria convert 'green apple-y' malic acid into 'creamy' lactic acid.

Wines are clarified, bottled, and released after a period of ageing.

AGLIANICO

🔊 'alli-yan-nico'
aka: Taurasi

PROFILE

FRUIT	●●●○○
BODY	●●●●●
TANNIN	●●●●●
ACIDITY	●●●●●
ALCOHOL	●●●●○

DOMINANT FLAVOURS

WHITE PEPPER — BLACK CHERRY — SMOKE — GAME — SPICED PLUM

POSSIBLE FLAVOURS

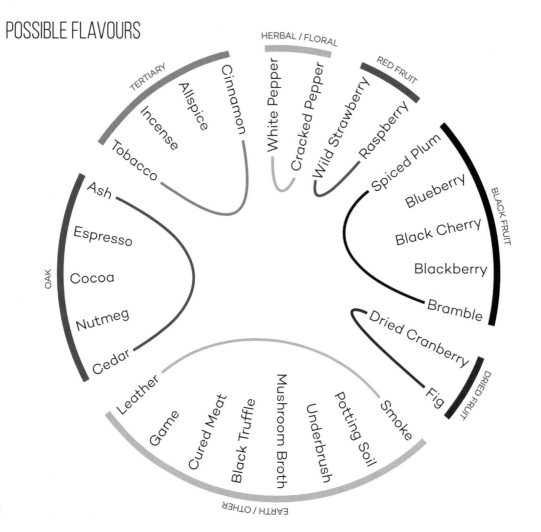

HERBAL / FLORAL
RED FRUIT
BLACK FRUIT
DRIED FRUIT
EARTH / OTHER
OAK
TERTIARY

Cinnamon
Allspice
Incense
Tobacco
Ash
Espresso
Cocoa
Nutmeg
Cedar
Leather
Game
Cured Meat
Black Truffle
Mushroom Broth
Underbrush
Potting Soil
Smoke
Fig
Dried Cranberry
Bramble
Blackberry
Black Cherry
Blueberry
Spiced Plum
Raspberry
Wild Strawberry
Cracked Pepper
White Pepper

📍 Origin: Southern Italy

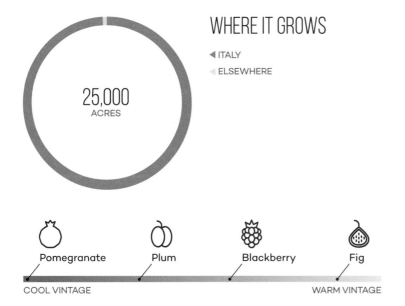

25,000
ACRES

WHERE IT GROWS

◄ ITALY
◄ ELSEWHERE

OVERSIZED

ROOM TEMP.

UP TO 15 YEARS

£ £ £ £ £
£10–£20

Pomegranate　　Plum　　Blackberry　　Fig

COOL VINTAGE　　　　　　　　WARM VINTAGE

winefolly.com / learn / winefolly.com / learn / variety / aglianico

Aglianico produces wines with a deep colour, high tannin and acidity. It is considered one of the classic wines of Southern Italy.

Decanting improves the taste of bold red wines like Aglianico. Decant this wine for at least 2 hours.

AGLIANICO WINES

AGLIANICO DEL VULTURE
Flavours of blackberry sauce, liquorice, and smoke. 100% Aglianico from Mount Vulture in Basilicata.

TAURASI
Flavours of black raspberry, smoked meats and cigar. Look for wines with around 10 years of age.

AGLIANICO DEL TABURNO
Flavours of black cherry, dried cranberry, cocoa powder, allspice and smoke. 100% Aglianico from the Taburno Mountains in Campania.

IRPINIA, BENEVENTANO, & CAMPANIA
Flavours of black fruits, green herbs and charcoal. Larger encompassing regions offer value alternatives. Have a decanter handy.

133

BORDEAUX BLEND

🔊 'bore-doe'
aka: Meritage, Cabernet-Merlot

PROFILE

FRUIT	●●●●○
BODY	●●●●●
TANNIN	●●●●●
ACIDITY	●●●○○
ALCOHOL	●●●●○

DOMINANT FLAVOURS

PLUM — BLACK CURRANT — VIOLET — GRAPHITE — CEDAR

POSSIBLE FLAVOURS

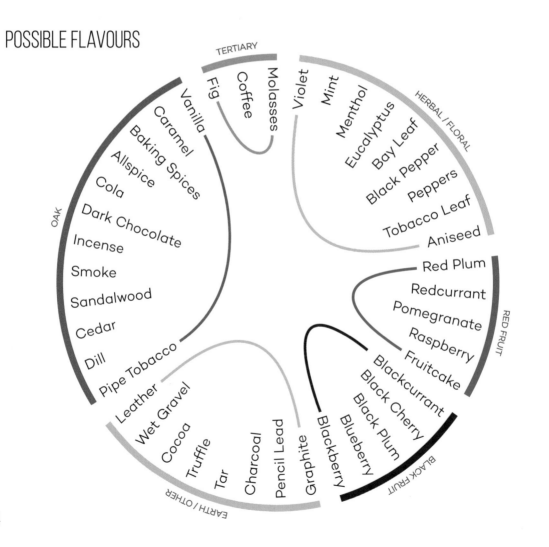

TERTIARY: Fig, Coffee, Molasses

HERBAL / FLORAL: Violet, Mint, Menthol, Eucalyptus, Bay Leaf, Black Pepper, Peppers, Tobacco Leaf, Aniseed

RED FRUIT: Red Plum, Redcurrant, Pomegranate, Raspberry, Fruitcake

BLACK FRUIT: Blackcurrant, Black Cherry, Black Plum, Blueberry, Blackberry

EARTH / OTHER: Graphite, Pencil Lead, Charcoal, Tar, Truffle, Cocoa, Wet Gravel, Leather

OAK: Vanilla, Caramel, Baking Spices, Allspice, Cola, Dark Chocolate, Incense, Smoke, Sandalwood, Cedar, Dill, Pipe Tobacco

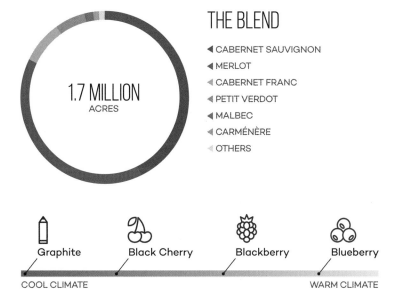

THE BLEND

◀ CABERNET SAUVIGNON
◀ MERLOT
◀ CABERNET FRANC
◀ PETIT VERDOT
◀ MALBEC
◀ CARMÉNÈRE
◀ OTHERS

1.7 MILLION
ACRES

OVERSIZED

ROOM TEMP.

UP TO 10 YRS

£10–£20

Graphite   Black Cherry   Blackberry   Blueberry

COOL CLIMATE   WARM CLIMATE

REGIONAL DIFFERENCES: When comparing Bordeaux blends from different regions, you'll notice some taste differences:

 BLACKBERRY, MENTHOL & CEDAR
Expect ripe black fruit with undertones of menthol, chocolate and allspice. Wines may be bolder with riper-tasting tannin.

● PASO ROBLES & NAPA, CA, USA
● AUSTRALIA
● MENDOZA, ARGENTINA
● SOUTH AFRICA
● TUSCANY, ITALY
● SPAIN

 BLACK CHERRY, VIOLET & BAY LEAF
Expect tart black and red fruit flavours with undertones of violet, black pepper and bay leaf. Wines may taste lighter due to higher acidity.

● BORDEAUX, FRANCE
● SOUTH WEST FRANCE
● CHILE
● VENETO, ITALY
● WASHINGTON STATE, USA
● COASTAL SONOMA, CA, USA
● MENDOCINO, CA, USA

Blends dominated by Cabernet Sauvignon typically have grippier tannin and green peppercorn notes, whereas Merlot blends have smoother tannins and more red fruit notes.

The first Bordeaux blend to become popular was not a red wine but a brilliant red rosé called Clairet ('Clair-ette'). Today, Clairet is rare but can still be found under the basic Bordeaux appellation.

CABERNET SAUVIGNON

PROFILE

FRUIT	● ● ● ● ○
BODY	● ● ● ● ●
TANNIN	● ● ● ● ○
ACIDITY	● ● ○ ○ ○
ALCOHOL	● ● ● ● ○

DOMINANT FLAVOURS

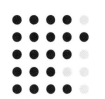

BLACK CHERRY · BLACKCURRANT · RED PEPPER · BAKING SPICES · CEDAR

POSSIBLE FLAVOURS

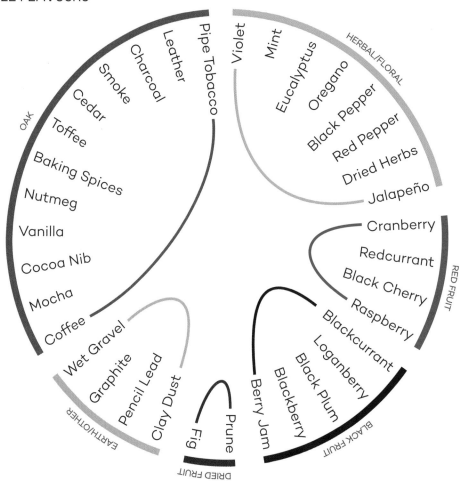

OAK: Pipe Tobacco, Leather, Charcoal, Smoke, Cedar, Toffee, Baking Spices, Nutmeg, Vanilla, Cocoa Nib, Mocha, Coffee

HERBAL/FLORAL: Violet, Mint, Eucalyptus, Oregano, Black Pepper, Red Pepper, Dried Herbs, Jalapeño

RED FRUIT: Cranberry, Redcurrant, Black Cherry, Raspberry

BLACK FRUIT: Blackcurrant, Loganberry, Black Plum, Blackberry, Berry Jam

DRIED FRUIT: Fig, Prune

EARTH/OTHER: Wet Gravel, Graphite, Pencil Lead, Clay Dust

136

📍 Origin: France

717,000
ACRES

WHERE IT GROWS

◀ FRANCE
◀ CHILE
◀ USA
◀ AUSTRALIA
◀ SPAIN
◀ CHINA
◀ ARGENTINA

◀ ITALY
◀ SOUTH AFRICA
◀ ELSEWHERE

OVERSIZED

ROOM TEMP.

UP TO 10 YRS

££££
£10–£20

Redcurrant — Blackcurrant — Black Cherry — Blackberry

COOL CLIMATE — WARM CLIMATE

REGIONAL DIFFERENCES: When comparing Cabernet Sauvignon wines from different regions, you'll notice some taste differences:

🫐 BLACK FRUITS, BLACK PEPPER AND COCOA POWDER
Warm climate regions lend to more fruit-forward wines with higher alcohol and ripe-tasting tannin.

- CALIFORNIA, USA
- AUSTRALIA
- ARGENTINA
- SOUTH AFRICA
- CENTRAL AND SOUTHERN ITALY
- SPAIN

🍒 RED FRUITS, MINT AND GREEN PEPPERCORN
Cool-climate Cabernet tends to exhibit red fruit flavours and a lighter body.

- BORDEAUX, FRANCE
- CHILE
- NORTHERN ITALY
- WASHINGTON STATE, USA
- NORTHERN CALIFORNIA, USA

Cabernet Sauvignon is a natural cross between Cabernet Franc and Sauvignon Blanc that first appeared in Bordeaux in the mid-1600s. Today, it is the most planted wine grape in the world.

winefolly.com/learn/winefolly.com/learn/variety/cabernet-sauvignon

MALBEC

🔊 'mal-bek'
aka: Côt

winefolly.com / learn / variety / malbec

PROFILE

FRUIT ●●●●●
BODY ●●●●○
TANNIN ●●●○○
ACIDITY ●●●○○
ALCOHOL ●●●●○

DOMINANT FLAVOURS

RED PLUM   BLUEBERRY   VANILLA   SWEET TOBACCO   COCOA

POSSIBLE FLAVOURS

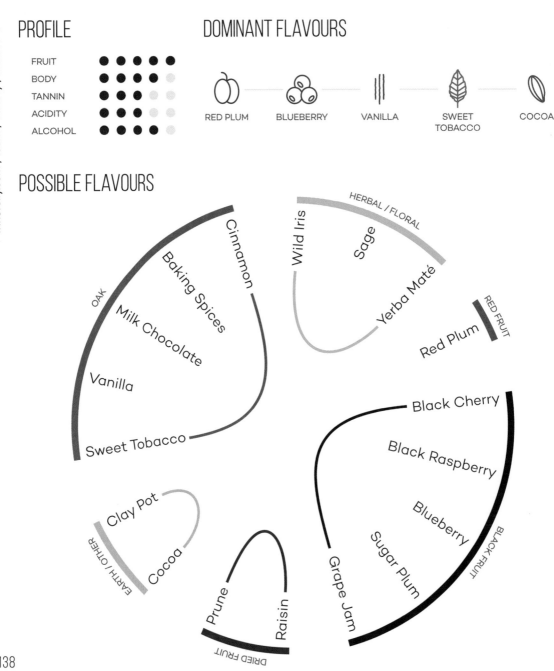

OAK

Cinnamon
Baking Spices
Milk Chocolate
Vanilla
Sweet Tobacco

HERBAL / FLORAL

Wild Iris
Sage
Yerba Maté

RED FRUIT

Red Plum

Black Cherry
Black Raspberry
Blueberry
Sugar Plum
Grape Jam

BLACK FRUIT

EARTH / OTHER

Clay Pot
Cocoa

Prune
Raisin

DRIED FRUIT

138

📍 Origin: South West France

WHERE IT GROWS

101,000
ACRES

◄ ARGENTINA
◄ FRANCE
◄ CHILE
◄ USA
◄ SOUTH AFRICA
◄ AUSTRALIA
◄ ITALY
◄ ELSEWHERE

Red Plum   Black Cherry   Sugar Plum   Blueberry

COOL CLIMATE   WARM CLIMATE

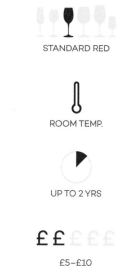

STANDARD RED

ROOM TEMP.

UP TO 2 YRS

£ £ £ £ £
£5–£10

winefolly.com / learn / winefolly.com / learn / variety / malbec

Malbec originated in South West France around Cahors but was never considered an important wine until Argentina revived the variety. Today, Argentina produces over 75% of the world's Malbec wines.

The majority of Malbec in Argentina comes from around Mendoza, with the best wines coming primarily from the high-elevation subregions of Uco Valley and Luján de Cuyo.

COMMON STYLES

BASIC MALBEC
A juicy style of Malbec with dominant red fruit flavours and balanced tannin, made with little to no oak ageing.

RESERVA MALBEC
Higher-end Malbec wines tend to age in oak longer and offer black fruit, chocolate, sweet tobacco and subtle notes of wild iris.

In Argentina, altitude is a key quality indicator for Malbec. Higher-elevation Malbec will have higher acidity, more tannin and additional flower and herb notes.

In France, Malbec is mostly from Cahors in the South West region. This wine, with a more earthy profile, is very different from Argentine Malbec. Expect higher tannin and flavours of red- and blackcurrant, smoke and liquorice.

139

MOURVÈDRE

PROFILE

FRUIT ●●●●○
BODY ●●●●●
TANNIN ●●●●●
ACIDITY ●●●●○
ALCOHOL ●●●●○

DOMINANT FLAVOURS

BLACKBERRY — BLACK PEPPER — COCOA — SWEET TOBACCO — ROASTED MEAT

POSSIBLE FLAVOURS

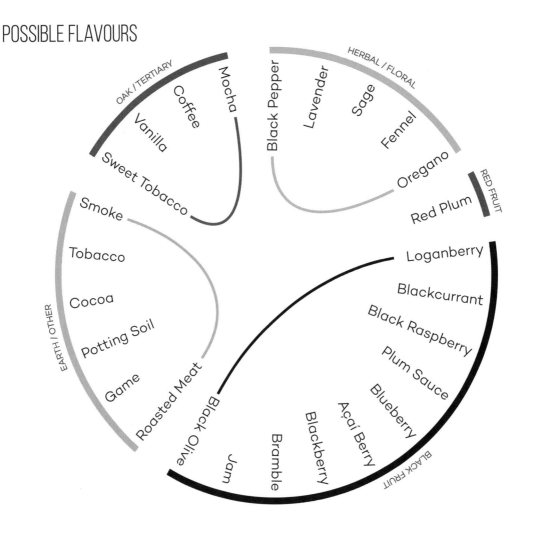

OAK / TERTIARY
- Mocha
- Coffee
- Vanilla
- Sweet Tobacco

HERBAL / FLORAL
- Black Pepper
- Lavender
- Sage
- Fennel
- Oregano

RED FRUIT
- Red Plum

EARTH / OTHER
- Smoke
- Tobacco
- Cocoa
- Potting Soil
- Game
- Roasted Meat

BLACK FRUIT
- Loganberry
- Blackcurrant
- Black Raspberry
- Plum Sauce
- Blueberry
- Açaí Berry
- Blackberry
- Bramble
- Jam
- Black Olive

📍 Origin: Spain

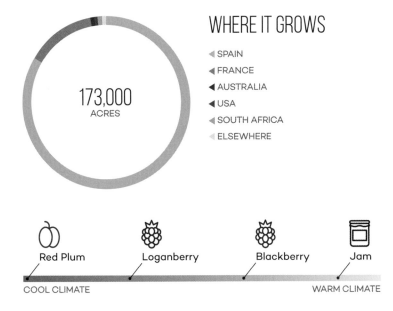

173,000
ACRES

WHERE IT GROWS

◀ SPAIN
◀ FRANCE
◀ AUSTRALIA
◀ USA
◀ SOUTH AFRICA
◀ ELSEWHERE

RED

ROOM TEMP.

UP TO 10 YRS

£ £ £ £ £
£5–£10

Red Plum

Loganberry

Blackberry

Jam

COOL CLIMATE   WARM CLIMATE

This variety is very old and may have been introduced to Spain by the Phoenicians who travelled into Catalonia around 500 BCE.

Mourvèdre is most commonly used as a blending grape, and is the 'M' in the Rhône/GSM blend. It adds colour, tannin structure and black fruit flavours.

🌍

REGIONS

SPAIN
Called Monastrell in Spain and found in Valencia, Jumilla, Yecla, Almansa and Alicante.

FRANCE
Single-varietal Mourvèdre wines are labelled 'Bandol', an appellation in Provence.

AUSTRALIA
Called Mataro and found in South Australia, where it's used in GSM blends.

Looking for value? Bottles of Spanish Monastrell are of superb value and don't require ageing. Decant Monastrell for at least 1 hour.

In Spain, Monastrell is used in Cava to make sparkling rosé.

In France, Mourvèdre is also made into a non-sparkling rosé. You can find this style in Bandol, Provence.

141

NEBBIOLO

🔊 'nebby-oh-low'

aka: Barolo, Barbaresco, Spanna, Chiavennasca

PROFILE

FRUIT	●●● ○ ○
BODY	●●●● ○
TANNIN	●●●●●
ACIDITY	●●●●●
ALCOHOL	●●●● ○

DOMINANT FLAVOURS

ROSE — CHERRY — LEATHER — CLAY POT — ANISE

POSSIBLE FLAVOURS

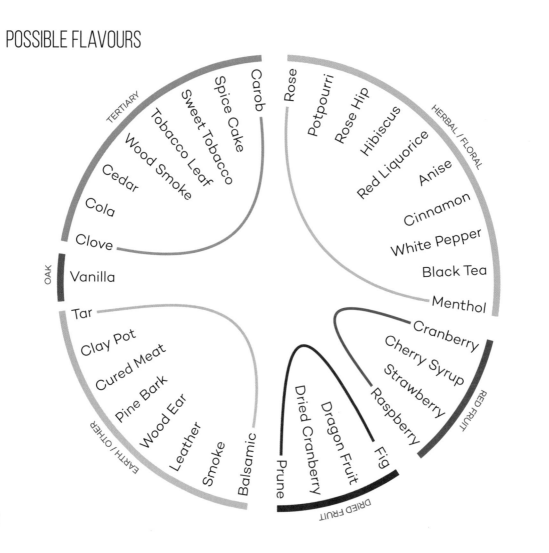

TERTIARY: Carob, Spice Cake, Sweet Tobacco, Tobacco Leaf, Wood Smoke, Cedar, Cola, Clove

OAK: Vanilla, Tar

EARTH / OTHER: Clay Pot, Cured Meat, Pine Bark, Wood Ear, Leather, Smoke, Balsamic

DRIED FRUIT: Prune, Dried Cranberry, Dragon Fruit, Fig

RED FRUIT: Raspberry, Strawberry, Cherry Syrup, Cranberry

HERBAL / FLORAL: Rose, Potpourri, Rose Hip, Hibiscus, Red Liquorice, Anise, Cinnamon, White Pepper, Black Tea, Menthol

142

📍 Origin: northern Italy

14,800
ACRES

WHERE IT GROWS

◀ ITALY
◀ MEXICO
◀ ARGENTINA
◀ AUSTRALIA
◀ USA
◀ OTHERS

AROMA COLLECTOR

CELLAR TEMP.

15+ YRS

£ £ £ £ £

£20

Cranberry   Cherry   Dried Dragon Fruit   Fruitcake

COOL VINTAGE   WARM VINTAGE

Nebbiolo is considered one of Italy's top red wines. It is perhaps more famously known by the names of its two top regions: Barolo and Barbaresco. Nebbiolo wines are pale-coloured and aromatic—*features of a light-bodied wine*—however, since Nebbiolo is naturally high in tannin, it can be characterized as a full-bodied red.

Nebbiolo wines improve with age and reveal subtle molasses, fig and leather flavours.

REGIONAL WINES: Nebbiolo is commonly labelled by its regional name. The following regions contain 70–100% Nebbiolo:

- Piedmont
  BAROLO
  BARBARESCO
  NEBBIOLO D'ALBA
  LANGHE NEBBIOLO
  ROERO
  GATTINARA
  CAREMA
  GHEMME

- Lombardy
  VALTELLINA & SFORZATO

Love Nebbiolo? Wines labelled as 'Langhe Nebbiolo' offer exceptional value on good vintages.

During the mid-1800s Barolo was a sweet red wine.

Barolo Chinato is a richly spiced red vermouth made with Nebbiolo.

143

NERO D'AVOLA

PROFILE

FRUIT
BODY
TANNIN
ACIDITY
ALCOHOL

DOMINANT FLAVOURS

BLACK CHERRY · BLACK PLUM · LIQUORICE · TOBACCO · CHILLI PEPPER

POSSIBLE FLAVOURS

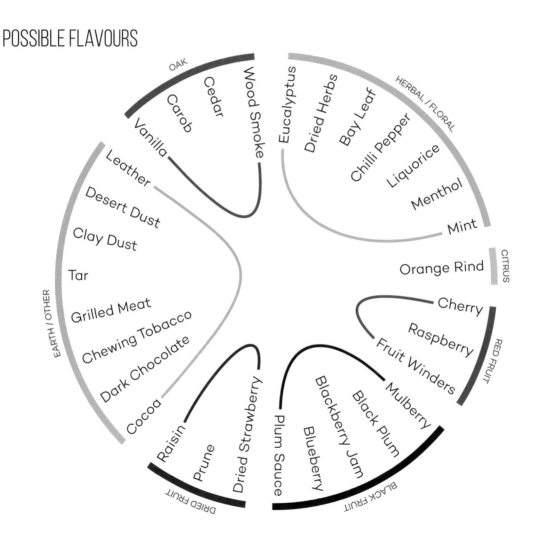

OAK
Wood Smoke
Cedar
Carob
Vanilla

HERBAL / FLORAL
Eucalyptus
Dried Herbs
Bay Leaf
Chilli Pepper
Liquorice
Menthol
Mint

CITRUS
Orange Rind

RED FRUIT
Cherry
Raspberry
Fruit Winders
Mulberry

EARTH / OTHER
Leather
Desert Dust
Clay Dust
Tar
Grilled Meat
Chewing Tobacco
Dark Chocolate
Cocoa

DRIED FRUIT
Raisin
Prune
Dried Strawberry

BLACK FRUIT
Plum Sauce
Blueberry
Blackberry Jam
Black Plum

144

📍 Origin: Sicily, Italy

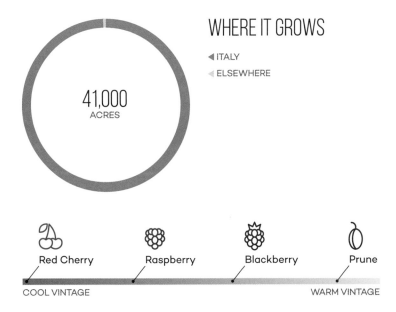

WHERE IT GROWS

◀ ITALY
◀ ELSEWHERE

41,000
ACRES

OVERSIZED

ROOM TEMP.

UP TO 10 YRS

£££££
£10–£15

Red Cherry

Raspberry

Blackberry

Prune

COOL VINTAGE

WARM VINTAGE

Nero d'Avola is the most planted red variety on the Island of Sicily. The wines have very bold sweet fruit flavours and often a subtly sweet smoky finish.

Quality Nero d'Avola wines are often described as having red fruit, black pepper, liquorice and spice cake flavours.

The spicy pepper flavours in Nero d'Avola become smoother with an hour of decanting.

If you like the candied red fruit flavours of Nero d'Avola, you might also enjoy other Sicilian red wines:

🍷 FRAPPATO
🍷 NERELLO MASCALESE

Try pairing Nero d'Avola with oxtail soup, beef and barley stew, or bacon burgers. Dishes with gamey and meaty flavours will bring out the wine's bright, sweet fruit flavours.

OXTAIL SOUP

BEEF AND BARLEY STEW

BACON BURGER

winefolly.com/learn/winefolly.com/learn/variety/nero-davola

145

PETIT VERDOT

PROFILE

FRUIT	● ● ● ● ○
BODY	● ● ● ● ●
TANNIN	● ● ● ● ●
ACIDITY	● ● ● ● ○
ALCOHOL	● ● ● ● ○

DOMINANT FLAVOURS

BLACK CHERRY   PLUM   VIOLET   LILAC   SAGE

POSSIBLE FLAVOURS

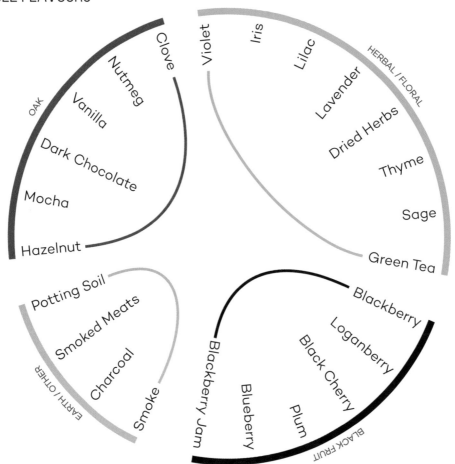

OAK: Clove, Nutmeg, Vanilla, Dark Chocolate, Mocha, Hazelnut

HERBAL / FLORAL: Violet, Iris, Lilac, Lavender, Dried Herbs, Thyme, Sage, Green Tea

EARTH / OTHER: Potting Soil, Smoked Meats, Charcoal, Smoke

BLACK FRUIT: Blackberry, Loganberry, Black Cherry, Plum, Blueberry, Blackberry Jam

📍 Origin: France

17,800
ACRES

WHERE IT GROWS

◄ SPAIN
◄ FRANCE
◄ AUSTRALIA
◄ USA
◄ SOUTH AFRICA
◄ CHILE
◄ ARGENTINA
◄ ELSEWHERE

OVERSIZED

ROOM TEMP.

UP TO 5 YRS

£ £ £ £ £

£10–£15

Dried Herbs

Black Cherry

Blueberry

Blackberry Jam

COOL CLIMATE   WARM CLIMATE

Petit Verdot is highly desired as a blending grape because of its deep purple colour, high tannin and floral aromas. You'll find this grape most commonly used in Bordeaux blends.

If you would like to taste a single-varietal Petit Verdot, look in Washington State, California, Spain and Australia, where conditions are sunny enough to properly ripen the grape.

REGIONS

SPAIN
Found in Castilla-La Mancha where it adds dark fruit flavours to Bordeaux blends.

BORDEAUX, FRANCE
The classic 'Left Bank' Bordeaux blend has about 1–2% Petit Verdot.

AUSTRALIA & USA
Single-varietal Petit Verdot wines taste of blueberry, vanilla and violets.

Looking for a bolder Bordeaux blend? Seek wines with a higher proportion of Petit Verdot and/or Petite Sirah.

The most famous Chilean Carménère, called 'Purple Angel', adds 10% Petit Verdot to embolden the wine with notes of dark fruit, chocolate and sage.

PETITE SIRAH

🔊 'peh-teet sear-ah'
aka: Durif, Petite Syrah

PROFILE

FRUIT	●●●●●
BODY	●●●●●
TANNIN	●●●●●
ACIDITY	●●●○○
ALCOHOL	●●●●●

DOMINANT FLAVOURS

SUGAR PLUM	BLUEBERRY	DARK CHOCOLATE	BLACK PEPPER	BLACK TEA

POSSIBLE FLAVOURS

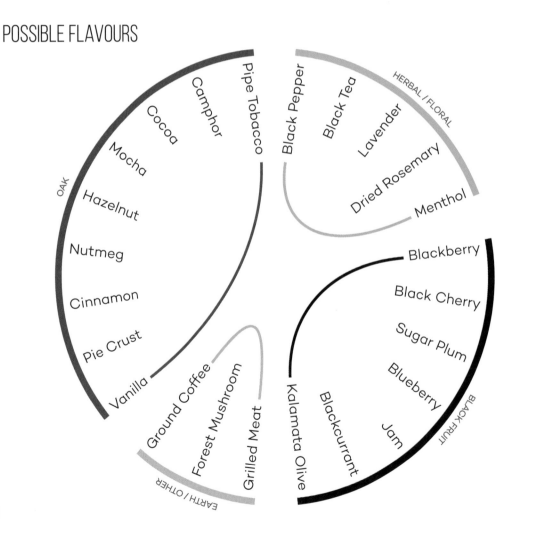

OAK: Pipe Tobacco, Camphor, Cocoa, Mocha, Hazelnut, Nutmeg, Cinnamon, Pie Crust, Vanilla

HERBAL / FLORAL: Black Pepper, Black Tea, Lavender, Dried Rosemary, Menthol

BLACK FRUIT: Blackberry, Black Cherry, Sugar Plum, Blueberry, Jam, Blackcurrant, Kalamata Olive

EARTH / OTHER: Ground Coffee, Forest Mushroom, Grilled Meat

148

📍 Origin: France

WHERE IT GROWS

◄ USA
◄ ELSEWHERE

9,800
ACRES

RED

ROOM TEMP.

UP TO 5 YRS

£ £ £ £ £
£5–£10

Black Cherry

Black Plum

Blackberry

Prune

COOL VINTAGE   WARM VINTAGE

Petite Sirah is the offspring grape of Syrah and a rare black grape from South West France called Peloursin.

Today, Petite Sirah grows primarily in California, where it's often used to add body to Cabernet Sauvignon and Zinfandel.

Petite Sirah is one of the best values for full-bodied red wine. Look for wines with extended oak ageing or a small percentage of Zinfandel, which acts to soften the high tannin.

Petite Sirah and other opaque, high-tannin red wines contain 2–3 times as many antioxidants as light, translucent red wines like Zinfandel and Gamay.

Petite Sirah will taste great alongside rich braised meats, barbecue, casseroles and meaty pasta dishes.

BARBECUE

MEATY PASTA DISHES

CASSEROLE

149

PINOTAGE

 'pee-no-taj'

PROFILE

FRUIT	●●●●○
BODY	●●●●●
TANNIN	●●●●○
ACIDITY	●●○○○
ALCOHOL	●●●●●

DOMINANT FLAVOURS

 BLACK CHERRY   BLACKBERRY   FIG   MENTHOL   ROASTED MEAT

POSSIBLE FLAVOURS

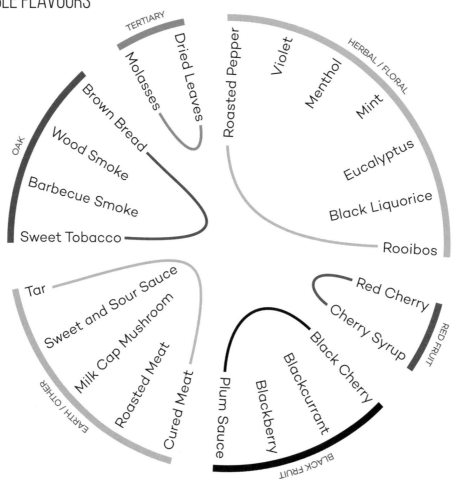

TERTIARY
- Dried Leaves
- Molasses

OAK
- Brown Bread
- Wood Smoke
- Barbecue Smoke
- Sweet Tobacco

HERBAL / FLORAL
- Roasted Pepper
- Violet
- Menthol
- Mint
- Eucalyptus
- Black Liquorice
- Rooibos

RED FRUIT
- Red Cherry
- Cherry Syrup

BLACK FRUIT
- Black Cherry
- Blackcurrant
- Blackberry
- Plum Sauce

EARTH / OTHER
- Tar
- Sweet and Sour Sauce
- Milk Cap Mushroom
- Roasted Meat
- Cured Meat

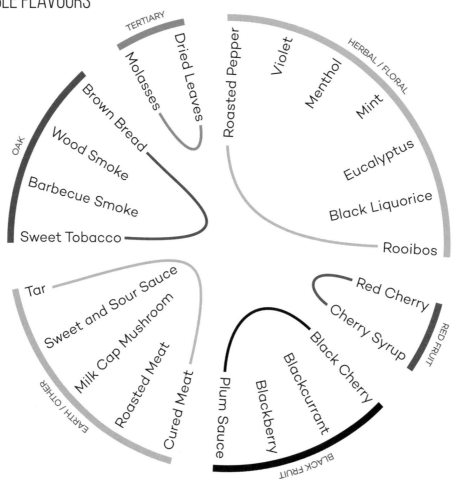

◆ Origin: South Africa

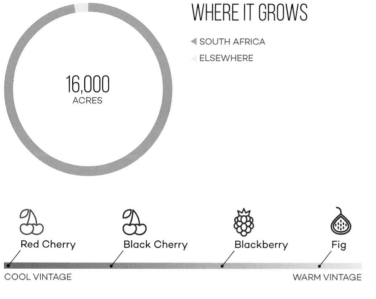

WHERE IT GROWS

16,000
ACRES

◀ SOUTH AFRICA
◀ ELSEWHERE

Red Cherry   Black Cherry   Blackberry   Fig

COOL VINTAGE   WARM VINTAGE

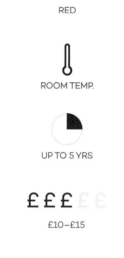

RED

ROOM TEMP.

UP TO 5 YRS

£ £ £ £ £
£10–£15

Pinotage is the 4th most planted red grape in South Africa. It was created by a scientist who crossed Cinsaut with Pinot Noir in 1925. The scientist, Abraham Izak Perold, was attempting to create a wine that tasted like Pinot Noir but was hardy enough to thrive in South Africa's climate.

Oddly enough, Pinotage tastes nothing like either of its progenitors. It is an enigma.

Look for Pinotage wines with descriptions of both red and black fruit flavours, a hint that suggests a wine with more balance and complexity.

Avoid low-quality bulk Pinotage. The wines can have a pungent note of tar and nail polish remover—a sign of volatile acidity.

SIMILAR WINES: If you like Australian Shiraz or American Petite Sirah, you will enjoy the black fruit flavours and sweet tobacco notes in South African Pinotage.

SOUTH AFRICAN
PINOTAGE

AMERICAN
PETITE SIRAH

AUSTRALIAN
SHIRAZ

SYRAH

🔊 'sear-ah'
aka: Shiraz

PROFILE

FRUIT
BODY
TANNIN
ACIDITY
ALCOHOL

DOMINANT FLAVOURS

BLUEBERRY　　PLUM　　MILK CHOCOLATE　　TOBACCO　　GREEN PEPPERCORN

POSSIBLE FLAVOURS

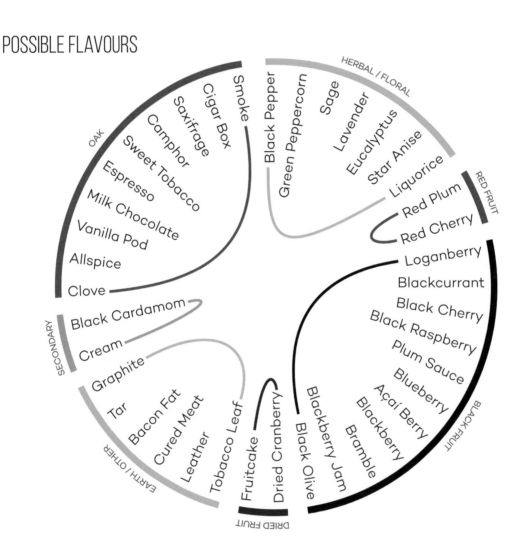

HERBAL / FLORAL
OAK
RED FRUIT
BLACK FRUIT
SECONDARY
EARTH / OTHER
DRIED FRUIT

Smoke
Cigar Box
Saxifrage
Camphor
Sweet Tobacco
Espresso
Milk Chocolate
Vanilla Pod
Allspice
Clove
Black Cardamom
Cream
Graphite
Tar
Bacon Fat
Cured Meat
Leather
Tobacco Leaf
Fruitcake
Dried Cranberry
Black Olive
Blackberry Jam
Blackberry
Bramble
Açaí Berry
Blueberry
Plum Sauce
Black Raspberry
Black Cherry
Blackcurrant
Loganberry
Red Cherry
Red Plum
Liquorice
Star Anise
Eucalyptus
Lavender
Sage
Green Peppercorn
Black Pepper

152

Origin: France

WHERE IT GROWS

459,000 ACRES

◄ FRANCE
◄ AUSTRALIA
◄ SPAIN
◄ ARGENTINA
◄ SOUTH AFRICA
◄ USA
◄ ITALY
◄ CHILE
◄ PORTUGAL
◄ ELSEWHERE

RED

ROOM TEMP.

UP TO 10 YRS

£ £ £ £ £
£5–£10

 Olive — Red Plum — Blueberry — Blackberry Jam

COOL CLIMATE   WARM CLIMATE

REGIONAL DIFFERENCES: When comparing Syrah wines from different regions, you'll notice some taste differences:

FRUIT-FORWARD BLACKBERRY, BLUEBERRY & SWEET TOBACCO

Full-bodied wines with fruit-forward flavours of blackberry, blueberry, sweet tobacco smoke, chocolate, baking spices and vanilla

● CALIFORNIA, USA
● SOUTH AUSTRALIA
● SPAIN
● ARGENTINA
● SOUTH AFRICA

SAVOURY PLUM, OLIVE & GREEN PEPPERCORN

Medium- to full-bodied wines with savoury flavours of plum, olive, loganberry, leather, green peppercorn, bacon fat and cocoa powder

● RHÔNE, FRANCE
● COLUMBIA VALLEY, WA, USA
● VICTORIA, AUSTRALIA
● WESTERN AUSTRALIA
● CHILE

Regions where Syrah is a single-varietal wine:

● SOUTH AUSTRALIA
● NORTHERN RHÔNE
● CALIFORNIA, USA
● COLUMBIA VALLEY, WA, USA

Regions where Syrah is blended with other varieties:

● CÔTES DU RHÔNE, FRANCE
● LANGUEDOC-ROUSSILLON, FRANCE
● CASTILLA-LA MANCHA, SPAIN
● EXTREMADURA, SPAIN
● CATALONIA, SPAIN
● VALENCIA, SPAIN
● ARAGON, SPAIN

TEMPRANILLO

🔊 'temp-rah-nee-oh'
aka: Cencibel, Tinta Roriz, Tinta
de Toro, Rioja, Ribera del Duero

PROFILE

FRUIT
BODY
TANNIN
ACIDITY
ALCOHOL

DOMINANT FLAVOURS

CHERRY — DRIED FIG — CEDAR — TOBACCO — DILL

POSSIBLE FLAVOURS

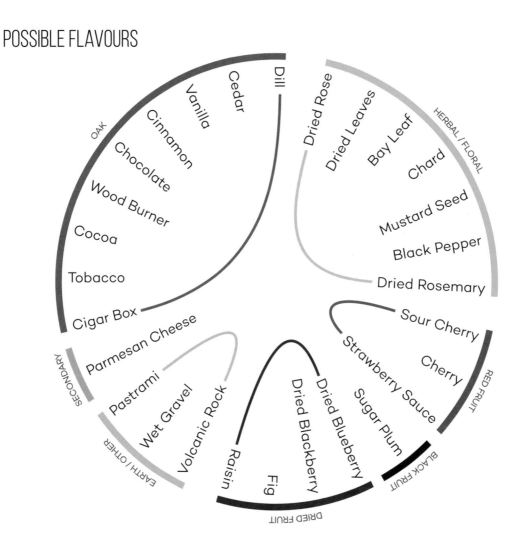

OAK
Dill
Cedar
Vanilla
Cinnamon
Chocolate
Wood Burner
Cocoa
Tobacco
Cigar Box

HERBAL / FLORAL
Dried Rose
Dried Leaves
Bay Leaf
Chard
Mustard Seed
Black Pepper
Dried Rosemary

RED FRUIT
Sour Cherry
Cherry
Strawberry Sauce
Sugar Plum

BLACK FRUIT
Dried Blueberry
Dried Blackberry

DRIED FRUIT
Fig
Raisin

SECONDARY
Parmesan Cheese
Pastrami

EARTH / OTHER
Wet Gravel
Volcanic Rock

📍 Origin: Spain

575,000
ACRES

WHERE IT GROWS

◁ SPAIN
◁ PORTUGAL
◁ ARGENTINA
◁ FRANCE
◁ AUSTRALIA
◁ ELSEWHERE

RED

CELLAR TEMP.

UP TO 10 YRS

£££££
£10–£15

winefolly.com/learn/winefolly.com/learn/variety/tempranillo

Sour Cherry   Strawberry Sauce   Dried Blackberry   Raisin

COOL VINTAGE   WARM VINTAGE

REGIONAL WINES: Tempranillo is Spain's top red wine. It's typically labelled by its regional name.

- La Rioja
  RIOJA

- Castilla y León
  RIBERA DEL DUERO
  CIGALES
  TORO

- La Mancha
  VALDEPEÑAS

- Extremadura
  RIBERA DEL GUADIANA

AGING TERMS: Spanish wines can be identified by ageing terms. Rules vary from region to region.

☑ ROBLE/TINTO
   Little to no oak ageing

☑ CRIANZA
   6–12 months ageing in oak

☑ RESERVA
   12 months oak ageing with up to 2 years of bottle ageing

☑ GRAN RESERVA
   18–24 months oak ageing with up to 4 years of bottle ageing

COMMON STYLES

YOUNG (ROBLE/CRIANZA)
Juicy red fruit flavours, herbs and a spicy kick

SOME AGING (RESERVA)
Red and black fruit flavours, dried roses and baking spices

LONG AGING (RESERVA+)
Dried red and black fruits, fig, cinnamon and cedar flavours with notes of leather and dusty dry leaves

155

TOURIGA NACIONAL

PROFILE

FRUIT ● ● ● ● ●
BODY ● ● ● ● ●
TANNIN ● ● ● ● ●
ACIDITY ● ● ● ● ○
ALCOHOL ● ● ● ●

DOMINANT FLAVOURS

VIOLET · BLUEBERRY · PLUM · MINT · WET SLATE

POSSIBLE FLAVOURS

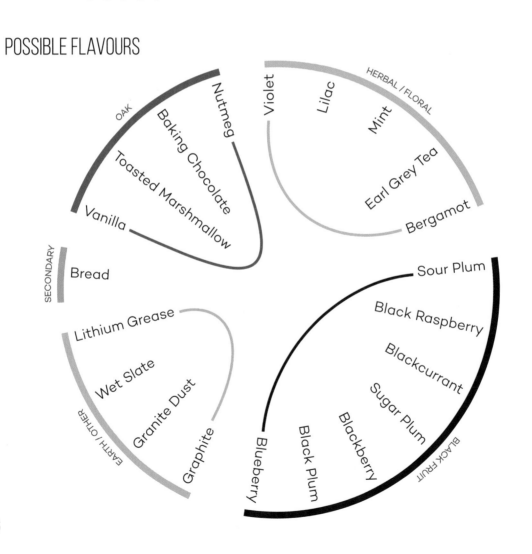

OAK: Nutmeg, Baking Chocolate, Toasted Marshmallow, Vanilla

HERBAL / FLORAL: Violet, Lilac, Mint, Earl Grey Tea, Bergamot

SECONDARY: Bread

EARTH / OTHER: Lithium Grease, Wet Slate, Granite Dust, Graphite

BLACK FRUIT: Sour Plum, Black Raspberry, Blackcurrant, Sugar Plum, Blackberry, Black Plum, Blueberry

📍 Origin: Portugal

winefolly.com/learn/winefolly.com/learn/variety/touriga-nacional

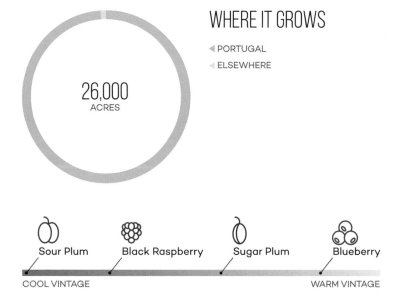

WHERE IT GROWS

26,000 ACRES

◀ PORTUGAL
◀ ELSEWHERE

GLASS TYPE

ROOM TEMP.

UP TO 5 YRS

£ £ £ £ £
£10–£15

Sour Plum | Black Raspberry | Sugar Plum | Blueberry

COOL VINTAGE

WARM VINTAGE

Touriga Nacional is a deeply coloured red wine grape that originated in the Douro Valley of Portugal. It has been traditionally used for Port wine, although several Portuguese winemakers have started to create dry red wines with Touriga Nacional and the other primary Port varieties.

Touriga Nacional wines are characterized by lush black fruit flavours, bold tannin and a subtle floral aroma of violets.

REGIONS

DOURO
Expect flavours of blueberry, blackcurrant, violets, vanilla and subtle notes of roasted meat. Wine is structured with fine gravelly tannins.

DÃO
The Dão is cooler and higher elevation than Douro and produces wines with more red fruit flavours, bergamot and violet supported by spicy acidity.

ALENTEJO
Alentejo produces a rich but juicy style with black and red fruit, violet, liquorice and usually a touch of vanilla from oak ageing.

There are just under 100 acres of Touriga Nacional in the US, found mostly in Lodi, CA.

Dessert Wine

MADEIRA

MARSALA

PORT

SAUTERNAIS

SHERRY

VIN SANTO

Dessert wines range in style from off-dry to very sweet. The sweetest and highest acidity of these dessert wines can be cellared for many years to develop subtle nutty flavours.

Some dessert wines are stabilized with the addition of brandy in a process called fortification. Fortified wines have high alcohol and can store open for up to a month.

This book includes examples of common dessert wines but there are many more variations found throughout the world.

TYPES OF DESSERT WINE

FORTIFIED WINE

Wines are preserved with the addition of spirits usually before all the grape sugar is fermented.

LATE-HARVEST WINE

Grapes are harvested late in the growing season when the sugar content is highest.

DRIED GRAPE WINE

Also known as Passito in Italy. Grapes are laid out to raisinate and lose up to 70% of their moisture content.

ICE WINE / EISWEIN

Grapes freeze while still on the vine and are picked and pressed before they thaw, making a very sweet wine.

'NOBLE ROT' WINE

Botrytis cinerea (aka 'noble rot') is a fungal rot that causes grapes to shrivel and sweeten with honey and ginger-like flavours.

MADEIRA

🔊 'mad-deer-uh'
Style: Fortified Wine

PROFILE

FRUIT	●●●○○
BODY	●●●●●
SWEET	●●●●○
ACIDITY	●●●●○
ALCOHOL	●●●●●

DOMINANT FLAVOURS

BURNT CARAMEL — WALNUT OIL — PEACH — HAZELNUT — ORANGE PEEL

POSSIBLE FLAVOURS

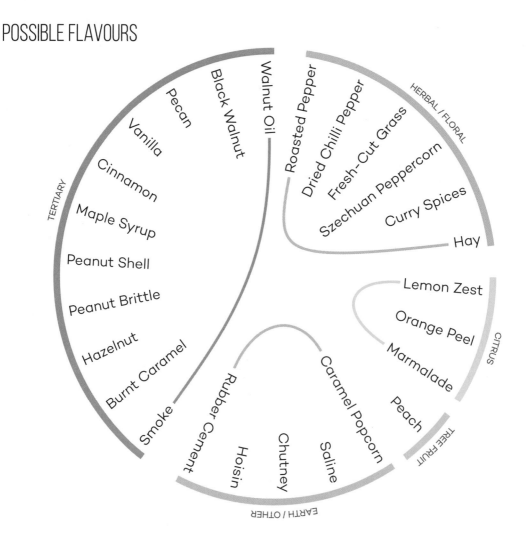

TERTIARY
- Walnut Oil
- Black Walnut
- Pecan
- Vanilla
- Cinnamon
- Maple Syrup
- Peanut Shell
- Peanut Brittle
- Hazelnut
- Burnt Caramel
- Smoke

HERBAL / FLORAL
- Roasted Pepper
- Dried Chilli Pepper
- Fresh-Cut Grass
- Szechuan Peppercorn
- Curry Spices
- Hay

CITRUS
- Lemon Zest
- Orange Peel
- Marmalade

TREE FRUIT
- Peach

EARTH / OTHER
- Rubber Cement
- Hoisin
- Chutney
- Saline
- Caramel Popcorn

📍 Origin: Madeira Island, Portugal

1,000
ACRES

- GUARANTEE

W.FOLLY
MADEIRA — PRODUCER
BUAL — STYLE
MEDIUM RICH — SWEETNESS
1990 — QUALITY & AGEING
COLHEITA

SWEETNESS LEVELS

- ⬡ EXTRA DRY: 0–50 g/L RS
- ⬡ DRY: 50–65 g/L RS
- ⬡⬡ MEDIUM DRY: 65–80 g/L RS
- ⬢ MEDIUM RICH/SWEET: 80–96 g/L RS
- ⬢ RICH/SWEET: 96+ g/L RS

WHERE IT'S MADE

◀ MADEIRA, PORTUGAL

QUALITY LEVELS & AGEING

NON-VINTAGE MADEIRA

FINEST/CHOICE/SELECT
Aged 3 yrs by Estufa & made with Tinta Negramoll.

RAINWATER
Medium-dry style aged 3 yrs and typically blended w/ T. Negramoll.

5-YEAR/RESERVE/MATURE
Aged 5–10 years and typically blended with Tinta Negramoll.

10-YEAR/SPECIAL RESERVE
Aged 10–15 years by Canteiro. Often a single variety.

15-YEAR/EXTRA RESERVE
Aged 15–20 years by Canteiro. Often a single variety.

VINTAGE MADEIRA

COLHEITA/HARVEST
A single vintage aged 5+ years by Canteiro. Often a single variety.

SOLERA
Multi-vintage blend by Canteiro. First year of solera is listed on the bottle but is no longer made.

FRASQUEIRA/GARRAFEIRA
Single vintage aged 20+ years by Canteiro method. Very rare.

WHITE OR DESSERT (75 ML)

CELLAR TEMP.

UP TO 2 YRS

£ £ £ £ £

£5–£10

⬭ ESTUFA METHOD
Wine is heated in tanks for a short period of time.

⬭ CANTEIRO METHOD
Wines age naturally in barrels in warm rooms or under the sun.

TYPES OF MADEIRA

🍷 TINTA NEGRAMOLL / RAINWATER
Dry-sweet and basic quality

🍷 SERCIAL
The lightest, extra-dry style (serve chilled)

🍷 VERDELHO
Light, aromatic & dry to med. dry wines (serve chilled)

🍷 BUAL / BOAL
Medium-sweet nutty wines

🍷 MALMSEY
The sweetest style

MARSALA

◀ 'mar-sal-uh'
Style: Fortified Wine

PROFILE

FRUIT
BODY
SWEET
ACIDITY
ALCOHOL

DOMINANT FLAVOURS

STEWED APRICOT — VANILLA — TAMARIND — BROWN SUGAR — TOBACCO

POSSIBLE FLAVOURS

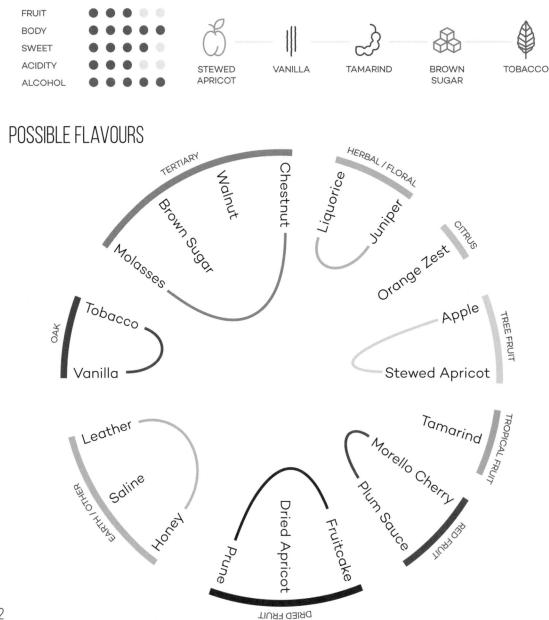

TERTIARY
Chestnut
Walnut
Brown Sugar
Molasses

HERBAL / FLORAL
Liquorice
Juniper

CITRUS
Orange Zest

OAK
Tobacco
Vanilla

TREE FRUIT
Apple
Stewed Apricot

TROPICAL FRUIT
Tamarind

EARTH / OTHER
Leather
Saline
Honey

RED FRUIT
Morello Cherry
Plum Sauce

DRIED FRUIT
Prune
Dried Apricot
Fruitcake

162

📍 Origin: Italy

WHERE IT'S MADE

◄ SICILY, ITALY

~100,000
ACRES

DESSERT (75 ML)

CELLAR TEMP.

UP TO 2 YRS

£ £ ~~£ £ £~~

£5–£10

STYLES OF MARSALA

GOLD (ORO)
Made with white grapes.

AMBER (AMBRA)
Made with white grapes
and cooked wine must.

ROSSO (RUBINO)
Rare. A red Marsala with up
to 30% white grapes.

MARSALA WINE GRAPES

GRILLO
CATTARATO
INZOLIA
GRECIANO

NERO D'AVOLA
PIGNATELLO
NERELLO MASCALESE

AGEING TERMS & STYLES

COOKING

FINE/FINE IP
All styles. Aged 1 year.

SUPERIOR
All styles. Aged 2 years.

DRINKING

SUPERIOR RESERVE
Dry to semisweet. Aged 4+
years.

VIRGIN/VIRGIN SOLERA
Dry. Aged 5+ years.

VIRGIN STRAVECCHIO/
VIRGIN RESERVE
Dry. Aged 10+ years.

SWEETNESS LEVELS

DRY (SECCO): 0–40 g/L RS

SEMISWEET (SEMISECCO):
40–100 g/L RS

SWEET/GD (DOLCE):
100+ g/L RS

MARSALA FOR COOKING

SWEET MARSALA
Use for sweet sauces with pork
and chicken or in desserts such as
zabaglione.

DRY MARSALA
Use for savoury courses, to add
nutty flavours in beef, mushrooms,
turkey or veal. Dry Marsala tends
to be the more versatile choice
to have on hand.

PORT

🔊 'port'
Style: Fortified Wine

PROFILE

FRUIT	● ● ● ● ●
BODY	● ● ● ● ●
TANNIN	● ● ● ● ●
ACIDITY	● ● ● ○ ○
ALCOHOL	● ● ● ● ●

DOMINANT FLAVOURS

RIPE BLACKBERRY — RASPBERRY SAUCE — CINNAMON — TOFFEE APPLE — STAR ANISE

POSSIBLE FLAVOURS

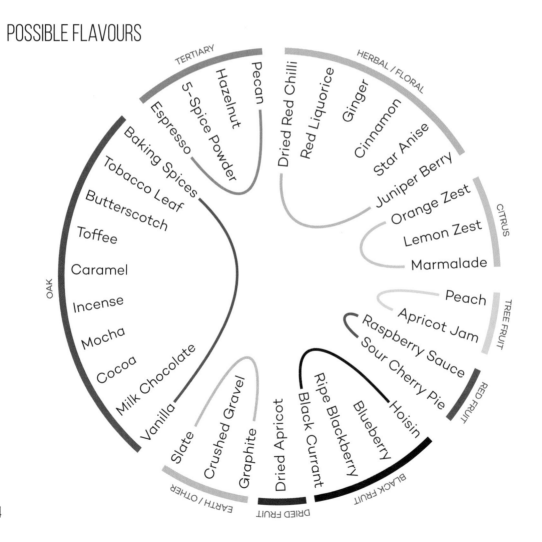

TERTIARY: Pecan, Hazelnut, 5-Spice Powder

HERBAL / FLORAL: Dried Red Chilli, Red Liquorice, Ginger, Cinnamon, Star Anise, Juniper Berry, Orange Zest

CITRUS: Lemon Zest, Marmalade

TREE FRUIT: Peach, Apricot Jam

RED FRUIT: Raspberry Sauce, Sour Cherry Pie, Hoisin

BLACK FRUIT: Blueberry, Ripe Blackberry, Black Currant

DRIED FRUIT: Dried Apricot

EARTH / OTHER: Graphite, Crushed Gravel, Slate

OAK: Espresso, Baking Spices, Tobacco Leaf, Butterscotch, Toffee, Caramel, Incense, Mocha, Cocoa, Milk Chocolate, Vanilla

♦ Origin: Portugal

111,000
ACRES

WHERE IT'S MADE

◀ DOURO, PORTUGAL

DESSERT (85 ML)

ROOM TEMP.

15+ YRS

£ £ £ £ £

£10–£20

YOUNG PORT

A youthful style of Port wine that's aged for a short time and designed to be drunk immediately. Wines tend to have more spice notes and tannin.

🍷 **RUBY**
Red fruit and chocolate flavours with spicy acidity.

🍷 **LBV (LATE BOTTLED VINTAGE)**
Red and black fruit flavours, spice and cocoa with high tannin and acidity.

🍷 **WHITE**
Dried peach, white pepper, tangerine zest and incense.

🍷 **ROSÉ**
Notes of strawberry, honey, cinnamon and framboise liqueur.

TAWNY PORT

Oak-aged Port wines that age for several years develop nutty flavours from oxidation. Since they are aged by the winery, they can be enjoyed immediately.

🍷 **10-YEAR**
Raspberry, dried blueberry, cinnamon, clove and caramel.

🍷 **20-YEAR**
Fig, raisin, caramel, orange zest, and cinnamon.

🍷 **40-YEAR**
Dried apricot, orange zest, caramel and toffee.

🍷 **COLHEITA**
Single-vintage tawny port. Flavours vary depending on the age of the wine.

AGE-WORTHY PORT

Stoppered with a standard cork and designed to age 40+ years.

🍷 **VINTAGE PORT**
Single-vintage Ports from exceptional years. Expect to age for a minimum of 10 years and ideally 30–50 years.

🍷 **CRUSTED PORT**
A multi-vintage Port designed to age just like vintage Port. Wines often develop a 'crust' and need to be decanted with a filter screen.

165

SAUTERNAIS

PROFILE

FRUIT ●●●●●
BODY ●●●○○
VERY SWEET ●●●●●
ACIDITY ●●●●●
ALCOHOL ●●●○○

DOMINANT FLAVOURS

LEMON CURD — APRICOT — QUINCE — HONEY — GINGER

POSSIBLE FLAVOURS

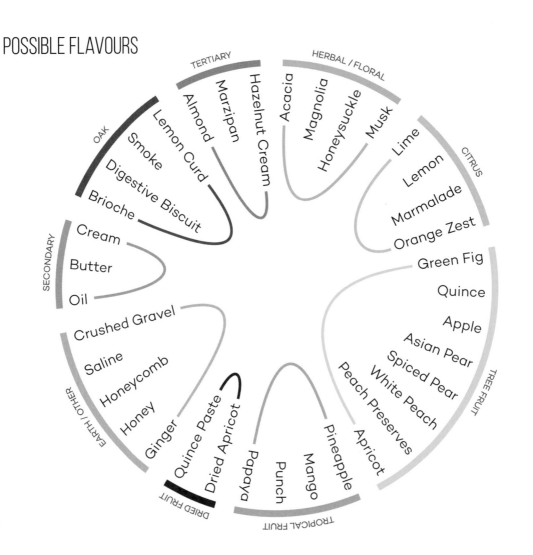

TERTIARY
Hazelnut Cream
Marzipan
Almond

OAK
Lemon Curd
Smoke
Digestive Biscuit
Brioche

SECONDARY
Cream
Butter
Oil

EARTH / OTHER
Crushed Gravel
Saline
Honeycomb
Honey
Ginger

DRIED FRUIT
Quince Paste
Dried Apricot

TROPICAL FRUIT
Papaya
Punch
Mango
Pineapple
Apricot

HERBAL / FLORAL
Acacia
Magnolia
Honeysuckle
Musk

CITRUS
Lime
Lemon
Marmalade
Orange Zest

TREE FRUIT
Green Fig
Quince
Apple
Asian Pear
Spiced Pear
White Peach
Peach Preserves

166

● Origin: France

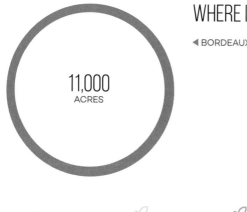

11,000
ACRES

WHERE IT'S MADE

◀ BORDEAUX, FRANCE

WHITE (100 ML)

COLD

15+ YRS

£10–£20

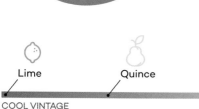

| Lime | Quince | Apricot | Papaya |

COOL VINTAGE   WARM VINTAGE

GRAPES: The sweet wines of Bordeaux are made exclusively with white grapes.

 SÉMILLON
The popular choice. Sémillon adds body and tropical fruit notes.

 SAUVIGNON BLANC
Adds lime and grapefruit notes with tingling acidity.

 MUSCADELLE
Typically only a small portion of the blend.

MAIN REGIONS: The name Sauternais refers to the dessert-wine-producing areas in Bordeaux that are typically found close to the river where grapes often develop noble rot (see Glossary).

● SAUTERNES
● BORDEAUX MOELLEUX
● BARSAC
● SAINTE-CROIX-DU-MONT
● LOUPIAC
● GRAVES SUPÉRIEURES
● PREMIÈRES CÔTES DE BORDEAUX
● CADILLAC

Some producers only produce sweet wines on vintages when white grapes develop noble rot.

An average glass of Sauternes has nearly 17 grams of sugar per 100 ml serving. However, due to the wine's high natural acidity, the sugar level tastes balanced.

winefolly.com / learn / winefolly.com / learn / wine / sauternais

SHERRY

🔊 'sherr-ee'
Style: Fortified Wine

PROFILE

FRUIT	●●○○○
BODY	●●●○○
OFF-DRY	●●○○○
ACIDITY	●●●●○
ALCOHOL	●●●●○

DOMINANT FLAVOURS

JACKFRUIT — SALINE — PRESERVED LEMON — BRAZIL NUT — ALMOND

POSSIBLE FLAVOURS

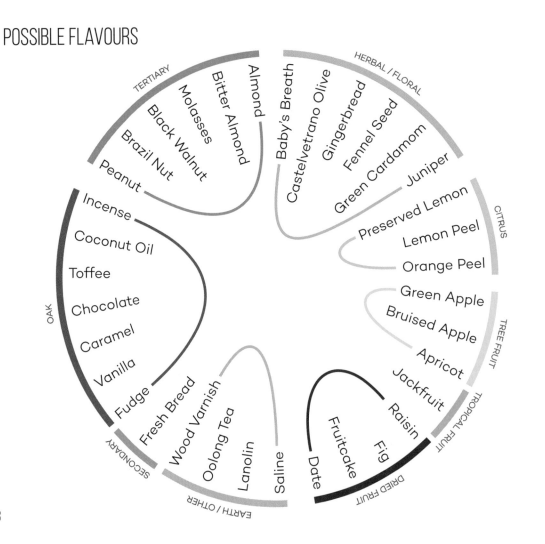

TERTIARY: Almond, Bitter Almond, Molasses, Black Walnut, Brazil Nut, Peanut

HERBAL / FLORAL: Baby's Breath, Castelvetrano Olive, Gingerbread, Fennel Seed, Green Cardamom, Juniper

CITRUS: Preserved Lemon, Lemon Peel, Orange Peel

TREE FRUIT: Green Apple, Bruised Apple, Apricot

TROPICAL FRUIT: Jackfruit

DRIED FRUIT: Raisin, Fig, Fruitcake, Date

EARTH / OTHER: Saline, Lanolin, Oolong Tea, Wood Varnish

SECONDARY: Fresh Bread

OAK: Incense, Coconut Oil, Toffee, Chocolate, Caramel, Vanilla, Fudge

📍 Origin: Spain

78,000
ACRES

WHERE IT'S MADE

◀ ANDALUCÍA, SPAIN

WHITE OR
DESSERT (3 OZ)

CELLAR TEMP.

UP TO 2 YRS

£ £ £ £ £

£10–£15

DRY SHERRY STYLES

These Sherry wines are made with Palomino Fino grapes and come in a range of styles depending on the winemaking method.

🍷 FINO & MANZANILLA
Very light styles with salty fruit flavours. Serve chilled.

🍷 AMONTILLADO
Slightly bolder nutty style in between Fino and Oloroso.

🍷 PALO CORTADO
Rich with roasted flavours of coffee and molasses.

🍷 OLOROSO
Dark nutty style from long-term oxidative aging.

SWEET SHERRY STYLES

Sweet Sherries are typically produced with Pedro Ximénez or Moscatel grapes.

🍷 PX (PEDRO XIMÉNEZ)
The sweetest style made of Pedro Ximénez with fig and date flavours.

🍷 MOSCATEL
A very sweet style made of Muscat of Alexandria with caramel flavours.

🍷 SWEETENED SHERRY
Typically made by blending Oloroso Sherry with PX.

⬡ DRY: 5–45 g/L RS
⬡ MEDIUM: 5–115 g/L RS
⬡⬡ PALE CREAM: 45–115 g/L RS
⬡ CREAM: 115–140 g/L RS
⬡ DULCE: 160+ g/L RS

SOLERA AGING

Sherry wines employ a unique multi-vintage ageing technique called a solera. Soleras are tiers of barrels with 3 to 9 steps called criaderas or scales:

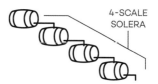

4-SCALE
SOLERA

New wine goes into the top scale, and finished wine is taken in small portions from the bottom scale. Wines 'run the scales' for at least 3 years up to 50 years (or more). There is also a rare vintage Sherry, Añada, that doesn't use a solera.

169

VIN SANTO

winefolly.com / learn / wine / vin-santo

PROFILE

FRUIT
BODY
VERY SWEET
ACIDITY
ALCOHOL

DOMINANT FLAVOURS

PERFUME — FIG — RAISIN — ALMOND — TOFFEE

POSSIBLE FLAVOURS

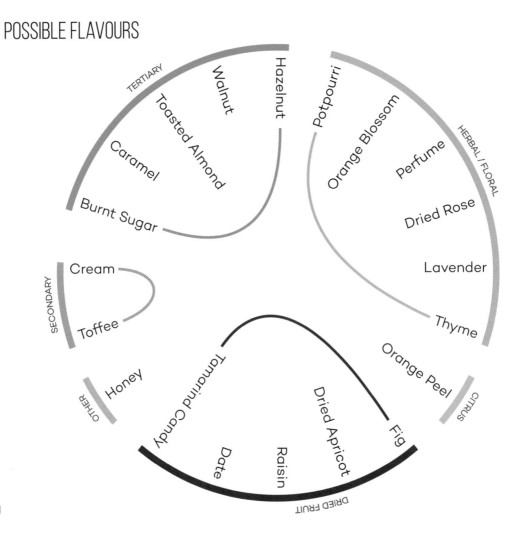

TERTIARY

Walnut
Hazelnut
Toasted Almond
Caramel
Burnt Sugar

Potpourri
Orange Blossom
Perfume
Dried Rose
Lavender
Thyme

HERBAL / FLORAL

SECONDARY

Cream
Toffee
Honey

OTHER

Tamarind Candy
Date
Raisin
Dried Apricot
Fig
Orange Peel

CITRUS

DRIED FRUIT

📍 Origin: Italy

58,000
ACRES

WHERE IT'S MADE

◀ CENTRAL ITALY

WHITE (100 ML)

CELLAR TEMP.

15+ YRS

££££ £

£15–£20

Vin Santo is made with the *appassimento* method. Grapes are harvested and laid out on straw mats for up to 6 months where they will dry and lose about 70% of their water content.

GRAPES   STRAW MATS   RAISINS

Then, the raisinated grapes are squeezed and put into oak or chestnut barrels to vinify. The fermentation is very slow and can take 4 years to complete.

COMMON STYLES

WHITE VIN SANTO
The most common type of Vin Santo has dried fig, almond and toffee flavours and is made primarily with Malvasia Bianca and Trebbiano.

RED VIN SANTO
A rare style of Vin Santo called Occhio di Pernice offers caramel, coffee and hazelnut flavours and is made with Sangiovese grapes.

Tuscany and Umbria are the main regions that produce Vin Santo in Italy. You can also find excellent passito-style aged Malvasia wines from Sicily called Malvasia delle Lipari.

Vin Santo is traditionally enjoyed during Easter week and paired with almond biscotti.

Wine Regions

Wine Regions

WINE REGIONS OF
THE WORLD

ARGENTINA

AUSTRALIA

AUSTRIA

CHILE

FRANCE

GERMANY

ITALY

NEW ZEALAND

PORTUGAL

SOUTH AFRICA

SPAIN

UNITED STATES

WINE REGIONS OF THE WORLD

There are over 90 countries making wine in the world. The 12 countries included in this book account for 80% of the wine produced in the world.

WORLD WINE PRODUCTION

6.8 BILLION
GALLONS OF WINE
ANNUALLY (2012)

◀ ITALY
◀ FRANCE
◀ SPAIN
◀ UNITED STATES
◀ ARGENTINA
◀ AUSTRALIA
◀ SOUTH AFRICA

◀ CHILE
◀ GERMANY
◀ PORTUGAL
◀ AUSTRIA
◀ NEW ZEALAND
◀ OTHERS

6.8 billion gallons of wine is enough to fill the area of 99 city blocks of Manhattan with 40 feet of wine.

COOL V. WARM CLIMATE WINE REGIONS

Climate affects the taste of wine. Generally, cool climates make wines with more tart flavours and hot climates make wines with more ripe flavours.

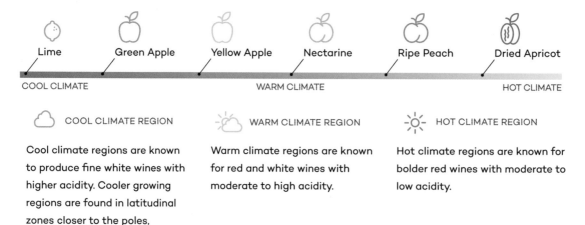

| Lime | Green Apple | Yellow Apple | Nectarine | Ripe Peach | Dried Apricot |

COOL CLIMATE   WARM CLIMATE   HOT CLIMATE

COOL CLIMATE REGION

Cool climate regions are known to produce fine white wines with higher acidity. Cooler growing regions are found in latitudinal zones closer to the poles, higher elevation areas, and areas affected by cooling breezes.

WARM CLIMATE REGION

Warm climate regions are known for red and white wines with moderate to high acidity.

HOT CLIMATE REGION

Hot climate regions are known for bolder red wines with moderate to low acidity.

WHERE WINE GROWS

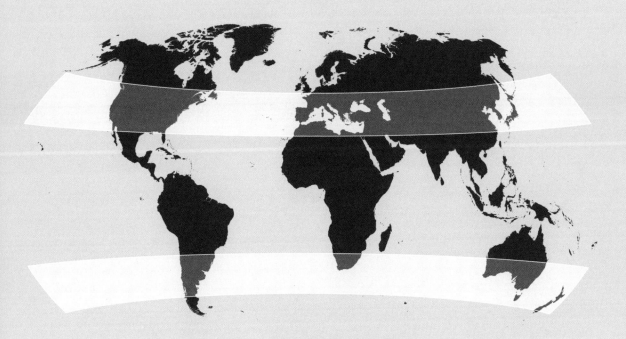

LATITUDINAL ZONES WHERE
WINE GRAPES GROW

The latitudinal zones above
illustrate a general overview of
where wine grapes grow. It's useful
to note that some regions outside
of these zones, including parts of
Brazil, Mexico and India, can also
make wine due to their unique
microclimates.

Argentina

Argentina is a New World region that is most known for a bold and fruity style of Malbec. The country accounts for over 75% of the world's Malbec wines.

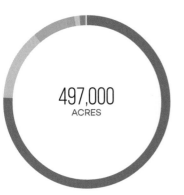

497,000
ACRES

WINE REGIONS BY SIZE

◀ MENDOZA
◀ SAN JUAN
◀ LA RIOJA
◀ PATAGONIA
◀ SALTA
◀ CATAMARCA
◀ TUCUMÁN

TOP WINES OF ARGENTINA

🍇 MALBEC

The country's top wine ranges in taste from juicy tart raspberry flavours to rich blueberry and sweet tobacco depending on vintage, quality and oak.

- MENDOZA — LUJÁN DE CUYO
- SALTA — UCO VALLEY

🍇 CABERNET SAUVIGNON

Argentine Cabernet Sauvignon offers rich black raspberry, mocha and tobacco leaf flavours with medium tannin and peppery acidity.

- MENDOZA — LUJÁN DE CUYO
           — MAIPÚ

🍇 BONARDA (DOUCE NOIR)

Also known as Charbono in California, Bonarda is the second most planted Argentine grape. Expect flavours of blackcurrant, liquorice and dried green herbs.

- LA RIOJA
- MENDOZA

🍇 SYRAH

Argentine Syrah offers full-bodied flavours of loganberry, liquorice, plum and cocoa. The best examples come from high elevation subregions.

- SAN JUAN
- UCO VALLEY (MENDOZA)
- CATAMARCA

🍇 TORRONTÉS

Argentina's own variety ranges in taste from dry and citrusy, to off-dry with rich aromas of peach and guava.

- SALTA
- CATAMARCA
- LA RIOJA
- MENDOZA

🍇 PINOT NOIR

Argentine Pinot Noir offers flavours of ripe raspberries, rhubarb, minerals and spiced plum.

- PATAGONIA
- UCO VALLEY (MENDOZA)

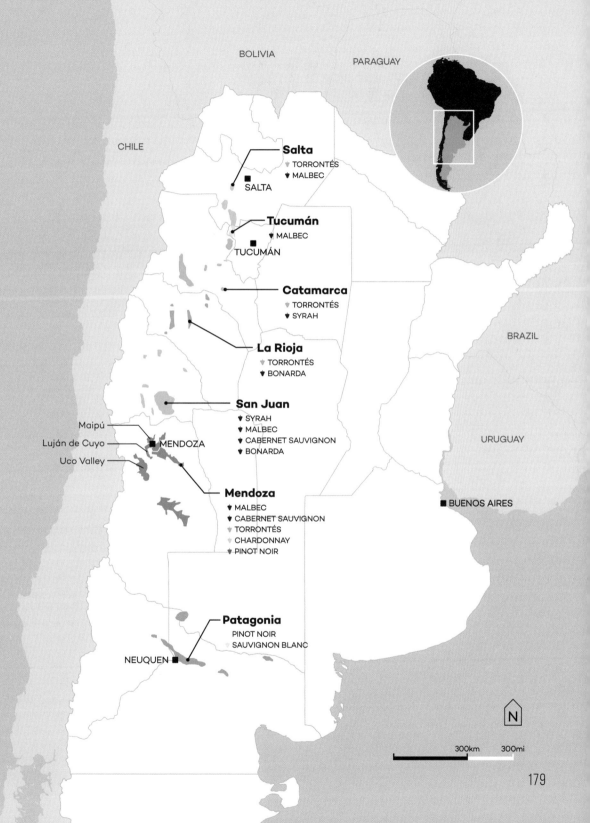

BOLIVIA

PARAGUAY

CHILE

Salta
▼ TORRONTÉS
♥ MALBEC

■ SALTA

Tucumán
♥ MALBEC

■ TUCUMÁN

Catamarca
▼ TORRONTÉS
♥ SYRAH

La Rioja
▼ TORRONTÉS
♥ BONARDA

San Juan
♥ SYRAH
♥ MALBEC
♥ CABERNET SAUVIGNON
♥ BONARDA

Maipú
Luján de Cuyo
Uco Valley

■ MENDOZA

Mendoza
♥ MALBEC
♥ CABERNET SAUVIGNON
▼ TORRONTÉS
♥ CHARDONNAY
♥ PINOT NOIR

BRAZIL

URUGUAY

■ BUENOS AIRES

Patagonia
PINOT NOIR
▼ SAUVIGNON BLANC

NEUQUEN ■

N

300km   300mi

179

Australia

Australia is most famous for Shiraz, a very rich, smoky, and fruit-forward style of Syrah. Australia has 3 distinct climate areas offering a range of wines.

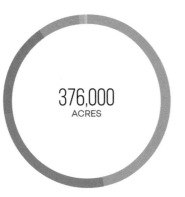

376,000
ACRES

WINE REGIONS BY SIZE

◀ SOUTH AUSTRALIA
◀ NEW SOUTH WALES
◀ VICTORIA
◀ WESTERN AUSTRALIA
◀ TASMANIA
◀ QUEENSLAND

WESTERN AUSTRALIA

WARM CLIMATE

Western Australia is famous for unoaked Chardonnay. However, the region makes quite a bit of lighter-bodied Cabernet Sauvignon, tasting of ripe black fruit and violets with persistent acidity.

- UNOAKED CHARDONNAY
- SAUVIGNON BLANC
- ELEGANT CABERNET & MERLOT BLENDS
- SHIRAZ

SOUTH AND CENTRAL

HOT CLIMATE

The largest area is famous for smoky and rich Shiraz, Sémillon and Chardonnay. Cooler micro regions produce excellent petrol-driven dry Rieslings and peachy Sauvignon Blanc.

- BOLD SHIRAZ
- BUTTERY CHARDONNAY
- DRY RIESLING

VICTORIA AND TASMANIA

COOL CLIMATE

A much cooler area produces Pinot Noir and Chardonnay with excellent acidity. This area tends to make leaner, more elegant red wines.

- PLUMMY PINOT NOIR
- CREAMY CHARDONNAY
- CITRUSY SAUVIGNON BLANC
- SPARKLING WINE

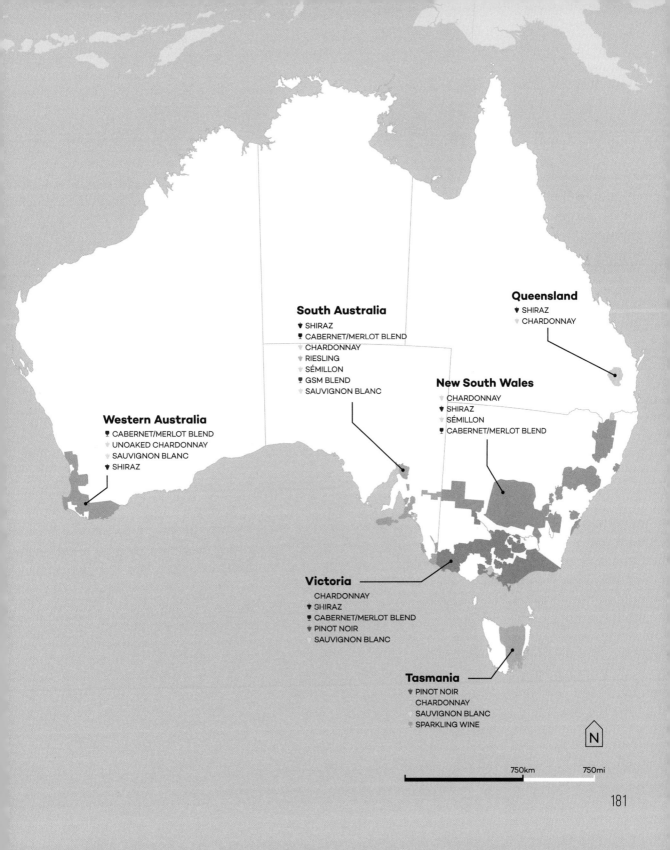

Queensland
- ♥ SHIRAZ
- ♥ CHARDONNAY

South Australia
- ♥ SHIRAZ
- ♥ CABERNET/MERLOT BLEND
- ♥ CHARDONNAY
- ♥ RIESLING
- ♥ SÉMILLON
- ♥ GSM BLEND
- SAUVIGNON BLANC

New South Wales
- ♥ CHARDONNAY
- ♥ SHIRAZ
- ♥ SÉMILLON
- ♥ CABERNET/MERLOT BLEND

Western Australia
- ♥ CABERNET/MERLOT BLEND
- ♥ UNOAKED CHARDONNAY
- ♥ SAUVIGNON BLANC
- ♥ SHIRAZ

Victoria
- CHARDONNAY
- ♥ SHIRAZ
- ♥ CABERNET/MERLOT BLEND
- ♥ PINOT NOIR
- SAUVIGNON BLANC

Tasmania
- ♥ PINOT NOIR
- CHARDONNAY
- SAUVIGNON BLANC
- ♥ SPARKLING WINE

N

750km   750mi

181

AUSTRALIA DETAIL

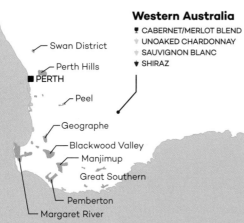

Swan District

Perth Hills

■ PERTH

Peel

Geographe

Blackwood Valley

Manjimup

Great Southern

Pemberton

Margaret River

Western Australia

♟ CABERNET/MERLOT BLEND

♟ UNOAKED CHARDONNAY

♟ SAUVIGNON BLANC

♥ SHIRAZ

Queensland
- ♥ SHIRAZ
- ▽ CHARDONNAY

South Burnett

BRISBANE ■

Granite Belt

New England
Australia

South Australia
- ♥ SHIRAZ
- ♟ CABERNET/MERLOT BLEND
- ▽ CHARDONNAY
- ♥ RIESLING
- ▽ SÉMILLON
- ♟ GSM BLEND

New South Wales
- ▽ CHARDONNAY
- ♥ SHIRAZ
- ▽ SÉMILLON
- ♟ CABERNET/MERLOT BLEND

Hastings River

Southern
Flinders
Ranges

Clare Valley

Barossa Valley

Eden Valley

Riverland

Mudgee

Orange

Cowra

Hunter Valley

Adelaide
Plains

ADELAIDE ■

Adelaide Hills

McLaren Vale

Langhorne Creek

Currency Creek

Southern Fleurieu

Kangaroo Island

Murray Darling

Swan Hill

Riverina

Hilltops

Gundagai

SYDNEY ■

Southern Highlands

Shoalhaven Coast

Canberra District

Tumbarumba

Mount Benson

Robe

Padthaway

Wrattonbully

Coonawarra

Mount Gambier

Heathcote

Bendigo

Macedon Ranges

Pyrenees

Grampians

Henty

MELBOURNE ■

Geelong

Sunbury

Mornington Peninsula

Yarra Valley

Pericoota

Goulburn Valley

Rutherglen

Glenrowan

Beechworth

Alpine Valleys

King Valley

Strathbogie Ranges

Gippsland

Upper Goulburn

Victoria
- CHARDONNAY
- ♥ SHIRAZ
- ♟ CABERNET/MERLOT BLEND
- ▽ PINOT NOIR
- ▽ SAUVIGNON BLANC

Tasmania
- ♥ PINOT NOIR
- CHARDONNAY
- SAUVIGNON BLANC
- SPARKLING WINE

North West

Pipers River

Tamar Valley

East Coast

Coal River Valley

Derwent Valley

Huon Valley

N

300km   300mi

Austria

Austria is a cool climate growing region famous for Grüner Veltliner wines. Austria is known for its minerally white wines and spicy red wines.

113,000
ACRES

WINE REGIONS BY SIZE

◄ NIEDERÖSTERREICH (LOWER AUSTRIA)
◄ BURGENLAND
◄ STEIERMARK (STYRIA)
◄ WIEN (VIENNA)
◄ OTHER

TOP WINES OF AUSTRIA

GRÜNER VELTLINER

The country's champion wine ranges from light peppery citrus flavours to richer Reserve level wines that are often oaked and have more tropical fruit flavours.

Peppery regions
└ ● NIEDERÖSTERREICH
    ├ ● WEINVIERTEL
    └ ● TRAISENTAL

Fruity regions
└ ● NIEDERÖSTERREICH
    ├ ● KREMSTAL
    ├ ● KAMPTAL
    ├ ● WAGRAM
    └ ● WACHAU

ZWEIGELT

('zz-Y-gelt') A light-bodied red with bold cherry flavours and a slight herbaceous bitter note on the finish. Rosé wines are fruity.

├ ● BURGENLAND
└ ● NIEDERÖSTERREICH
    ├ ● CARNUNTUM
    └ ● THERMENREGION

BLAUER PORTUGIESER

Simple light red wines tasting of red berries and woody herbs with lighter tannin and acidity.

└ ● NIEDERÖSTERREICH
    ├ ● THERMENREGION
    └ ● WEINVIERTEL

BLAUFRÄNKISCH

('blao-frankish') A spicy medium red wine with red forest-berry flavours and dry tannin.

├ ● BURGENLAND
└ ● NIEDERÖSTERREICH
    ├ ● CARNUNTUM
    └ ● THERMENREGION

PINOT BLANC

Known as Weissburgunder, this wine offers floral aromas with a dry herbal minerally taste.

├ ● NIEDERÖSTERREICH
└ ● LEITHABERG (BURGENLAND)

CZECH
REPUBLIC

SLOVAKIA

Weinviertel

Kamptal

Kremstal

Wachau

Wagram

■ LINZ

Traisental

Niederösterreich
- GRÜNER VELTLINER
- BLAUER PORTUGIESER
- RIESLING
- ZWEIGELT
- BLAUFRÄNKISCH
- PINOT BLANC

Wien
- GEMISCHTER SATZ (BLEND)

■ VIENNA

Carnuntum

Neusiedlersee

Thermenregion

EISENSTADT ■

Neusiedlersee-Hügelland
(Leithaberg)

Burgenland
- BLAU FRÄNKISCH
- ZWEIGELT
- PINOT BLANC

Mittelburgenland

Südburgenland

Steiermark
- PINOT BLANC
- SAUVIGNON BLANC
- MÜLLER-THURGAU

Süd-Oststeiermark

Weststeiermark

Südsteiermark

N

SLOVENIA

50km   50mi

185

Chile

Chile is a cool climate region most known for its lean and fruity Bordeaux blends. Chile is divided into 3 areas from the coast to the Andes Mountains.

276,000
ACRES

WINE REGIONS BY SIZE

◀ CENTRAL VALLEY
◀ ACONCAGUA
◀ SOUTH
◀ COQUIMBO
◀ AUSTRAL
◀ ATACAMA

COASTAL CHILE

 COOL CLIMATE

Coastal Chile is chilled by the frigid Humboldt current. Wines that thrive here include slightly saline citrus-driven white wines and juicy Pinot Noir.

- CHARDONNAY
- SAUVIGNON BLANC
- PINOT NOIR

INLAND VALLEYS

 WARM CLIMATE

The inland valleys include the Central Valley Region and are known for elegant red wines. The zone focuses on red Bordeaux blends with red fruit flavours and heightened acidity.

- BORDEAUX BLEND
- PETIT VERDOT
- SYRAH
- CARMÉNÈRE
- CARIÑENA (CARIGNAN)

THE ANDES

 WARM CLIMATE

The higher elevation vineyards in the foothills of the Andes produce red wines with tannin structure and, on good vintages, offer plentiful ripe fruit flavours along with heightened acidity.

- SYRAH
- CABERNET SAUVIGNON
- CABERNET FRANC
- CARMÉNÈRE

Atacama ─────── ■ COPIAPÓ
 🍷 PISCO (BRANDY) ────── Copiapó Valley

──── Huasco Valley

Coquimbo Region ─────── LA SERENA ■ ──── Elqui Valley
 CHARDONNAY
 SAUVIGNON BLANC
 🍷 SYRAH ──── Limari Valley

──── Choapa Valley

Aconcagua Region ─────── ──── Aconcagua Valley
 SAUVIGNON BLANC ──── Casablanca Valley
 CHARDONNAY VALPARAISO ■ ──── San Antonio Valley
 🍷 PINOT NOIR ■ SANTIAGO
 Leyda Valley ──── ──── Maipo Valley

■ RANCAGUA
──── Cachapoal Valley
Central Valley Region ─────── ──── Colchagua Valley
 🍷 BORDEAUX BLEND
 🍷 CARMÉNÈRE ──── Curico Valley
 🍷 CARIÑENA ■ TALCA
 🍷 PETIT VERDOT ──── Maule Valley
 🍷 SYRAH

──── Itata Valley
CONCEPCIÓN ■

South Region ─────── ──── Bío-Bío Valley
 🍷 PAÍS ──── Malleco Valley
 CHARDONNAY
 🍷 PINOT NOIR
■ TEMUCO

──── Cautín Valley

Austral Region ───────
 🍷 PINOT NOIR ■ OSORNO
 CHARDONNAY ──── Osorno Valley

N

200km 200mi

187

France

A wine region known for earthy and mineral-driven wines with heightened acidity. The country can be divided into three zones by the climate.

2 MILLION
ACRES

WINE REGIONS BY SIZE

◀ LANGUEDOC-ROUSSILLON
◀ BORDEAUX
◀ RHÔNE VALLEY
◀ LOIRE VALLEY
◀ SOUTH WEST
◀ PROVENCE
◀ CHAMPAGNE

◀ BURGUNDY
◀ BEAUJOLAIS
◀ ALSACE
◀ CORSICA

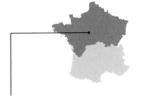

NORTHERN FRANCE

 COOL CLIMATE

Northern French wines have very high acidity, tart fruit and mineral flavours.

REGIONAL PRODUCTION:

- CHAMPAGNE
- MUSCADET
- LOIRE SAUVIGNON BLANC
- BURGUNDY CHARDONNAY
- LOIRE CHENIN BLANC
- ALSACE RIESLING
- BURGUNDY PINOT NOIR

CENTRAL FRANCE

 WARM CLIMATE

Central France wines have moderate acidity, tart fruit and soil flavours.

REGIONAL PRODUCTION:

- BORDEAUX SÉMILLON
- BEAUJOLAIS GAMAY
- RED BORDEAUX BLEND
- NORTHERN RHÔNE SYRAH
- SAUTERNAIS

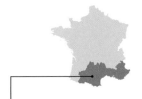

MEDITERRANEAN FRANCE

 WARM CLIMATE

Mediterranean French wines have medium acidity, ripe fruit and rustic earthy flavours.

REGIONAL PRODUCTION:

- LIMOUX SPARKLING
- PROVENCE ROSÉ
- RHÔNE/GSM BLEND
- CORBIERES CARIGNAN & GSM
- CAHORS MALBEC

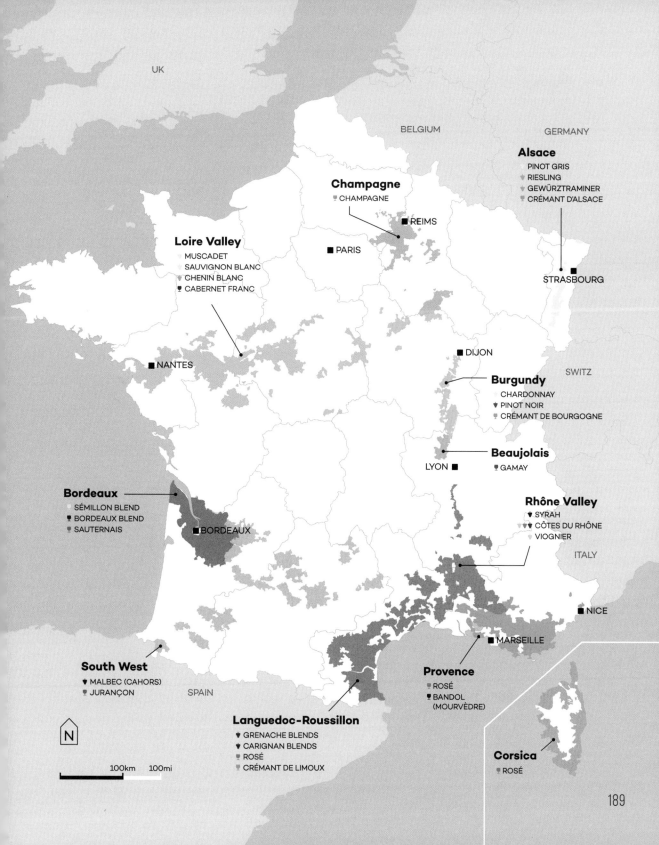

Champagne
- CHAMPAGNE

Alsace
- PINOT GRIS
- RIESLING
- GEWÜRZTRAMINER
- CRÉMANT D'ALSACE

Loire Valley
- MUSCADET
- SAUVIGNON BLANC
- CHENIN BLANC
- CABERNET FRANC

Burgundy
- CHARDONNAY
- PINOT NOIR
- CRÉMANT DE BOURGOGNE

Beaujolais
- GAMAY

Bordeaux
- SÉMILLON BLEND
- BORDEAUX BLEND
- SAUTERNAIS

Rhône Valley
- SYRAH
- CÔTES DU RHÔNE
- VIOGNIER

South West
- MALBEC (CAHORS)
- JURANÇON

Provence
- ROSÉ
- BANDOL (MOURVÈDRE)

Languedoc-Roussillon
- GRENACHE BLENDS
- CARIGNAN BLENDS
- ROSÉ
- CRÉMANT DE LIMOUX

Corsica
- ROSÉ

UK

BELGIUM

GERMANY

REIMS

PARIS

STRASBOURG

DIJON

NANTES

SWITZ

LYON

BORDEAUX

ITALY

NICE

MARSEILLE

SPAIN

N

100km 100mi

189

FRANCE: BORDEAUX

Merlot and Cabernet Sauvignon originate in Bordeaux and are blended into the eponymous Bordeaux Blend. Red wines make up nearly 90% of the production.

CLASSIFICATION OF RED BORDEAUX

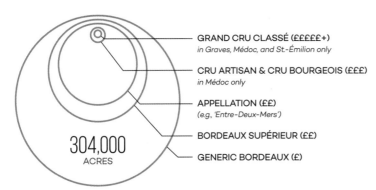

GRAND CRU CLASSÉ (£££££+)
in Graves, Médoc, and St-Émilion only

CRU ARTISAN & CRU BOURGEOIS (£££)
in Médoc only

APPELLATION (££)
(e.g. 'Entre-Deux-Mers')

BORDEAUX SUPÉRIEUR (££)

GENERIC BORDEAUX (£)

304,000 ACRES

FINDING QUALITY

Pay attention to vintage and look for wines labelled by their sub-appellation. If you see the term 'Grand Vin de Bordeaux' printed on the label, this is typically a producer's best wine.

GOOD VINTAGES:
2010, 2009, 2008, 2005, 2003
2000, 1998, 1990, 1989

TOP WINES OF BORDEAUX

🍷 'LEFT BANK' BORDEAUX

The west side of the Garonne River is predominantly Cabernet Sauvignon. The wines taste of blackcurrant, pencil lead, violet, tobacco, cocoa and liquorice with dense structured tannins. Many will age 20 years.

🥂 BORDEAUX BLANC

This blend is mostly Sémillon and Sauvignon Blanc and tastes of citrus, chamomile, grapefruit and beeswax. Bolder Bordeaux Blanc come from Pessac-Léognan and Graves. Lighter Bordeaux Blanc come from Entre-Deux-Mers.

🍷 'RIGHT BANK' BORDEAUX

The east side of the Garonne River is predominantly Merlot blended with Cabernet Franc. Wines taste of leather, strawberry, fig, plum, vanilla, grilled almonds and smoke with silky refined tannins. Some will age 30 years.

🥂 ROSÉ AND CLAIRET

Rich and deeply coloured dry rosé wines with flavours of redcurrant, wild strawberry, peony, and rose hips. Clairet ('Clair-ett') was the original style of Bordeaux during the 18th and 19th centuries.

🍷 CÔTES DE BORDEAUX

Areas close to rivers are called 'Côtes' meaning 'slope'. Wines are Merlot blends that taste of spicy red fruits, green pepper, and herbs with grippy bold tannin. Wines age 10 years.

🍷 SAUTERNAIS

A group of dessert wine regions can be found along the Garonne River. The largest appellation is Sauternes, which produces viscous, honeyed, waxy and peachy Sémillon-based wines.

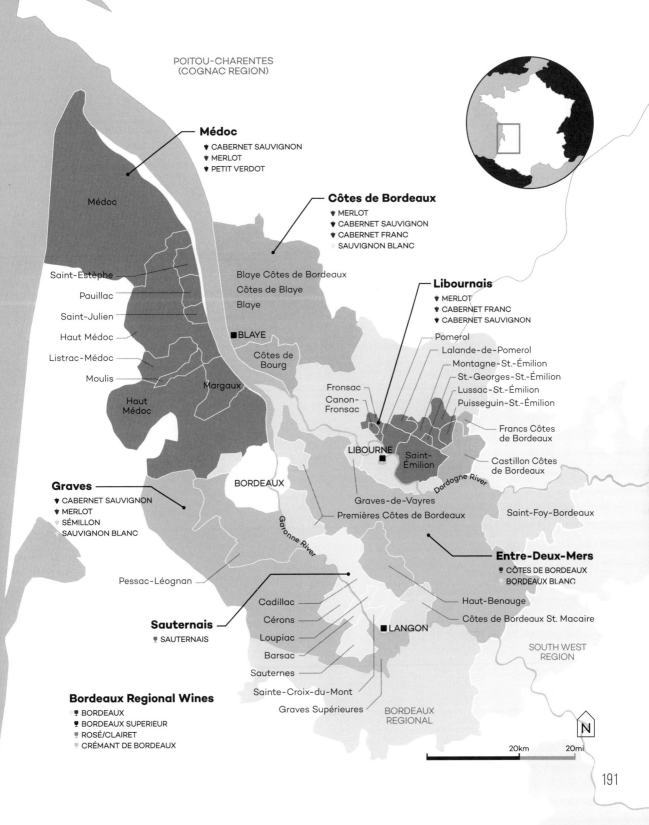

POITOU-CHARENTES
(COGNAC REGION)

Médoc
- ♥ CABERNET SAUVIGNON
- ♥ MERLOT
- ♥ PETIT VERDOT

Médoc

Côtes de Bordeaux
- ♥ MERLOT
- ♥ CABERNET SAUVIGNON
- ♥ CABERNET FRANC
- ⚬ SAUVIGNON BLANC

Saint-Estèphe
Pauillac
Saint-Julien
Haut Médoc
Listrac-Médoc
Moulis

Haut
Médoc

Margaux

Blaye Côtes de Bordeaux
Côtes de Blaye
Blaye

■ BLAYE

Côtes de
Bourg

Libournais
- ♥ MERLOT
- ♥ CABERNET FRANC
- ♥ CABERNET SAUVIGNON

Pomerol
Lalande-de-Pomerol
Montagne-St.-Émilion
St.-Georges-St.-Émilion
Lussac-St.-Émilion
Puisseguin-St.-Émilion

Fronsac
Canon-
Fronsac

Francs Côtes
de Bordeaux

LIBOURNE ■

Saint-
Émilion

Castillon Côtes
de Bordeaux

Graves
- ♥ CABERNET SAUVIGNON
- ♥ MERLOT
- ⚬ SÉMILLON
- ⚬ SAUVIGNON BLANC

BORDEAUX

Graves-de-Vayres

Premières Côtes de Bordeaux

Dordogne River

Saint-Foy-Bordeaux

Garonne River

Pessac-Léognan

Entre-Deux-Mers
- ♥ CÔTES DE BORDEAUX
- ⚬ BORDEAUX BLANC

Sauternais
- ⚬ SAUTERNAIS

Cadillac
Cérons
Loupiac
Barsac
Sauternes
Sainte-Croix-du-Mont
Graves Supérieures

Haut-Benauge
Côtes de Bordeaux St. Macaire

■ LANGON

SOUTH WEST
REGION

BORDEAUX
REGIONAL

Bordeaux Regional Wines
- ♥ BORDEAUX
- ♥ BORDEAUX SUPERIEUR
- ♥ ROSÉ/CLAIRET
- ⚬ CRÉMANT DE BORDEAUX

N

20km   20mi

FRANCE: BURGUNDY

Chardonnay and Pinot Noir come from Burgundy. The production is about 60% Chardonnay but Burgundy is most known for floral and earthy Pinot Noir.

CLASSIFICATION OF BURGUNDY WINES

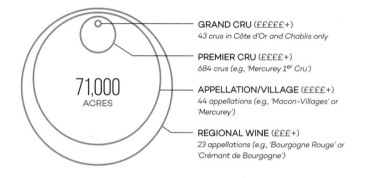

71,000 ACRES

GRAND CRU (£££££+)
43 crus in Côte d'Or and Chablis only

PREMIER CRU (££££+)
684 crus (e.g., 'Mercurey 1ᵉʳ Cru')

APPELLATION/VILLAGE (££££+)
44 appellations (e.g., 'Macon-Villages' or 'Mercurey')

REGIONAL WINE (£££+)
23 appellations (e.g., 'Bourgogne Rouge' or 'Crémant de Bourgogne')

TERMS

Domaine: a winery with vineyards

Negociant: a brand that buys grapes or wine

Clos: a walled vineyard

Lieu-dit/Climat: vineyard plot name listed on the label

GOOD VINTAGES:
2013, 2012, 2011, 2010, 2009, 2005

TOP WINES OF BURGUNDY

CHABLIS
Chablis produces mainly unoaked Chardonnay. Wines taste of yellow apple, passion fruit and citrus, with high acidity. At the Grand Cru level, Chablis is made more toasty with oak.

PINOT NOIR (CÔTE D'OR)
At the Village level, wines taste rustic with notes of mushrooms, potting soil and tart berries. Premier Cru and Grand Cru wines have moderate tannin with flavours of dried cranberry, candied hibiscus, vanilla and rose.

CHARDONNAY (CÔTE D'OR)
The Côte d'Or produces mainly oaked Chardonnay. Wines taste of yellow apple, lemon curd, quince tart, vanilla and hazelnut. Look in the Côte de Beaune for high-quality Chardonnays produced in this style.

CHARDONNAY (MÂCONNAIS)
The Mâconnais makes a light unoaked style of Chardonnay with flavours of ripe yellow apple with hints of lemon zest, apricot and a zesty finish. Pouilly-Fuissé, Saint-Véran and Viré-Clessé are the largest wine villages.

CRÉMANT DE BOURGOGNE
A sparkling wine appellation that produces white and rosé bubbly wines with the same method as Champagne. The regional appellation offers exceptional quality for the price.

PINOT NOIR (OTHER REGIONS)
Côte Chalonnaise also produces Pinot Noir with plummy fruit, Loganberries and clove, along with rustic earthy notes of dried leaves and potting soil. Look for Givry and Mercurey.

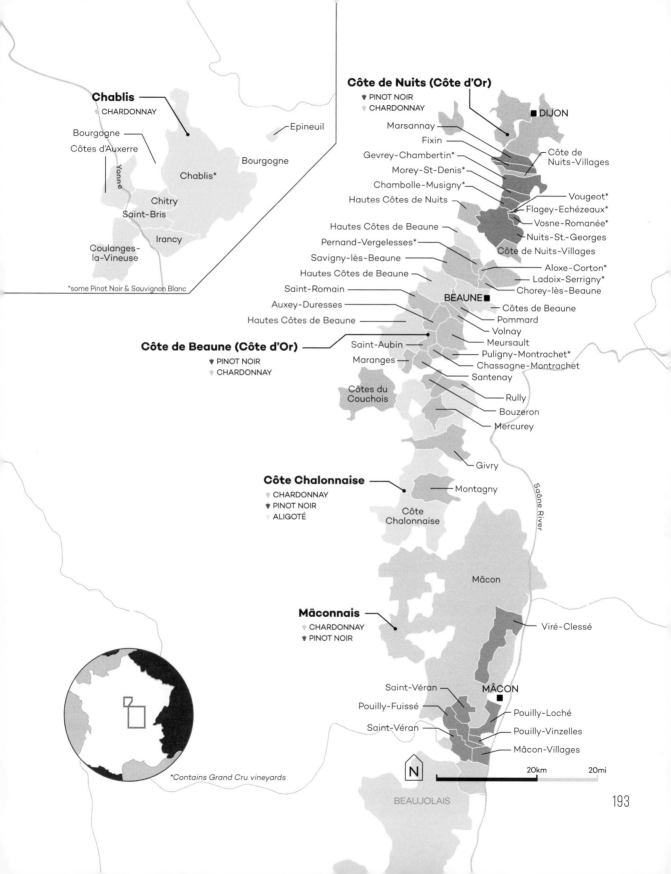

Chablis
  ᵪ CHARDONNAY

Bourgogne
Côtes d'Auxerre

Epineuil

Bourgogne

Chablis*

Yonne

Chitry
Saint-Bris

Irancy

Coulanges-
la-Vineuse

*some Pinot Noir & Sauvignon Blanc

Côte de Nuits (Côte d'Or)
  ♥ PINOT NOIR
  ᵪ CHARDONNAY

DIJON

Marsannay
Fixin
Gevrey-Chambertin*
Morey-St-Denis*
Chambolle-Musigny*
Hautes Côtes de Nuits

Côte de
Nuits-Villages

Vougeot*
Flagey-Echézeaux*
Vosne-Romanée*
Nuits-St.-Georges
Côte de Nuits-Villages

Hautes Côtes de Beaune
Pernand-Vergelesses*
Savigny-lès-Beaune
Hautes Côtes de Beaune
Saint-Romain
Auxey-Duresses
Hautes Côtes de Beaune

Aloxe-Corton*
Ladoix-Serrigny*
Chorey-lès-Beaune

BEAUNE

Côtes de Beaune
Pommard
Volnay
Meursault
Puligny-Montrachet*
Chassagne-Montrachet
Santenay
Rully
Bouzeron
Mercurey

Côte de Beaune (Côte d'Or)
  ♥ PINOT NOIR
  ᵪ CHARDONNAY

Saint-Aubin
Maranges

Côtes du
Couchois

Givry

Côte Chalonnaise
  ᵪ CHARDONNAY
  ♥ PINOT NOIR
  ᵪ ALIGOTÉ

Montagny

Côte
Chalonnaise

Saône River

Mâcon

Mâconnais
  ᵪ CHARDONNAY
  ♥ PINOT NOIR

Viré-Clessé

Saint-Véran
Pouilly-Fuissé
Saint-Véran

MÂCON

Pouilly-Loché
Pouilly-Vinzelles
Mâcon-Villages

N

*Contains Grand Cru vineyards

20km   20mi

BEAUJOLAIS

FRANCE: RHÔNE VALLEY

The Rhône Valley is most known for leathery and fruity Southern Rhône red blends and savoury herbaceous Northern Rhône Syrahs.

CLASSIFICATION OF RHÔNE WINES

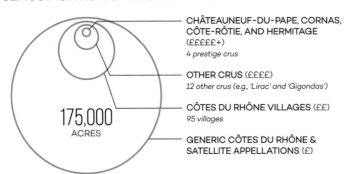

175,000 ACRES

CHÂTEAUNEUF-DU-PAPE, CORNAS, CÔTE-RÔTIE, AND HERMITAGE (£££££+)
4 prestige crus

OTHER CRUS (££££)
12 other crus (e.g., 'Lirac' and 'Gigondas')

CÔTES DU RHÔNE VILLAGES (££)
95 villages

GENERIC CÔTES DU RHÔNE & SATELLITE APPELLATIONS (£)

FINDING QUALITY

Value-driven wines vary in taste year to year, so look for trends on the quality of the vintage overall. You'll see less variation and more ageability from higher quality producers, particularly in the northern Rhône and the crus.

GOOD VINTAGES:
2012, 2010, 2009, 2007, 2005, 2001, 2000

TOP WINES OF THE RHÔNE VALLEY

🍷 CÔTES DU RHÔNE RED

Some of the highest acclaimed southern Rhône reds have higher proportions of Grenache in the blend. As bold as these wines can be, they're rarely oaked. Flavours range from sweet candied raspberries to leather and bacon fat.

🍷 CHÂTEAUNEUF-DU-PAPE

One of the boldest age-worthy southern Rhône blends are made with no less than 13 different grapes. The dominant varieties include Grenache, Syrah, Mourvèdre and Cinsault.

🍷 RHÔNE ROSÉ & TAVEL ROSÉ

Rhône rosé bursts with wild strawberry and red currant flavours. The deeply coloured rosés of Tavel are said to have been a favourite of the writer and man's man, Ernest Hemingway.

🍷 NORTHERN RHÔNE SYRAH

The birthplace of Syrah offers rich and dense wines that typically have a meaty edge to them along with loads of blackcurrant, liquorice, plums and olives. The finest wines can age for 20 years.

🍷 CÔTES DU RHÔNE WHITE

Marsanne and Viognier are the champion grapes of Rhône White. Wines are often citrusy with notes of apple, beeswax and granite-like minerals. Northern Rhône delivers the boldest whites with notes of almond, white peach and orange blossom.

🍷 MUSCAT BEAUMES DE VENISE

A rarity, Muscat Blanc goes into what the French call a VDN or 'Vin doux Naturels'—a fortified dessert wine. Wines are rich with aromas of orchids, candied orange, honey and tropical fruits.

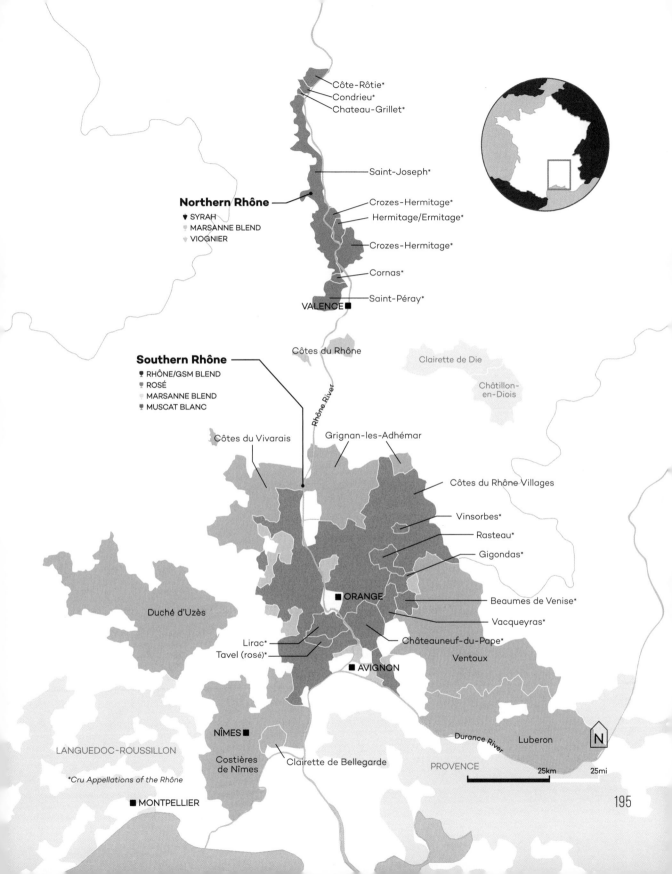

Côte-Rôtie*
Condrieu*
Chateau-Grillet*

Saint-Joseph*

Northern Rhône

♥ SYRAH
♟ MARSANNE BLEND
♠ VIOGNIER

Crozes-Hermitage*
Hermitage/Ermitage*

Crozes-Hermitage*

Cornas*

Saint-Péray*

VALENCE ■

Côtes du Rhône

Clairette de Die

Châtillon-en-Diois

Southern Rhône

♟ RHÔNE/GSM BLEND
♟ ROSÉ
♠ MARSANNE BLEND
♟ MUSCAT BLANC

Côtes du Vivarais

Grignan-les-Adhémar

Rhône River

Côtes du Rhône Villages

Vinsorbes*

Rasteau*

Gigondas*

Beaumes de Venise*

ORANGE ■

Vacqueyras*

Duché d'Uzès

Châteauneuf-du-Pape*

Lirac*
Tavel (rosé)*

Ventoux

AVIGNON ■

NÎMES ■

Durance River

Luberon

N

LANGUEDOC-ROUSSILLON

Costières de Nîmes

Clairette de Bellegarde

PROVENCE

25km   25mi

*Cru Appellations of the Rhône

■ MONTPELLIER

195

Germany

Germany is a cool climate growing region known mostly for Riesling as well as ripe and rustic Pinot Noir.

250,000
ACRES

WINE REGIONS BY SIZE

◄ RHEINHESSEN
◄ PFALZ
◄ BADEN
◄ WÜRTTEMBERG
◄ MOSEL
◄ FRANKEN
◄ NAHE

◄ RHEINGAU
◄ SAALE-UNSTRUT
◄ AHR
◄ SACHSEN
◄ MITTELRHEIN
◄ HESSISCHE BERGSTRASSE

TOP WINES OF GERMANY

RIESLING

The top German grape, known for aromatic wines that range in style from dry or 'trocken' to sweet ice wine or 'eiswein'.

- MOSEL
- RHEINGAU
- RHEINHESSEN
- MITTELRHEIN

MÜLLER-THURGAU

A simple aromatic white wine with peach and floral flavours that is often a touch sweet.

- RHEINHESSEN
- FRANKEN
- PFALZ

PINOT NOIR

Pinot Noir (Spätburgunder) offers cranberry, cherry and subtle earthy flavours. Wines are often likened to red Burgundy.

- BADEN
- FRANKEN
- AHR

DORNFELDER

A simple medium red wine with sweet red fruit flavours, an herbaceous green note, medium tannin and spicy acidity.

- RHEINHESSEN
- PFALZ

PINOT GRIS & PINOT BLANC

Germany produces a rich style of Pinot Blanc (Weissburgunder) and Pinot Gris (Grauburgunder) with white peach, citrus and subtle notes of honeycomb.

- BADEN

SILVANER

A light dry white wine with high acidity and flavours of citrus zest and green apple.

- RHEINHESSEN
- FRANKEN

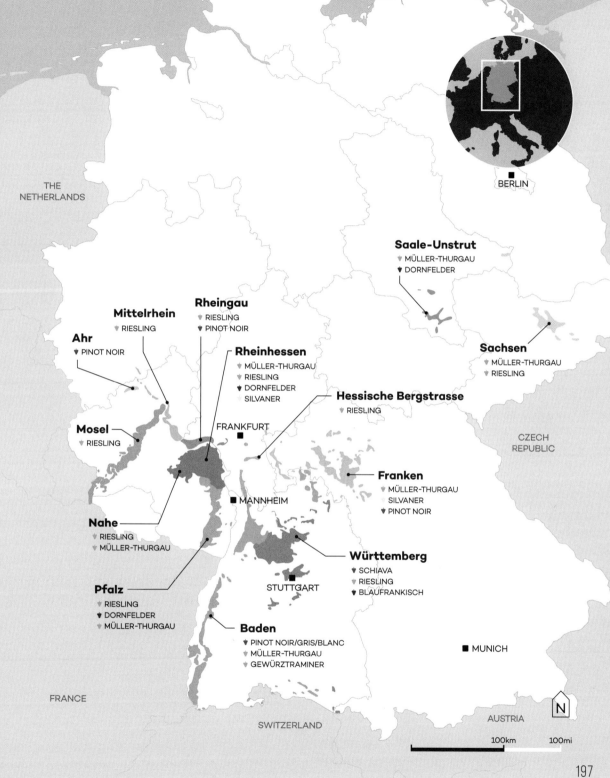

THE NETHERLANDS

BERLIN

Saale-Unstrut
♀ MÜLLER-THURGAU
♥ DORNFELDER

Sachsen
♀ MÜLLER-THURGAU
♀ RIESLING

Mittelrhein
♀ RIESLING

Rheingau
♀ RIESLING
♥ PINOT NOIR

Ahr
♥ PINOT NOIR

Rheinhessen
♀ MÜLLER-THURGAU
♀ RIESLING
♥ DORNFELDER
SILVANER

Hessische Bergstrasse
♀ RIESLING

Mosel
♀ RIESLING

FRANKFURT

Franken
♀ MÜLLER-THURGAU
SILVANER
♥ PINOT NOIR

CZECH
REPUBLIC

Nahe
♀ RIESLING
♀ MÜLLER-THURGAU

MANNHEIM

Württemberg
♥ SCHIAVA
♀ RIESLING
♥ BLAUFRÄNKISCH

Pfalz
♀ RIESLING
♥ DORNFELDER
♀ MÜLLER-THURGAU

STUTTGART

Baden
♥ PINOT NOIR/GRIS/BLANC
♀ MÜLLER-THURGAU
♀ GEWÜRZTRAMINER

■ MUNICH

FRANCE

SWITZERLAND

AUSTRIA

N

100km   100mi

197

Italy

Italy is known for its concentrated rustic wines. The country can be divided into three major areas, each with a different climate.

WINE REGIONS BY SIZE

1.5 MILLION ACRES

◀ SICILY
◀ PUGLIA
◀ VENETO
◀ TUSCANY
◀ EMILIA-ROMAGNA
◀ PIEDMONT
◀ ABRUZZO

◀ CAMPANIA
◀ LOMBARDY
◀ FRIULI-VENEZIA GIULIA
◀ SARDEGNA
◀ MARCHE
◀ LAZIO
◀ TRENTINO-ALTO ADIGE

◀ UMBRIA
◀ CALABRIA
◀ MOLISE
◀ BASILICATA
◀ LIGURIA
◀ VALLE D'AOSTA

NORTHERN ITALY

 COOL CLIMATE

Northern Italian wines have higher acidity, tart fruit and herb flavours.

REGIONAL PRODUCTION:

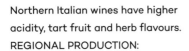

- 🍷 PROSECCO
- 🍷 MOSCATO D'ASTI
- 🍷 PINOT GRIGIO
- 🍷 SOAVE
- 🍷 BARBERA
- 🍷 VALPOLICELLA
- 🍷 BAROLO (NEBBIOLO)

CENTRAL ITALY

 WARM CLIMATE

Central Italian wines have higher acidity, ripe fruit, leather and clay flavours.

REGIONAL PRODUCTION:

- 🍷 LAMBRUSCO
- 🍷 VERMENTINO
- 🍷 CHIANTI (SANGIOVESE)
- 🍷 SUPER TUSCAN (BORDEAUX BLEND)
- 🍷 MONTEPULCIANO
- 🍷 VIN SANTO

SOUTHERN ITALY / ISLANDS

 HOT CLIMATE

Southern Italian wines have medium acidity, sweet fruit and leather flavours.

REGIONAL PRODUCTION:

- 🍷 VERMENTINO
- 🍷 CANNONAU (GRENACHE)
- 🍷 PRIMITIVO
- 🍷 NEGROAMARO
- 🍷 NERO D'AVOLA
- 🍷 MARSALA

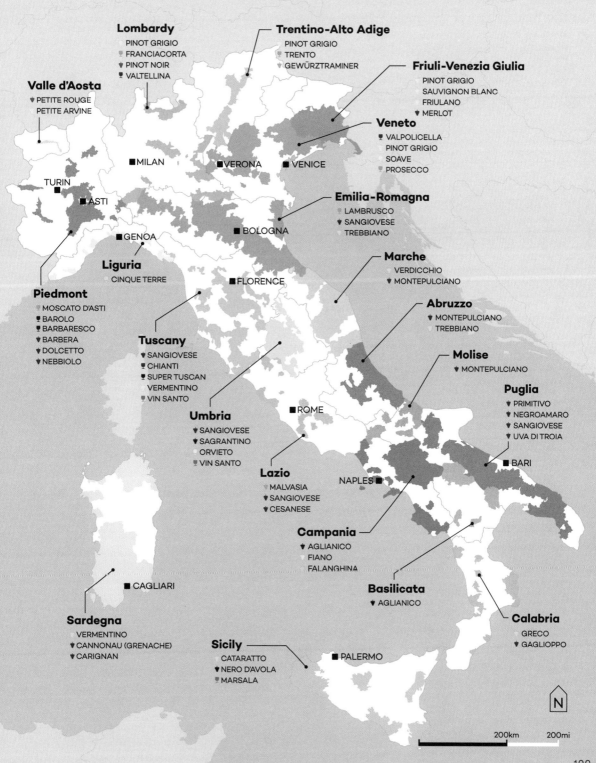

Valle d'Aosta
- PETITE ROUGE
- PETITE ARVINE

Lombardy
- PINOT GRIGIO
- FRANCIACORTA
- PINOT NOIR
- VALTELLINA

Trentino-Alto Adige
- PINOT GRIGIO
- TRENTO
- GEWÜRZTRAMINER

Friuli-Venezia Giulia
- PINOT GRIGIO
- SAUVIGNON BLANC
- FRIULANO
- MERLOT

Veneto
- VALPOLICELLA
- PINOT GRIGIO
- SOAVE
- PROSECCO

Emilia-Romagna
- LAMBRUSCO
- SANGIOVESE
- TREBBIANO

Marche
- VERDICCHIO
- MONTEPULCIANO

Abruzzo
- MONTEPULCIANO
- TREBBIANO

Molise
- MONTEPULCIANO

Puglia
- PRIMITIVO
- NEGROAMARO
- SANGIOVESE
- UVA DI TROIA

Piedmont
- MOSCATO D'ASTI
- BAROLO
- BARBARESCO
- BARBERA
- DOLCETTO
- NEBBIOLO

Liguria
- CINQUE TERRE

Tuscany
- SANGIOVESE
- CHIANTI
- SUPER TUSCAN
- VERMENTINO
- VIN SANTO

Umbria
- SANGIOVESE
- SAGRANTINO
- ORVIETO
- VIN SANTO

Lazio
- MALVASIA
- SANGIOVESE
- CESANESE

Campania
- AGLIANICO
- FIANO
- FALANGHINA

Basilicata
- AGLIANICO

Calabria
- GRECO
- GAGLIOPPO

Sardegna
- VERMENTINO
- CANNONAU (GRENACHE)
- CARIGNAN

Sicily
- CATARATTO
- NERO D'AVOLA
- MARSALA

MILAN
VERONA
VENICE
TURIN
ASTI
GENOA
BOLOGNA
FLORENCE
ROME
NAPLES
BARI
CAGLIARI
PALERMO

200km   200mi

ITALY: TUSCANY

The region of Italy that specializes in Italy's most planted grape: Sangiovese. Wines are spicy and herbaceous when young and more fig-like as they age.

WHAT TUSCANY GROWS

148,000 ACRES

◀ SANGIOVESE

◀ MERLOT, CABERNET SAUVIGNON, CABERNET FRANC, & SYRAH

◀ CANAIOLO NERO

◀ VERMENTINO

◀ MALVASIA *(used in Vin Santo)*

◀ CHARDONNAY

◀ OTHERS

CHIANTI AGING

2.5 YRS: 'GRAN SELEZIONE'
Chianti Classico only

2 YRS: 'RISERVA'
Riserva wines from all 8 subzones

1 YR: CLASSICO, FIORENTINI, RUFINA
Plus, other subzones labelled as 'Superiore'

9 MO: CHIANTI MONTESPERTOLI

6 MO: CHIANTI
Chianti, Ch. Colli Arentini, Ch. Colline Pisane, Ch. Colli Senesi and Ch. Montalbano

GOOD VINTAGES:
2010, 2009, 2006, 2004
2001, 2000, 1999, 1997

TOP DRY WINES OF TUSCANY

🍷 CHIANTI

Sangiovese-dominant blend. Aged Chianti wines taste of preserved cherry, oregano, clay pot, sweet balsamic, espresso and sweet tobacco. Value Chianti tastes spicy and herbaceous with notes of game, red fruits and tomato.

🍷 SUPER TUSCAN BLEND

The colloquial name for a blend that includes non-indigenous grapes such as Merlot and Cabernet Franc. Wines are identifiable from other Tuscan wines by their unique made-up label names.

🍷 BRUNELLO DI MONTALCINO

100% Sangiovese with a regional clone called Prugnolo Gentile. Brunello is aged for 4+ years. Wines taste of liquorice, cedar, vanilla, fig and sweet red berries, supported by spicy acidity and moderate tannin.

🍷 VERNACCIA DI SAN GIMIGNANO

The 'Fiore' Vernaccia wines are dry and minerally, with flavours of lemon, apple blossom and pear. 'Tradizionale' wines are similar to 'Fiore' but usually feature a bitter almond note on the finish.

🍷 OTHER TUSCAN SANGIOVESE

While Chianti and Brunello are the most well-known Sangiovese wines of Tuscany, there are several other regional designations that also make great Sangiovese:

CARMIGNANO
Blended 10–20% Cabernet Franc/Cab. Sauvignon.

MONTECUCCO
18 months ageing & 34 months ageing for Riserva.

VINO NOBILE DI MONTEPULCIANO
Aged for 24 months & 34 months for Riserva

MORELLINO DI SCANSANO
Aged for 8 months & 24 months for Riserva

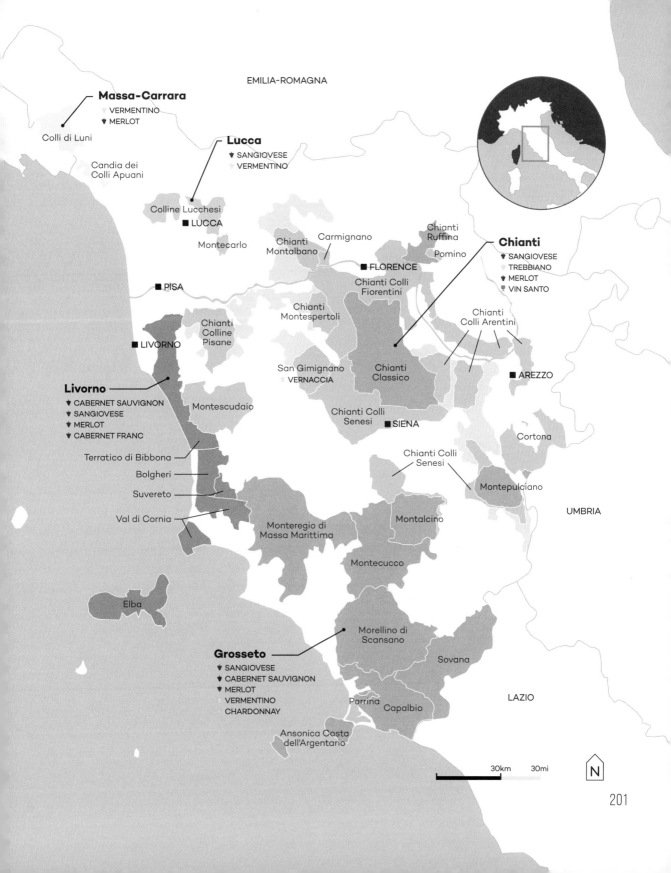

EMILIA-ROMAGNA

Massa-Carrara
  ♥ VERMENTINO
  ♥ MERLOT

Colli di Luni

Candia dei
Colli Apuani

Lucca
  ♥ SANGIOVESE
  ♥ VERMENTINO

Colline Lucchesi

■ LUCCA

Montecarlo

Chianti
Montalbano

Carmignano

Chianti
Ruffina

Pomino

Chianti
  ♥ SANGIOVESE
  ♥ TREBBIANO
  ♥ MERLOT
  ♥ VIN SANTO

■ FLORENCE

Chianti Colli
Fiorentini

Chianti
Montespertoli

Chianti
Colli Arentini

■ PISA

Chianti
Colline
Pisane

San Gimignano
  VERNACCIA

Chianti
Classico

■ AREZZO

■ LIVORNO

Cortona

Livorno
  ♥ CABERNET SAUVIGNON
  ♥ SANGIOVESE
  ♥ MERLOT
  ♥ CABERNET FRANC

Montescudaio

Chianti Colli
Senesi

■ SIENA

Terratico di Bibbona

Bolgheri

Suvereto

Val di Cornia

Chianti Colli
Senesi

Montepulciano

UMBRIA

Montalcino

Monteregio di
Massa Marittima

Montecucco

Elba

Morellino di
Scansano

Grosseto
  ♥ SANGIOVESE
  ♥ CABERNET SAUVIGNON
  ♥ MERLOT
  ♥ VERMENTINO
  CHARDONNAY

Sovana

LAZIO

Parrina

Capalbio

Ansonica Costa
dell'Argentario

30km   30mi

N

New Zealand

New Zealand is a cool climate region most known for its intensely flavoured Sauvignon Blanc. Expect wines to taste tart, light-bodied and elegant.

220,000 ACRES

WINE REGIONS BY SIZE

◄ MARLBOROUGH

◄ HAWKE'S BAY

◄ CENTRAL OTAGO

◄ GISBORNE

◄ CANTERBURY/WAIPARA VALLEY

◄ NELSON

◄ WAIRARAPA

◄ AUCKLAND

◄ WAIKATO/BAY OF PLENTY

◄ NORTHLAND

TOP WINES OF NEW ZEALAND

SAUVIGNON BLANC

The most important wine of New Zealand explodes with flavours of gooseberry, passion fruit, lime, tomato stalk and grapefruit.

- MARLBOROUGH
- NELSON
- HAWKE'S BAY

PINOT NOIR

Marlborough tends to offer tart red fruit flavours, whereas Central Otago produces wines with ripe raspberry flavours.

- CENTRAL OTAGO
- WAIRARAPA
- MARLBOROUGH

CHARDONNAY

Bold lemon and tropical fruit flavours with crisp acidity and usually a touch of oak, which adds toasty caramel and vanilla flavours.

- HAWKE'S BAY
- GISBORNE
- MARLBOROUGH

PINOT GRIS

Both dry and off-dry styles with notes of apple, pear, honeysuckle and spice bread.

- GISBORNE
- CANTERBURY/WAIPARA VALLEY
- NELSON

RIESLING

Wines range from bone-dry with lime notes to lusciously sweet and tasting of apricots and honey.

- MARLBOROUGH
- CENTRAL OTAGO
- NELSON

BORDEAUX BLEND

A light fruity style with juicy aromas of ripe black cherry, baking spices and coffee.

- HAWKE'S BAY
- NORTHLAND
- AUCKLAND

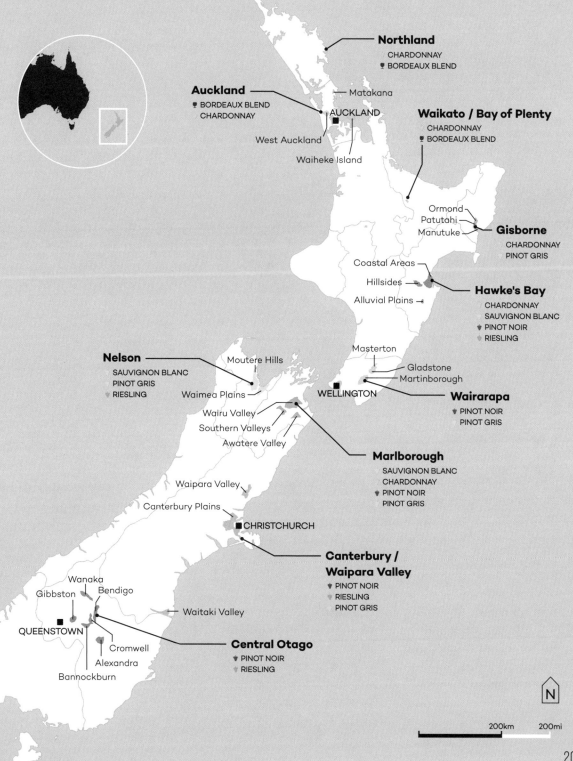

Northland
CHARDONNAY
🍷 BORDEAUX BLEND

Auckland
🍷 BORDEAUX BLEND
CHARDONNAY

Matakana

AUCKLAND

West Auckland

Waiheke Island

Waikato / Bay of Plenty
CHARDONNAY
🍷 BORDEAUX BLEND

Ormond
Patutahi
Manutuke

Gisborne
CHARDONNAY
PINOT GRIS

Coastal Areas

Hillsides

Alluvial Plains

Hawke's Bay
CHARDONNAY
SAUVIGNON BLANC
🍷 PINOT NOIR
🍷 RIESLING

Nelson
SAUVIGNON BLANC
PINOT GRIS
🍷 RIESLING

Moutere Hills

Waimea Plains

Masterton

Gladstone
Martinborough

WELLINGTON

Wairarapa
🍷 PINOT NOIR
PINOT GRIS

Wairu Valley
Southern Valleys
Awatere Valley

Marlborough
SAUVIGNON BLANC
CHARDONNAY
🍷 PINOT NOIR
PINOT GRIS

Waipara Valley

Canterbury Plains

CHRISTCHURCH

**Canterbury /
Waipara Valley**
🍷 PINOT NOIR
🍷 RIESLING
PINOT GRIS

Wanaka
Bendigo
Gibbston

Waitaki Valley

QUEENSTOWN

Cromwell
Alexandra
Bannockburn

Central Otago
🍷 PINOT NOIR
🍷 RIESLING

N

200km   200mi

Portugal

Portugal is most famous for Port but also produces excellent dry wines with more than 200 native wine grapes.

554,000
ACRES

WINE REGIONS BY SIZE

◀ DOURO VALLEY
◀ MINHO
◀ BEIRA INTERIOR
◀ LISBOA
◀ ALENTEJO
◀ DÃO
◀ TEJO/RIBATEJO

◀ SETÚBAL
◀ BEIRA ATLÂNTICO
◀ TERRAS DE CISTER
◀ ALGARVE
◀ TRANSMONTANO
◀ MADEIRA

TOP DRY WINES OF PORTUGAL

❦ TOURIGA NACIONAL

Quite possibly Portugal's most important grape, used in Port and dry red blends. Wines offer flavours of black plum, blackberry, mint and violet.

├─● DOURO
└─● DÃO

❦ TEMPRANILLO

Tempranillo is labelled as 'Aragonez' in southern Portugal and 'Tinta Roriz' in the north. Wines offer smoky red fruit flavours, cinnamon and bittersweet chocolate.

└─● ALL OF PORTUGAL

❦ ALICANTE BOUSCHET

A rare wine grape that has red skins and red flesh. Wines offer bold black fruit and black pepper flavours with a sweet smoky tobacco finish.

├─● ALENTEJO
└─● LISBOA

❦ TRINCADEIRA

Unique woodsy-tasting wines with notes of red fruit, barbecue smoke, hickory, plum sauce, raisins, kerosene and chocolate.

├─● ALENTEJO
└─● LISBOA

❦ ARINTO

When young, wines are lean with citrus pith flavours. As they age, they develop flavours of lemon, almond and honeycomb. Arinto is sometimes aged in oak.

└─● ALL OF PORTUGAL

❦ FERNÃO PIRES

An aromatic wine with perfumed floral aromas. Wines are sometimes blended with Viognier to add richer flavours of peaches and honeysuckle.

├─● LISBOA
└─● TEJO

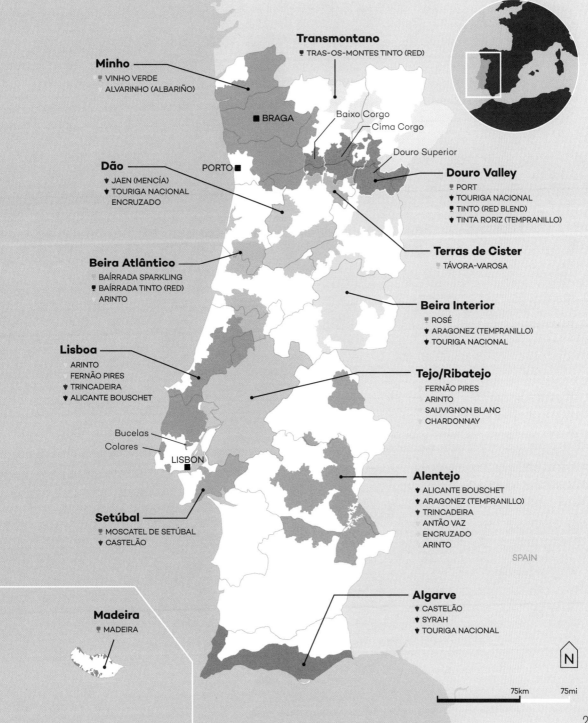

Transmontano
- 🍷 TRAS-OS-MONTES TINTO (RED)

Minho
- 🥂 VINHO VERDE
  ALVARINHO (ALBARIÑO)

■ BRAGA

Baixo Corgo
Cima Corgo
Douro Superior

Dão
- 🍷 JAEN (MENCÍA)
- 🍷 TOURIGA NACIONAL
  ENCRUZADO

PORTO ■

Douro Valley
- 🍷 PORT
- 🍷 TOURIGA NACIONAL
- 🍷 TINTO (RED BLEND)
- 🍷 TINTA RORIZ (TEMPRANILLO)

Terras de Cister
- 🥂 TÁVORA-VAROSA

Beira Atlântico
- 🥂 BAÍRRADA SPARKLING
- 🍷 BAÍRRADA TINTO (RED)
  ARINTO

Beira Interior
- 🍷 ROSÉ
- 🍷 ARAGONEZ (TEMPRANILLO)
- 🍷 TOURIGA NACIONAL

Lisboa
- ARINTO
- FERNÃO PIRES
- 🍷 TRINCADEIRA
- 🍷 ALICANTE BOUSCHET

Tejo/Ribatejo
- FERNÃO PIRES
- ARINTO
- SAUVIGNON BLANC
- CHARDONNAY

Bucelas
Colares

■ LISBON

Alentejo
- 🍷 ALICANTE BOUSCHET
- 🍷 ARAGONEZ (TEMPRANILLO)
- 🍷 TRINCADEIRA
- ANTÃO VAZ
- ENCRUZADO
- ARINTO

Setúbal
- 🍷 MOSCATEL DE SETÚBAL
- 🍷 CASTELÃO

SPAIN

Algarve
- 🍷 CASTELÃO
- 🍷 SYRAH
- 🍷 TOURIGA NACIONAL

Madeira
- 🍷 MADEIRA

75km   75mi

N

205

South Africa

South Africa is a hot climate region known for full-bodied savoury reds and rich fruity whites. Much of South Africa's wine grapes are used for brandy.

250,000
ACRES

WINE REGIONS BY SIZE

◀ STELLENBOSCH

◀ PAARL

◀ SWARTLAND/MALMESBURY

◀ ROBERTSON

◀ BREEDEKLOOF

◀ OLIFANTS RIVER VALLEY

◀ WORCESTER

◀ ORANGE RIVER VALLEY

◀ KLEIN KAROO

◀ OTHERS

TOP WINES OF SOUTH AFRICA

CHENIN BLANC

The country's top wine offers 6 main styles: fresh & fruity; rich & unoaked; rich & oaked; rich & sweet; very sweet; and a sparkling style called Cap Classique.

- PAARL
- SWARTLAND
- STELLENBOSCH

CABERNET SAUVIGNON

Wines are bold and herbaceous with flavours of black pepper, blackcurrant and earthy notes of graphite and clay.

- STELLENBOSCH
- PAARL

PINOTAGE

Quality producers offer wines with blackberry, raspberry and plum sauce with a smoky sweet tobacco finish.

- PAARL
- STELLENBOSCH
- SWARTLAND

SHIRAZ/SYRAH

Bolder Syrah wines with spicy flavours of black pepper, liquorice, raspberry and plum sauce.

- STELLENBOSCH
- PAARL
- SWARTLAND

CHARDONNAY

Chardonnay grows well in the cooler southern parts. Wines have baked apple notes, lemon zest and vanilla flavours from oak ageing.

- WALKER BAY
- ELGIN (NW OF WALKER BAY)

SÉMILLON

Wines are rich and full-bodied with flavours of Meyer lemon, yellow apple, wax lips and creamy hazelnut.

- FRANSCHHOEK
- STELLENBOSCH

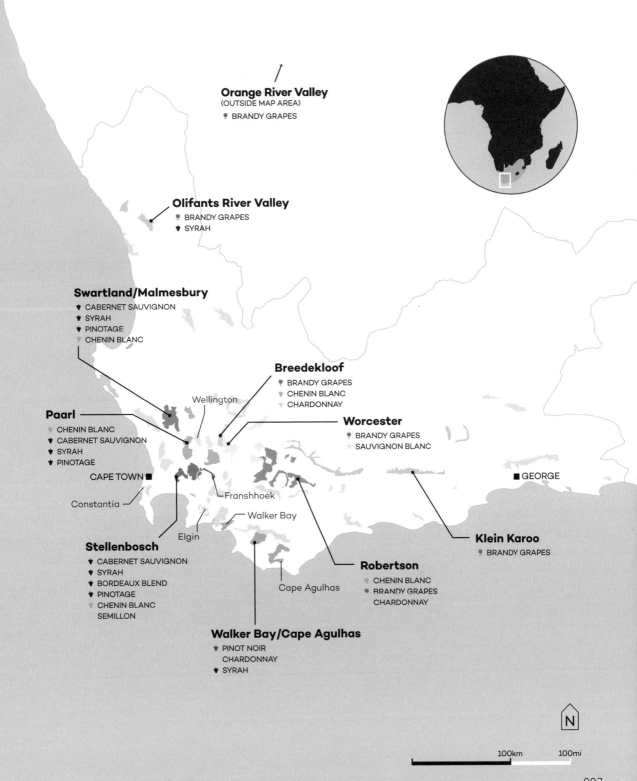

Orange River Valley
(OUTSIDE MAP AREA)
- ♟ BRANDY GRAPES

Olifants River Valley
- ♟ BRANDY GRAPES
- ♥ SYRAH

Swartland/Malmesbury
- ♥ CABERNET SAUVIGNON
- ♥ SYRAH
- ♥ PINOTAGE
- ♥ CHENIN BLANC

Wellington

Breedekloof
- ♟ BRANDY GRAPES
- ♥ CHENIN BLANC
- ♥ CHARDONNAY

Paarl
- ♥ CHENIN BLANC
- ♥ CABERNET SAUVIGNON
- ♥ SYRAH
- ♥ PINOTAGE

Worcester
- ♟ BRANDY GRAPES
- ♥ SAUVIGNON BLANC

CAPE TOWN ■

■ GEORGE

Constantia

Franshhoek

Walker Bay

Klein Karoo
- ♟ BRANDY GRAPES

Elgin

Stellenbosch
- ♥ CABERNET SAUVIGNON
- ♥ SYRAH
- ♥ BORDEAUX BLEND
- ♥ PINOTAGE
- ♥ CHENIN BLANC
  SEMILLON

Robertson
- ♥ CHENIN BLANC
- ♟ BRANDY GRAPES
  CHARDONNAY

Cape Agulhas

Walker Bay/Cape Agulhas
- ♥ PINOT NOIR
  CHARDONNAY
- ♥ SYRAH

N

100km   100mi

207

Spain

A region most known for its full-bodied fruity wines with subtle claylike earth notes. The country can be divided into three major climates.

2.5 MILLION
ACRES

WINE REGIONS BY SIZE

◄ CASTILLA-LA MANCHA
◄ VALENCIA
◄ EXTREMADURA
◄ RIOJA / NAVARRA
◄ CASTILLA / LEON
◄ CATALONIA
◄ ARAGON

◄ ANDALUCÍA
◄ GALICIA
◄ PAÍS VASCO
◄ THE ISLANDS

GREEN SPAIN

 COOL CLIMATE

Northwest Spanish wines have high acidity, tart fruit and mineral flavours.

REGIONAL PRODUCTION:

🍷 ALBARIÑO
🍷 MENCÍA

NORTHERN SPAIN

 WARM CLIMATE

Northern Spanish wines have medium acidity, ripe fruit and mineral flavours.

REGIONAL PRODUCTION:

🍷 CAVA
🍷 VERDEJO
🍷 GARNACHA (GRENACHE)
🍷 CARIGNAN
🍷 PRIORAT (GSM BLEND)
🍷 RIOJA (TEMPRANILLO)
🍷 RIBERA DEL DUERO (TEMPRANILLO)

SOUTHERN SPAIN

 HOT CLIMATE

Southern Spanish wines have medium acidity, sweet fruit and rustic clay flavours.

REGIONAL PRODUCTION:

🍷 GARNACHA (GRENACHE)
🍷 MONASTRELL (MOURVÈDRE)
🍷 SHERRY

208

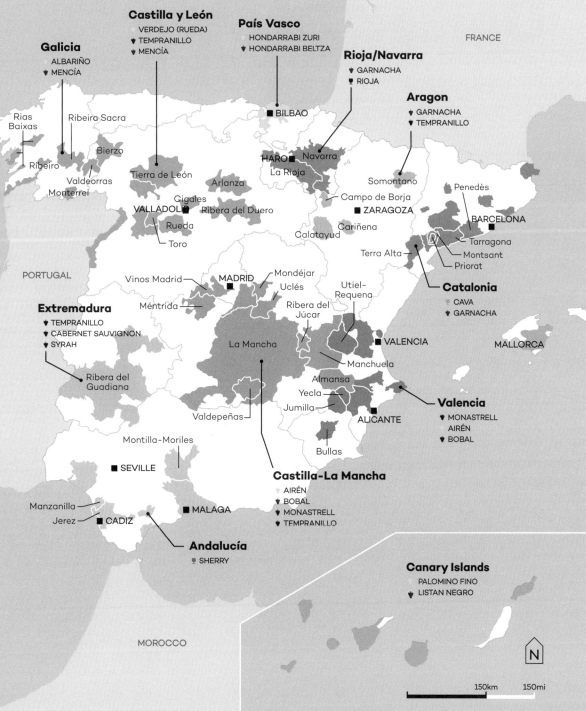

Galicia
- ALBARIÑO
- MENCÍA

Rias Baixas
Ribeira Sacra
Ribeiro
Bierzo
Valdeorras
Monterrei

Castilla y León
- VERDEJO (RUEDA)
- TEMPRANILLO
- MENCÍA

Tierra de León
Arlanza
Cigales
VALLADOLID
Ribera del Duero
Rueda
Toro

País Vasco
- HONDARRABI ZURI
- HONDARRABI BELTZA

BILBAO

Rioja/Navarra
- GARNACHA
- RIOJA

HARO
Navarra
La Rioja

FRANCE

Aragon
- GARNACHA
- TEMPRANILLO

Somontano
Campo de Borja
ZARAGOZA
Cariñena
Calatayud
Terra Alta

Penedès
BARCELONA
Tarragona
Montsant
Priorat

Catalonia
- CAVA
- GARNACHA

PORTUGAL

Extremadura
- TEMPRANILLO
- CABERNET SAUVIGNON
- SYRAH

Ribera del Guadiana

Vinos Madrid
MADRID
Méntrida
Mondéjar
Uclés
Ribera del Júcar

Utiel-Requena

La Mancha
Manchuela
VALENCIA

MALLORCA

Valdepeñas
Almansa
Yecla
Jumilla
ALICANTE
Bullas

Valencia
- MONASTRELL
- AIRÉN
- BOBAL

Montilla-Moriles

SEVILLE

Castilla-La Mancha
- AIRÉN
- BOBAL
- MONASTRELL
- TEMPRANILLO

Manzanilla
Jerez
CADIZ
MALAGA

Andalucía
- SHERRY

Canary Islands
- PALOMINO FINO
- LISTAN NEGRO

MOROCCO

N

150km   150mi

209

United States

The United States is most known for its bold, fruity red and white wines. Three regions produce the majority of US wine.

564,000
ACRES

WINE REGIONS BY SIZE

◀ CALIFORNIA
◀ NORTHWEST
◀ NORTHEAST
◀ MIDWEST
◀ SOUTHEAST
◀ SOUTHWEST

WHAT IS AN AVA?

American Viticultural Areas (AVA) are grape-growing regions with distinguishing features that allow people to identify quality or taste or other traits of a wine that are unique to its geographic origin. There are over 200 AVAs.

CALIFORNIA

 WARM/HOT CLIMATE

California wines have rich ripe fruit flavours and medium acidity. The coastal areas are cool enough for Pinot Noir and Chardonnay.

- CHARDONNAY
- CABERNET SAUVIGNON
- MERLOT
- PINOT NOIR
- ZINFANDEL

THE NORTHWEST

 WARM/COOL CLIMATE

A slightly cooler region than California, producing red wines with higher acidity and ripe fruit flavours.

- BORDEAUX BLEND
- PINOT NOIR
- CHARDONNAY
- RIESLING
- PINOT GRIS

THE NORTHEAST

 COOL CLIMATE

A cool climate region most known for its native American hybrid grapes that survive icy winters. Reds range from slightly sweet to dry and rustic. Whites are zesty.

- CONCORD
- NIAGARA
- ROSÉ
- MERLOT
- RIESLING

CANADA

SEATTLE

Northwest

BOSTON

CHICAGO

Northeast

NYC

California

SAN FRANCISCO

Midwest

Southeast

LOS ANGELES

Southwest

DALLAS

MIAMI

MEXICO

N

750km   750mi

USA DETAIL

Okanagan Valley
Similkameen Valley

Washington
- BORDEAUX BLEND
- RIESLING
- SYRAH

CANADA

■ SEATTLE

Yakima Valley
Horse Heaven Hills
Columbia Valley
PORTLAND ■
Walla Walla

Willamette Valley

Oregon
- PINOT NOIR
- PINOT GRIS
- CHARDONNAY
- RIESLING

Umqua Valley

Snake River Valley

Mendocino County
Lake County
Napa Valley
Sonoma County
Sierra Foothills
Lodi

SAN FRANCISCO ■

California
- CHARDONNAY
- CABERNET SAUVIGNON
- ZINFANDEL
- PINOT NOIR
- SYRAH
- MERLOT

Grand Valley

DENVER ■

West Elks

Madera

Monterey

Paso Robles

Southwest
- BORDEAUX BLEND
- RIESLING
- SPARKLING WINE
- VIOGNIER

Santa Barbara

■ LOS ANGELES

Temecula Valley

■ ALBUQUERQUE

■ SAN DIEGO

■ PHOENIX

Middle Rio
Grande Valley

Texoma

Sonoita

Texas High Plains

Escondido Valley

Texas Hill Country

Texas
- BORDEAUX BLEND
- TEMPRANILLO
- MOURVÈDRE

MEXICO

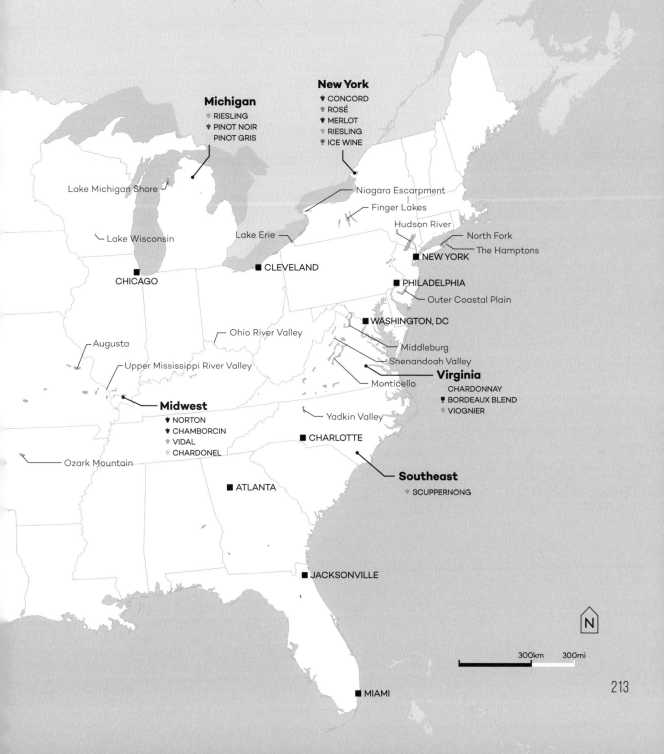

Michigan
- ♥ RIESLING
- ♥ PINOT NOIR
- PINOT GRIS

New York
- ♥ CONCORD
- ♥ ROSÉ
- ♥ MERLOT
- ♥ RIESLING
- ♥ ICE WINE

Lake Michigan Shore

Niagara Escarpment

Finger Lakes

Hudson River

Lake Wisconsin

Lake Erie

North Fork

The Hamptons

CLEVELAND

NEW YORK

CHICAGO

PHILADELPHIA

Outer Coastal Plain

WASHINGTON, DC

Ohio River Valley

Middleburg

Augusta

Shenandoah Valley

Upper Mississippi River Valley

Virginia
- CHARDONNAY
- ♥ BORDEAUX BLEND
- ♥ VIOGNIER

Monticello

Midwest
- ♥ NORTON
- ♥ CHAMBORCIN
- ♥ VIDAL
- ♥ CHARDONEL

Yadkin Valley

Ozark Mountain

CHARLOTTE

ATLANTA

Southeast
- ♥ 3CUPPERNONG

JACKSONVILLE

N

300km   300mi

MIAMI

USA: CALIFORNIA

A large and varied region known for bold fruit-forward wines. Three regions make most of California's wine, and each region is suited for different wines.

WINE REGIONS BY SIZE

491,000 ACRES

◀ INLAND VALLEYS
◀ NORTH COAST
◀ CENTRAL COAST
◀ SIERRA FOOTHILLS
◀ OTHERS

TOP CALIFORNIA REGIONS

● NORTH COAST

The North Coast contains Napa and Sonoma and can be split into two climate areas: the cooler coastal areas and the warmer inland valleys and hillsides.

 WARM CLIMATE
Inland areas of Napa, Sonoma, & Lake County

- ❧ CABERNET SAUVIGNON
- ❧ ZINFANDEL
- ❧ SYRAH

 COOLER CLIMATE
Coastal areas of Sonoma, Napa, & Mendocino County

- ❧ PINOT NOIR
- ❧ CHARDONNAY
- ❧ MERLOT

● CENTRAL COAST

The Central Coast can be separated into two distinct climate areas: coastal valleys that receive morning fog, and hot, dry inland areas.

 HOT CLIMATE
Inland areas such as Santa Barbara & Paso Robles

- ❧ CABERNET SAUVIGNON
- ❧ SYRAH
- ❧ ZINFANDEL

 COOLER CLIMATE
Coastal areas of San Luis Obispo & Santa Barbara

- ❧ PINOT NOIR
- ❧ CHARDONNAY
- ❧ SYRAH

● INLAND VALLEYS

The Inland Valleys are hot and dry regions most known for large-scale commercial wine production. The AVAs of Madera and Lodi make 75% of the wine in this area. The region has many old vineyard plantings of Zinfandel, Petite Sirah, Portuguese varieties like Touriga Nacional, and Muscat of Alexandria that have potential.

- ❧ ZINFANDEL
- ❧ PETITE SIRAH
- ❧ MUSCAT OF ALEXANDRIA
- ❧ BRANDY GRAPES

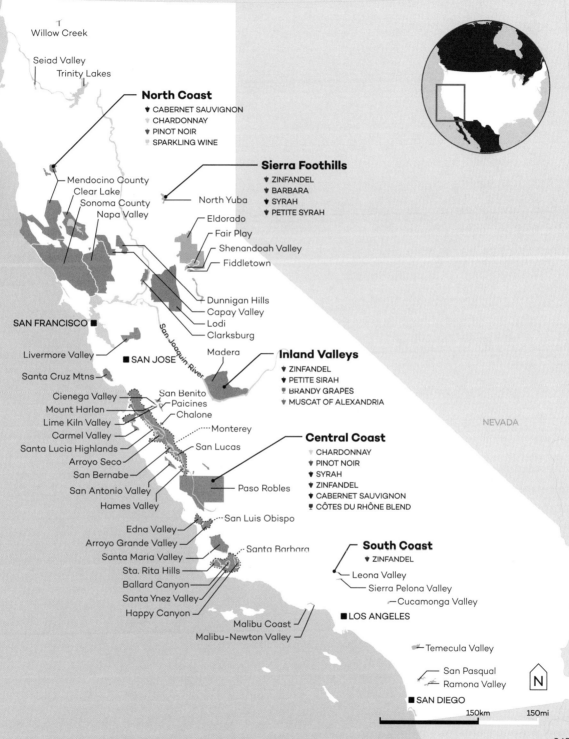

Willow Creek

Seiad Valley
Trinity Lakes

North Coast
- ♥ CABERNET SAUVIGNON
- ♥ CHARDONNAY
- ♥ PINOT NOIR
- ♥ SPARKLING WINE

Sierra Foothills
- ♥ ZINFANDEL
- ♥ BARBARA
- ♥ SYRAH
- ♥ PETITE SYRAH

North Yuba

Mendocino County
Clear Lake
Sonoma County
Napa Valley

Eldorado
Fair Play
Shenandoah Valley
Fiddletown

Dunnigan Hills
Capay Valley
Lodi
Clarksburg

SAN FRANCISCO ■

Madera

Inland Valleys
- ♥ ZINFANDEL
- ♥ PETITE SIRAH
- ♥ BRANDY GRAPES
- ♥ MUSCAT OF ALEXANDRIA

San Joaquin River

Livermore Valley

■ SAN JOSE

Santa Cruz Mtns

NEVADA

Cienega Valley
Mount Harlan
Lime Kiln Valley
Carmel Valley
Santa Lucia Highlands
Arroyo Seco
San Bernabe
San Antonio Valley
Hames Valley

San Benito
Paicines
Chalone

Monterey

San Lucas

Central Coast
- ♥ CHARDONNAY
- ♥ PINOT NOIR
- ♥ SYRAH
- ♥ ZINFANDEL
- ♥ CABERNET SAUVIGNON
- ♥ CÔTES DU RHÔNE BLEND

Paso Robles

Edna Valley
Arroyo Grande Valley
Santa Maria Valley
Sta. Rita Hills
Ballard Canyon
Santa Ynez Valley
Happy Canyon

San Luis Obispo

Santa Barbara

South Coast
- ♥ ZINFANDEL

Leona Valley
Sierra Pelona Valley
Cucamonga Valley

■ LOS ANGELES

Malibu Coast
Malibu-Newton Valley

Temecula Valley

San Pasqual
Ramona Valley

N

■ SAN DIEGO

150km   150mi

215

USA: NORTHWEST

The Northwest is characterized by fruit-forward wines with moderate acidity. The region can be split into two major regions by climate.

WASHINGTON

 WARM CLIMATE

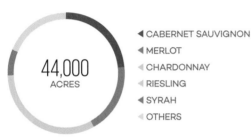

44,000
ACRES

◄ CABERNET SAUVIGNON
◄ MERLOT
◄ CHARDONNAY
◄ RIESLING
◄ SYRAH
◄ OTHERS

OREGON

 COOL CLIMATE

25,000
ACRES

◄ PINOT NOIR
◄ PINOT GRIS
◄ CHARDONNAY
◄ SYRAH
◄ RIESLING
◄ OTHERS

TOP WINES OF WASHINGTON

🍷 BORDEAUX BLEND

Bordeaux blends from the dry and sunny Columbia Valley area usually taste of raspberry, blackberry, milk chocolate and mint. Wines tend to have higher acidity, making them taste lighter bodied. High-quality examples will age 10+ years.

🍷 RIESLING

Ranging from dry to sweet, Washington Rieslings offer mouth-quenching acidity and flavours of yellow peach, honey and limeade.

🍷 SYRAH

At their best, Washington Syrahs offer bold blackberry flavours with notes of olive, black pepper, vanilla, clove and bacon. The region also produces Red Rhône blends with Grenache and Mourvèdre.

TOP WINES OF OREGON

🍷 PINOT NOIR

At its best, Oregon Pinot Noir has rich spicy flavours of cranberry, cherry, vanilla and allspice with subtle notes of tarragon. The best wines can be found in the sub-appellations of the Willamette Valley.

🍷 PINOT GRIS

Oregon Pinot Gris offers delicate aromas of pear, white nectarine and peony. The wines are typically made in a dry style that is zesty and refreshing.

🍷 CHARDONNAY

The cooler climate of the Willamette Valley produces Chardonnay with flavours of yellow apple, lemon and pineapple with high acidity and cream flavours from oak ageing. Unoaked Chardonnay delivers flavours of honeydew, pear and apple.

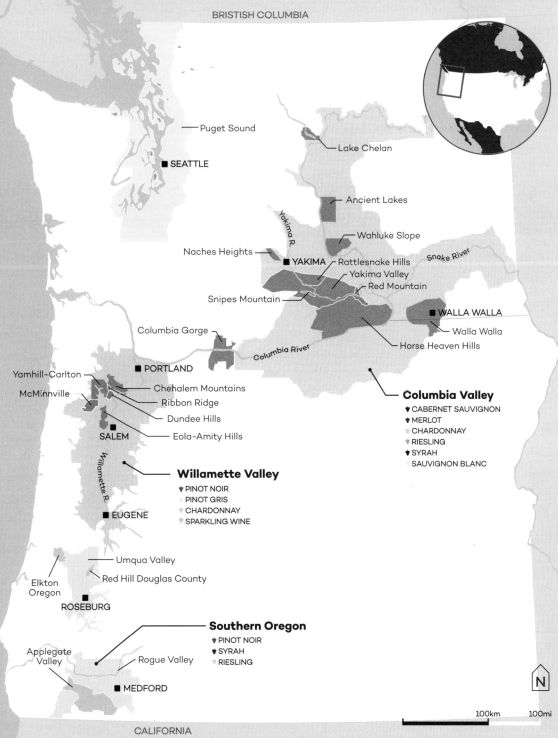

BRISTISH COLUMBIA

Puget Sound

■ SEATTLE

Lake Chelan

Ancient Lakes

Yakima R.

Wahluke Slope

Naches Heights

■ YAKIMA

Rattlesnake Hills

Yakima Valley

Snake River

Red Mountain

Snipes Mountain

■ WALLA WALLA

Walla Walla

Horse Heaven Hills

Columbia Gorge

Columbia River

Yamhill-Carlton

■ PORTLAND

Chehalem Mountains

McMinnville

Ribbon Ridge

Dundee Hills

Columbia Valley

SALEM

Eola-Amity Hills

❦ CABERNET SAUVIGNON

❦ MERLOT

CHARDONNAY

RIESLING

❦ SYRAH

SAUVIGNON BLANC

Willamette R.

Willamette Valley

❦ PINOT NOIR

PINOT GRIS

CHARDONNAY

SPARKLING WINE

■ EUGENE

Umqua Valley

Red Hill Douglas County

Elkton
Oregon

ROSEBURG

Southern Oregon

❦ PINOT NOIR

❦ SYRAH

RIESLING

Applegate
Valley

Rogue Valley

■ MEDFORD

N

100km   100mi

CALIFORNIA

217

GLOSSARY

♀ ABV

The abbreviation of alcohol by volume, listed by per cent on a wine label (e.g., 13.5% ABV).

⚗ Acetaldehyde

A toxic organic chemical compound that is produced in our bodies in order to metabolize ethyl alcohol. It is the cause of alcohol poisoning.

⊖ Acidification

A wine additive process common in warm and hot climate growing regions to increase acidity by adding tartaric or citric acid. Acidification is less common in EU countries and more common in USA, Australia and Argentina.

⚗ Amino Acids

Organic compounds that act as building blocks of proteins. Red wine contains 300–1,300 mg/L of which proline accounts for up to 85%.

✆ Appellation

A legally defined geographical location used to identify where the grapes in a wine are grown.

⚗ Aroma Compounds

Chemical compounds with very low molecular weights making it possible for them to be carried into the upper nasal passage.

Aroma compounds are derived from grapes and fermentation and are volatilized by the evaporation of alcohol.

♀ Astringent

A drying mouthfeel typically caused by tannins that bind to salivary proteins causing them to depart the tongue/mouth. It results in a rough sandpapery sensation in the mouth.

⊖ Brix (symbol °Bx)

Relative density scale for sucrose dissolved in grape juice used for determining the potential alcohol level of a wine. ABV is about 55–64% of the Brix number. For example, 27°Bx will result in a dry wine with 14.9–17.3% ABV.

⊖ Carbonic Maceration

A winemaking method where uncrushed grapes are placed in a sealed vat and topped with carbon dioxide. Wines created without oxygen have low tannin and colour with juicy fruit flavours and bold yeast aromas. This practice is common with entry-level Beaujolais wines.

⊖ Chaptalization

A wine additive process common in cool climates where sugar is added when grape sweetness isn't high enough to produce the minimum alcohol level. Chaptalization is illegal in the United States and common in parts of France.

⊖ Clarification/Fining

A process after fermentation where proteins and dead yeast cells are removed. To clarify, either a protein, such as casein (from milk) and egg whites or a vegan clay-based agent like bentonite or kaolin clay are added. These fining agents bind to the particles and pull them from the wine, making it clear.

♀ Cru

A French term meaning 'growth' which signifies a vineyard area of recognized quality.

⚗ Diacetyl

An organic compound found in wine that tastes like butter. Diacetyl comes from oak aging and malolactic fermentation.

⚗ Esters

Esters are one type of aroma compound found in wine that are caused by alcohol reacting with acids in wine.

♀ Fortified Wine

A wine that has been preserved by the addition of spirits, typically made of neutral-tasting grape brandy. For example, about 30% of Port wine is spirits that raises the ABV to 20%.

⚗ Glycerol

A colourless, odourless, viscous, sweet-tasting liquid that is a by-product of fermentation. In red wines there are about 4–10 g/L and noble rot wines contain 20+ g/L. Glycerol has been considered to add a positive, rich, oily mouthfeel to wine, however, studies have shown that other traits, like alcohol level and residual sugar, have a greater effect on mouthfeel.

♉ Grape: Clone

Wine grapes are cloned for their beneficial traits much like other agricultural products. For example, there are over 1,000 registered clones of the Pinot cultivar.

♉ Grape Must

Freshly pressed grape juice that still contains the seeds, stems and skins of grapes.

⑧ Lees Aging

Sediment left in wine after the fermentation from dead yeast particles.

⑧ Malolactic Fermentation (MLF)

MLF is technically not fermentation but a bacterial conversion of one type of acid (malic) to another type of acid (lactic). MLF is common on nearly all red wines and some white wines, like Chardonnay. It is responsible for creating the compound diacetyl, which smells and tastes like butter.

♀ Minerality

Minerality is not thought to be presence of trace minerals in wine but more likely the presence of sulphur compounds, which sometimes taste like chalk, flint or gravel.

♀ Noble Rot

Noble rot is a fungal infection caused by *Botrytis cinerea*, common in areas with high humidity. It is considered a flaw in red grapes and wines, but in white grapes it is appreciated for adding flavours of honey, ginger, marmalade and chamomile, making wines sweeter.

⑧ Oak: American

American white oak (*Quercus alba*) grows in the eastern United States and is primarily used in the Bourbon industry. American oak is known for adding flavours of coconut, vanilla, cedar and dill. Since American oak tends to be more loose grained, it's known to impart robust flavours.

⑧ Oak: European

European oak (*Quercus robur*) is sourced primarily in France and Hungary. Depending on where it is grown it can range from medium grained to very fine grained. European oak is known for adding flavours of vanilla, clove, allspice and cedar.

♀ Off-Dry

A term to describe a wine that is slightly sweet.

♀ Oxidation

When wine is exposed to too much oxygen, a chain of chemical reactions occurs that alters the compounds in the wine. One of the obvious changes you can sense is an increased level of acetaldehyde, which smells similar to bruised apples in white wine and artificial raspberry flavour and nail polish remover in red wines. Oxidation is the opposite of reduction.

⚗ pH

A figure that expresses the acidity or alkalinity in a substance numbered from 1–14 where 1 is acid, 14 is alkaline, and 7 is neutral. The average range for wine is about 2.5–4.5 pH, and a wine with a pH of 3 is ten times more acidic than a wine with a pH of 4.

winefolly.com/learn/winefolly.com/learn/basics/wine-terms

⚗ Phenols

A group of several hundred chemical compounds found in wine that affect the taste, colour, and mouthfeel. Tannin is a type of phenol called a polyphenol.

♀ Reduction

When wine doesn't receive enough air during fermentation, the yeast will substitute its need for nitrogen with amino acids (found in grapes). This creates sulphur compounds that can smell like rotten eggs, garlic, burnt matches, rotten cabbage, or sometimes positive traits like passion fruit or wet flint rocks. Reduction is not caused by 'sulphites' being added to wine.

♀ Residual Sugar (RS)

The sugar from grapes left over in a wine after fermentation stops. Some wines are fermented completely dry, and some are stopped before all the sugar is converted to alcohol to create a sweet wine. Residual Sugar ranges from nothing to about 220 g/L (which is viscous and sweet like syrup).

⚗ Sulphites

Sulphites or SO_2 is a preservative that is either added to wine or present on grapes before fermentation. Wines range from about 10 ppm (parts per million) to 350ppm—the legal US limit. Comparatively, bacon contains nearly double that of wine and chips contain about 2,000 ppm SO_2.

⚗ Sulphur Compounds

Sulphur compounds affect the aroma and taste of wine. In low levels they offer positive aromas of minerals or some tropical fruits. In high levels they smell of rotten eggs, garlic or rotten cabbage.

♀ Terroir

('Tear-woh') Originally a French word that is used to describe how a particular region's climate, soils, aspect (terrain) and traditional winemaking practices affect the taste of the wine.

♀ Typicity

A wine that is typical of a particular region or style.

⚗ Vanillin

The primary extract of the vanilla bean is also found in oak.

♀ Vinified

The creation of wine by fermentation of grape juice.

♀ Volatile Acidity (VA)

Acetic acid is the volatile acid in wine that turns wine to vinegar. In small levels it adds to the complexity of flavour and in high levels it causes the wine to spoil.

INDEX

▤ Sources

Ahn, Y., Ahnert, S. E., Bagrow, J. P., Barabási, A., 'Flavor network and the principles of food pairing' *Scientific Reports*. 15 Dec. 2011. 20 Oct. 2014. <http://www.nature.com/srep/2011/111215/srep00196/full/srep00196.html>.

Anderson, Kym. *What Winegrape Varieties are Grown Where? A Global Empirical Picture*. Adelaide: University Press. 2013.

Klepper, Maurits de. 'Food Pairing Theory: A European Fad'. Gastronomica: *The Journal of Critical Food Studies*. Vol. 11, No. 4 Winter 2011: pp. 55-58.

Lipchock, S V., Mennella, J.A., Spielman, A.I., Reed, D.R. 'Human Bitter Perception Correlates with Bitter Receptor Messenger RNA Expression in Taste Cells 1,2,3.' *Am. Jour. of Clin. Nutrition*. Oct. 2013: pp. 1136–1143.

Pandell, Alexander J. 'How Temperature Affects the Aging of Wine' *The Alchemist's Wine Perspective*. 2011. 1 Nov. 2014. <http://www.wineperspective.com/STORAGE%20TEM-PERATURE%20&%20AGING.htm>.

'pH Values of Food Products'. *Food Eng.* 34(3): pp. 98-99.

'Table 3: World Wine Production by Country: 2009-2012 and % Change 2012/2009' *The Wine Institute*. 2014. 3 March 2015. <http://www.wineinstitute.org/files/2012_Wine_Production_by_Country_California_Wine_Institute.pdf>.

♡ Special Thanks

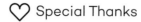

⌂ Kym Anderson
Director of Wine Economics, University of Adelaide

⌂ Andrew L. Waterhouse
Professor of Enology, UC, Davis

⌂ Luke Wohlers
Sommelier

⌂ Tony Polzer
Italian Wine Expert

⌂ Geoff Kruth
Master Sommelier

⌂ Beth Hickey
Sommelier

⌂ Rina Bussell
Sommelier

⌂ Sam Keirsey
Washington Winemaker

⌂ Cristian Ridolfi
Italian Winemaker

⌂ Jeffrey and Sandy

⌂ Margaret and Bob

⌂ Chad Wasser
Critique

🏛 University of Adelaide

🏛 University of California, Davis